Praise for *In Late Winter We Ate Pears*

"This winning little tome will convince you that the owners of Woodstock's Pane e Salute are bringing true Italian sensibility to this snowy northern state with their osteria."

—*Epicurious*

"In our mad-rush society, these enchanting essays and delicious recipes remind us of what Italians have always known: one of life's greatest pleasures is to linger at the table with good food and the company of loved ones. And now Deirdre Heckin and Caleb Barber have given us a truly original guide that teaches us, once again, to taste, to savor, to love."

—JOHN SEARLES, author of
Boy Still Missing

"The vignettes of their working Italian sojourns, during which they absorbed many secrets of kitchen and culture, bring a vivid allure to their narrative, just as the fruits of their experience are everywhere apparent in their marvelous osteria."

—*The Common Reader*

"As beautifully and evocatively written as any novel."

—*Hartford Courant*

"Not just a cookbook but a love story—between a man and a woman, a couple and two countries, a chef and a writer and the food they love. Deirdre Heekin and Caleb Barber understand the meaning of nurture, and they serve their readers lavishly, inviting us into their story and their kitchen. We savor the flavor of their lives and their table in prose that is good enough to eat."

—JULIA ALVAREZ, author of *In the Time of
the Butterflies* and *A Cafecito Story*

"A winning and well-written volume full of honest Italian cooking and memories."

—*Publishers Weekly*

"Just right! An inspiring and informative personal quest and a deeply felt journey into the heart and soul of Italian artisanal cuisine."
—ANTHONY BOURDAIN, author of *A Cook's Tour* and *Kitchen Confidential*

"Enchanting!"
—JOAN NATHAN, author of *Jewish Cooking in America*

"A treat for the senses. The writing will encourage all readers to sit down and savor. You can almost taste the recipes as you read them. Simple and clear instructions will bring Italy into the kitchens of even the most faint-hearted of cooks."
—BILL EICHNER, author of *The New Family Cookbook*

"I was charmed by the devotion of these two young Americans to the cuisine and customs of Italy. Deirdre Heekin's thoughtful narrative captures the essence of my country so that I'm made to see it through fresh eyes."
—FRANCESCA DURANTI, author of *Left-Handed Dreams* and *The House on Moon Lake*

In Late Winter We Ate Pears

In Late Winter
We Ate Pears
A YEAR OF HUNGER AND LOVE

DEIRDRE HEEKIN AND CALEB BARBER

CHELSEA GREEN PUBLISHING
WHITE RIVER JUNCTION, VERMONT

Printed in the United States of America.
First printing April, 2009
10 9 8 7 6 5 4 3 2 1   09 10 11 12 13

In Late Winter We Ate Pears was first published in 2002 as
Pane e Salute: Food and Love in Italy and Vermont.

"If You Look on a Map" appeared in another form in
The Vermont Standard, 2 June 2000, Woodstock, Vermont.

The authors acknowledge the following sources:

Martino, Maestro. *"Il Libro de arte coquinaria."* In *Arte della cucina, Libri di ricette: Testi sopra lo scalco,
il trinciante e i vini dal XIV al XIX secolo.* Edited by Emilio Faccioli, 1: 115-204. Milan: Il Polifilo, 1966.

Piras, Claudia, and Eugenio Medagliani, eds. *Culinaria Italy.*
Cologne: Könemann Verlagsgesellschaft mbH, 2000.

Quasimodo, Salvatore. *"Antico inverno."* In *Introduction to Italian Poetry: A Dual-Language Book.*
Edited by Luciano Rebay. New York: Dover Publications, 1969.

Redon, Odile, Francoise Sabban, and Silvano Serventi. *The Medieval Kitchen: Recipes from
France and Italy.* Translated by Edward Schneider. Chicago: The University of Chicago Press, 1998.

Tihany, Adam D., Francesco Antonucci, and Florence Fabricant. *Venetian Taste.*
New York: Abbeville Press Publishers, 1994

Book design and composition by Tim Jones for Sterling Hill Productions
Illustrations by Mary Elder Jacobsen

Our Commitment to Green Publishing
Chelsea Green sees publishing as a tool for cultural change and ecological stewardship. We strive
to align our book manufacturing practices with our editorial mission and to reduce the impact of
our business enterprise in the environment. We print our books and catalogs on chlorine-free recycled paper, using vegetable-based inks whenever possible. This book may cost slightly more because we use recycled paper, and we hope you'll agree that it's worth it. Chelsea Green is a
member of the Green Press Initiative (www.greenpressinitiative.org), a nonprofit coalition of publishers, manufacturers, and authors working to protect the world's endangered forests and con-
serve natural resources. *In Late Winter We Ate Pears* was printed on Natures Smooth Antique, a
30-percent postconsumer recycled paper supplied by RR Donnelley.

Library of Congress Cataloging-in-Publication Data on file with the publisher

Chelsea Green Publishing Company
Post Office Box 428
White River Junction, VT 05001
(802) 295-6300
www.chelseagreen.com

All of us surely house within ourselves another unwritten book. This would consist of an account of ourselves as eaters, recording the development of our palates, telling over like the beads of a rosary the memories of the best meals of our lives.

CLIFTON FADIMAN, 1954

contents

CONTENTS

list of recipes

SPRING

Contorni

Dolci

SUMMER

Antipasti

Primi

Secondi

∽◌

AUTUMN

Contorni

Dolci

WINTER

Antipasti

Primi

Secondi

Contorni

Dolci

BREAD

Appendix

foreword

IN RECENT YEARS, after many decades of looking to France for culinary inspiration, Americans turned toward Italy. France offered a sophisticated and elaborate approach to cuisine—the chef as performer—but Italy offered something quite different. If French cooking was like a Broadway production, with lavish costumes and a cast of thousands, in this new arena the sets were minimal and the players wore little, if anything. Pure forms revealed, they *were* the art, and their success depended upon the acumen of the chef's direction and casting.

In this thrilling and intimate culinary style, now such a vital part of the American food landscape, the eater is drawn into a bond with the ingredients themselves and, beyond them, with the earth that nurtured those ingredients. Inevitably, it is a celebration of place—of specific places, and the things they have to tell us about living on the earth. I can't think of a better emissary for this grounded lifestyle than the book you hold in your hands.

Too often cookbooks simply present a laundry list of recipes shorn of any real-life context. But food isn't like that. Food is always of a place and of a time. Now, when most foods in the supermarket have had their identities wiped as clean as those of participants in the Witness Protection Program, it is too easy to forget that even they had a life in a particular place and season.

Many of us were never really comfortable losing touch with that seasonality. After being briefly seduced by the novelty and freedom of year-round produce, we found that our old marriage to the seasons had been more rewarding than we'd realized. It gave texture to our year. Given the opportunity to walk out the door, we turned around and came right back to the kitchen. America's new interest in regional foods and seasonal menus is a most heartening development, but it had Italian roots, and Caleb Barber and Deirdre Heekin have been at the vanguard of that movement.

In their Woodstock osteria, Pane e Salute; in their gardens and vineyard on the slopes of Mount Hunger, which burst with miraculous fruits and herbs; and in the elegant essays and recipes in this book, Caleb and Deirdre exemplify a way of living—once second nature but now a revelation to many—in which food, love, work, and adventure are all a seamless part of the day, the month, the year. Somehow they manage to serve up discernment without pretension, a blend that is virtually impossible to find in this country. They humbly make food and art that is not humble at all—or, rather, it is, in the word's original meaning: of the *humus,* the earth.

This is an earthy book, and a sexy one. Savoring olive oil from ancient terra-cotta urns in a crumbling estate in the hills of Tuscany, rolling pizza dough by night while wild dogs bay in the distance, or gliding through the Venetian Carnivale in masks, they celebrate a life lived with the senses wide open, an engagement with the world and all its fruitfulness. It's a life they generously share in these pages, and we are well fortified by it.

—Rowan Jacobsen, author of
A Geography of Oysters and
American Terroir

preface: a personal note

THE DAY AFTER WE GOT MARRIED, my husband Caleb and I flew on one-way tickets and moved to Italy. While Caleb had been to Europe, been to Italy, I had never crossed the Atlantic before, and I was no seasoned traveler. At twenty-five, we were embarking on an unusual yearlong honeymoon, settling in a small town southeast of Florence.

We went to Italy looking for the romance and history of a place. We were searching for adventure, a sensibility captured like an old-fashioned snapshot. I imagined a moment of suspension where we'd see ourselves staring into the camera as if it might have been sixty years ago—the look on our faces so distant and youthful—thinking that the expression in our eyes and mouths said, "This is the time of our lives," but knowing with the passage of time that what we really felt was hunger.

Our time spent living in, leaving, and returning to Italy follows a map laid out by that hunger, the known and lesser known roads that took us to kitchens warmed by wood-fired ovens where we learned to roast chestnuts; to tables set with linen and somebody's best—but well-loved, used, and so chipped—china; to cantinas in old abandoned abbeys to drink red wine; and to eat from the hands of Generosity herself. In following the way of hunger, we began to understand how commingled it is with basic wants: for love, for warmth, for hope, for transformation. How hard to isolate one experience and say, "Oh, yes, it was that which changed me forever." But I do know that on our way to Italy, our experiences took us from a known world and disassembled our assumptions, and it was the food of Italy that put us back together, that taught us a new way to study, to love, to eat and drink, to be ourselves.

Hunger pushes you from place to place. At each watering hole you hope to be satisfied. Hunger is like traveling, and traveling is inherently about searching for something outside ourselves and letting it work its way in; it's about the length of a journey and what happens when you stay somewhere for a while. These elements of hunger are the reasons why Caleb and I opened a bakery and restaurant in Vermont that we named *Pane e Salute,* which means "bread and health," a toast to the essence of living. Our bakery has grown into an *osteria,* and this word is crucial. *Osteria* encompasses all we hope to offer at our table; it is a place of hospitality, a place where you can get a dish of handmade pasta, a bowl of soup, a glass of wine or beer. In the Middle Ages, *osteria* was defined as an inn, a tavern where you could eat a warm meal, be warmed by wine, and find a warm bed. While now it is more loosely defined (we offer two of the three), the sensibility of the word remains the same, stemming from its Latinate root "to host."

We returned to the States from Italy informed by our hunger. After reestablishing our lives here, we wanted to feed and refresh our own memory, our nostalgia for the Italian way of life that had affected us so. We wanted to return the hospitality and generosity we found in Italy in order to honor our hosts, and we wanted to offer those same things to others here. These are still our wants.

Without knowing it, shortly after arriving in Italy that first time together, we were already learning the lesson that ultimately led us to cook and feed people in the manner of Italy: When at the table, all else is suspended. This was the moment of suspension we'd sought, that sense of time delayed. Caleb and I paused at a trattoria near Lago Trasimeno with two friends and their family. And here was that illusive snapshot: we made a convivial crew, laughing at slightly bawdy jokes and listening to a captivating lecture on the painter Signorelli. We delighted in our food, the ability of our cooks, the generosity of our hosts. Caleb and I were there and not there; we were learning to be ghosts; we'd exited our previous lives and stepped into the world of central Italy. How had we somehow appeared at this table with this family eating together near the end of a long, hot summer? We didn't belong through nature, we were related to no one. The odds against us sitting there—of even making this move to another country—were so improbable, so steep, we felt like apparitions.

In my partial memory of this scene, the earthy colors somehow seem to have washed over into blue-green and white. As if we sat next to the sea, light refracting all over and around us, during that meal, the lines of our bodies turn, fading in and out, but we are arriving there, like a slowly accumulating yet flickering transmission of information, emotion, matter, and exhaustion, until we are finally present at the table. Aside from the shapes of our faces and the flurry of a hand in the air or a finger tracing the rim of a wineglass, there is a certain veracity in all our expressions: the concerns, trepidations, and loves spinning in our heads are gone for those few hours. We could do only one thing: take the day in through the aperture of our mouths.

In the end, this is a book about romance—a place, cuisine, art, and history — and a book about the *other* side of romance: the hard work, the ruthlessness of progress, and the choices born out of the contrast between context and content, choices that are defining the reality of living in Italy today. It is a fierce reality of people who must work, for all the same reasons we all must work, but also because theirs is a culture built on centuries of hard work. This is a book about preservation.

This book is also a true collaboration. Caleb and I have taken this journey together: in work, in love, and in adventure. In our efforts to share our experiences, we have included both our perspectives here, and as a result the book is divided into two first-person narratives. My voice informs the essays; Caleb's the recipes.

So, this is a book about the food we've eaten in Italy, about a risotto made with saffron and *parmigiano*, about a biscotto made with anise and almonds taken with a small glass of sweet wine. About leaving home, about finding a place to stay, this is a book born out of desire or parts of desire: hunger and love.

a note on our recipes

As DEIRDRE AND I have been developing this book, we have come to understand that its purpose is an extension of the mission at our restaurant: to communicate the style of life we learned in Italy. We are still learning.

Our restaurant has become a way to preserve not only part of our past, but a larger historical past that is still important to the present: Italy. So much of the Western world can be illuminated and explained by what you will find in Italy, especially when it comes to art.

We met a winemaker, Massimo Martinelli, from the Piemonte who has written a book called *Il Barolo Come lo Sento Io.* Although the title of the English version has been translated as *Barolo and How I Know It,* the original *sento* comes from the verb *sentire,* meaning "to sense." We believe cooking is an art form like any other: you learn the techniques, you learn what those techniques feel like, and then you learn by intuition, instinct, repetition, and your senses. This is an Italian philosophy we have observed in action countless times. This is how we approach the preparation and eating of food, and it is a method of success we've been taught by our Italian hosts and mentors, and how I encourage you to approach your time in the kitchen: Trust your senses and pay attention to the information they provide. Listen to the food sizzling in the oil—and adjust the flame. Taste the sauce—salt will bring out its flavor. See the color of the meat—a few more minutes in the pan will bring it to perfection. Touch the dough—its movement and lightness tell you it has risen enough to go into the oven. Trust yourself. Smell the wine . . .

Then trust your judgment as you respond to that information and draw upon the memories of other dishes you have prepared (either with success or—even more valuable—failure) and eaten and the memories of dishes prepared by others. Memory may prove over time to be your most useful tool while you work in your kitchen and become an ever more confident cook.

But then there is the actual cooking . . .

Recipes are simply guides, records of how a dish has been prepared in the past. It's interesting that the English word "recipe" is actually the imperative form of the Latin verb *recipere,* meaning "to take," a command to collect the goods with which to make a meal. Our modern definition of the English noun "recipe" now includes both a list of ingredients and a set of instructions. Armed with these two things, we still cannot be assured of success.

The cooking of a dish is a sequence of physical and sensory experiences guiding us from one technical step to the next. It is to these experiences that we must pay attention, because they will embed themselves more deeply in our memory than "what to do next." They become part of us, the dish becomes part of us, and we become connected to something outside of us: the history of the dish and all the people who have prepared and eaten it before us. We are having the same experiences they have had in another time and place. This is how a dish becomes classic.

Temperature, humidity, the ripeness of a vegetable, the cook's sense of timing—all play a part in what is placed on the table, and each is a variable. Your awareness of the state of your cooking environment and your responsiveness to those factors will elevate what comes to the table.

Nature is primary to cooking well. Just as recipes are a guide and your senses are the gauge, ingredients are the essence of cooking. Many people plan a meal ahead of time, make their shopping list, then go out and gather the ingredients. But what if it's January and the tomatoes are not very good that day? In Italy, a meal is approached from the other side. You go to the market first—old-fashioned, year-round, outdoor markets where the vendors bring their produce, meats, and cheeses. You see what looks best, and then you plan the meal around these things. Usually what's best is what's grown not too far away and is in season. This still holds true. Peaches aren't available in March or November. But fava beans are ready in March, spring green and waiting to be shelled. Chestnuts naturally fall from the tree in late October and early November, a treat that heralds the coming of winter.

In order to highlight this principle of seasonal cooking we've divided this book into four sections, four seasons. For each season the recipes focus on dishes that use ingredients available at that time of the year. Within each of these four sections we offer enough recipes so that the reader can choose to create a four-course meal appropriate to a particular season. Each season is also divided into sections: *antipasti* (appetizers), *primi* (first courses), *secondi* (second courses), *contorni* and *insalate* (side dishes and salads to be served with or after the second course), and *dolci* (desserts).

The recipes we offer here ask something of the cook in exchange: to work by the senses; to pay attention; to seek a balance and completion of the senses when you and your guests sit down; to enjoy the meal you've prepared with family or friends. These recipes are for simple, comforting, and graceful food.

a note on the recipe

Add a Dash of History

IMAGINE A MAN SMALL IN STATURE, his eyes the color of caramel, his hair the electric blue-black of an eel. His eyebrows grow thick above soft eyes, his bushy mustache is curled and groomed to cover a harelip, wrinkles crease around his mouth and on his forehead.

Imagine the year is 1452, the time of the Renaissance, forty years before Genova's Columbus will appeal to Spain's Queen Isabella for the funds to sail to the New World, forty years before she will grant this conqueror's wish. Our man too thinks of sailing sloops or frigates heavy with treasure: clove, cinnamon, anise, saffron. See him wearing blue silk stockings and a white linen shirt made by Spanish court tailors. Not a wealthy man himself, he works for a wealthy man—the Patriarch of Aquileia in the Friuli—he does, however, have his own dominion, a vast, wide space separate from the Patriarch's red velvet receiving rooms, the Patriarch's frescoed *salotto*, the Patriarch's sea-green ballroom; this man has a kitchen.

Enter his kitchen. Watch his large hands dance around the fire, his thick-muscled fingers slice, stir, whisk, shape. But his capable hands are gentle with a precise and quiet touch. Think of him later, there, behind the bed curtain. In bed with his lover, he rolls her hips as if he were kneading the morning's bread dough. The next day he will make a sky-blue sauce for summer, an orange omelette for harlots and ruffians, goat roasted in gold. His name is Maestro Martino.

No images or written descriptions of Maestro Martino survive (I conjured him for myself), only his own handwritten recipes clearly marked on thin, onion-skin pages and a reputation that hails him as one of the greatest cooks of the fifteenth century.

I met Maestro Martino in the Biblioteca Nazionale Braidense in Milan on a summer-warm April morning, only because Caleb and I went looking for him. Long before we decided to pull together a collection of recipes and vignettes rooted in our experiences of living, traveling, eating, and learning in Italy, and after we began infusing those experiences into the spirit and food of our own restaurant back in the States, we wanted to know the history behind the cuisine that had seduced us: How had certain dishes developed? How did the nature of Italian cooking become so closely linked to its people and then culture? How did this food and the Italian philosophy of cooking inform the grace of the Italian day? A friend had told us the library in Milan had a worthy collection of books on the history of Italian cookery. To Milan we went.

In Milan, an arts school accommodates the library, which is reached after passing through a light-filled courtyard followed by a high-ceilinged stone hallway whose tall, heavy wooden doors are locked because studio classes are in session. Halfway up two flights of Palladian-style steps, visitors must stop to duck into a small chamber where any carryalls are placed in bright blue and chrome metal lockers. Like a museum, no satchels or packs are allowed.

Beyond glass doors, inside the library, all the books on every shelf are leatherbound and old, all the ceilings are impossibly high.

We thumbed our way through the card catalogs making a long list of titles and their call numbers. *La Cucina e La Tavola, Il Cuoco Piemontese Perfezionato a Parigi, Libri di Ricette Testi Sopra la Scuola Il Trinciante e I Vini dal xiv al xix Secolo.* We settled on about fifteen books we wanted to check out but were told by a brusque young woman at the circulation desk that we could only check three books at a time. We gave her our requests and she gave us each a number as though we were in line at a New York deli.

In about ten minutes, after an elaborate choreography of staff and books, Caleb and I were handed our requests. We brought our finds to the Study where we spread our books before us like booty retrieved from sunken treasure. Around us, bookshelves rose up into an arced ceiling covered with paintings of queens and princes. At the back of the room hung a large painting of a man standing against the dark green velvet background of the artist's studio; he wore draped red robes with a narrow ermine collar. Joseph II, the son of Maria Theresa, the brother of Marie Antoinette, a member of the the royal Hapsburg family that once ruled northern Italy, would watch over our introduction to the medieval world of Maestro Martino and the history of the Italian cookbook.

While the Middle Ages did not invent what we consider classical Italian cooking, there is not much recorded in the way of recipes or cooking guides before the fourteenth century. At least one intact record has come down through antiquity, the famous culinary and dietetic treatise by the Roman Apicius, a compendium arranged in the late fourth century A.D., but a long dry period with little written record falls between Apicius's work and the arrival of the medieval cookbook at the beginning of the 1300s. Much changed in terms of the availability of foods and the implements used to prepare them across this nine-hundred-year period.

The Middle Ages typically calls forth an indelicate image of the baronial lord at his table supping gluttonously on large legs of gamy fowl or rotting meat drenched in a thick layer of spices to squelch the stench. The lord sits next to his tankard of brew, grease from his food slathers his mouth and jowls. In truth, the late Middle Ages bore a very aristocratic cuisine, providing a history of fine meals rather than ordinary eating. By the fifteenth century, Maestro Martino, our hailed chef, laid down the principles of a cuisine amid the cultural inventions of the time: the polyphonic music of the *ars nova,* the frescoes of Pisanello and Massaccio, and Lorenzo de Medici's humanistic ventures that would define the spirit of the Italian Renaissance. In the previous century, Dante had written his *La Vita Nuova* and his masterwork, *The Divine Comedy,* and Boccaccio created the tales of *The Decameron.*

Giotto broke from the Byzantine with his mastery of painted movement and the initial attempts at true perspective. Given two centuries of such creativity, why would we draw such an unsophisticated image—that of greedy baronial lord—to portray medieval cooking and dining?

During this time, Italian cooking strove to go beyond the limitations established by climate and custom on their local offerings. Italy of the Middle Ages did not rely on many of the ingredients we think of today as staples in Italian cookery: the tomato and the potato weren't available, not having arrived in Europe from the Americas until quite recently. Likewise, there was no corn, no succulent pepper, no chili, no coffee, no tobacco. However, there was much wine (usually thinned with a little water, a tradition still kept today in provincial households), and cooks aspired to create a subtle balance between the oriental spices, costly though light to transport, that came to Italy through the trade routes webbing out from Venice to and from China and India: saffron, black pepper, cinnamon, ginger, clove, and rose water.

Italian, and indeed all European, cuisine owes a great deal to this connection with the Orient. In thirteenth-century Peking, Marco Polo, who was the favorite of Kublai Khan, served the ruler in China, India, and Southeast Asia. Stories say that in 1295, when Polo returned to Venice, he brought back trunks full of all those exotic perfumed spices and began to introduce these heady flavors into Venetian cooking.

While spices dominated the style of medieval cooking, almonds and citrus fruit from northern Italy, were also essentials. Actual recipes traveled too, and many of the roots of medieval cuisine can be theoretically traced abroad—the correlations between Arabic traditions and modern cuisines show a perfect example. A layered Turkish pastry made from leavened dough shaped like a crescent, the symbol of Turkish power, made its way into the Italian *cornetto* and the French croissant, the only difference between recipes in the amount of butter and eggs used.

Several splits in the history of Italian cooking occurred: Antiquity to Medieval to the Renaissance to the Baroque to the Enlightenment to Modern. The initial break from the antique kitchen of the Romans developed slowly between the seventh and eleventh centuries. A similar methodical break in the style of cookery happened again in the seventeenth century, a time marked by a movement not only toward a French-dominated way of thinking and style, but a Frenchified Italian cuisine. Oriental spices were all but abandoned, except for black pepper. Native aromatic vegetables and herbs gained popularity, and a love affair with chocolate and sugar began. By the 1600s a greater diversity of cooking fats entered the kitchen. All these changes still influence contemporary Italian tastes.

Modern traditional Italian cooking, the cooking of the common folk of the eighteenth and nineteenth centuries, really became the identity of Italian food at the turn of the twentieth century, yet another gradual adaptation of the new, when a man named Pellegrino Artusi brought forward his collection of recipes in *The Art of Eating Well*. No easy connections between this style of cooking and that of medieval cuisine can be drawn. The differences between the two styles seem extreme. But this evolution of the way people cooked transpired over a thousand years, and by the time the seventeenth, eighteenth, and nineteenth centuries rolled around, cooking for all levels of society had become incredibly refined.

Yet it was in the fourteenth and fifteenth centuries when Italian cooking most significantly matured, making a break with the gastronomy of antiquity based on its new exposure to the Arabic diet, which had reached Italy via the Iberian peninsula and Sicily.

The literature of Italian cookbooks is first and foremost a technical literature. But in the early Middle Ages, books on medicines, herbs, hunting, and agriculture created a genre based on dietetic suggestions. The twelfth-century masters of the Scuola di Salerno wrote one of the first of this genre, *Regimen sanitatis*, which was a book written to embrace the Arabic and Hebraic scientific culture—as in the study of their medicine, herbs, plants, and animals. Designed for the layman, the *Regimen* called upon an Arabic manuscript by Abul-Mutarrif Ald el Balman Ibn Wafid, translated into Latin by Gherardo da Cremona, also of the early twelfth century.

This period saw many translations: *Il Liber de Ferculis et Condimentis* by Maestro Jambobin, also of Cremona, *De cibis et medicinis simplicibus et compositui* by Gege, a "son of Algazeal," and the celebrated *Tacuinium sanitatis in medicina* by Albusi, rewritten at the beginning of the fourteenth century into vernacular Italian by an unknown translator.

Later books of the thirteenth century show little having changed in their format: not entirely technical, these books focus on science and medicinal disciplines and their effects on health and diet rather than on actual recipes. In many respects, medieval cooking implemented a system of health through diet. Pietro de' Crescenzi's *ll liber ruralium commodorum* provides a continuing example of this interest, and such composite editions such as *La lettura didattica anglo-francese* by Brunetto Latini, a highly popular vernacular compendium written from the Latin books of Bono Giamboni and Vivald Belcazer, followed suit. *De proprietatibus rerum* was another vernacular translation from the original Latin of a man named Bartolomeo Anglico.

Finally, two books arrived, smilarly titled: *Il Libro per Cuoco* by an unknown Venetian author, and the anonymous Tuscan-language *Liber de coquina*. These two were the only major treatises of this period devoted solely to the preparation of food. Recipes came from fragments of other minor recipe pamphlets rather than any translations found in Latin manuals. They contained instructions for dishes like pear *minestra,* a pear broth, the fruit poached with saffron and onions, or pear soup cooked in almond milk and sugar; nut and onion breads, sweet fried dough with sugar and apples, or another soup not unlike a thick Roman *stracciatella,* a mixture of bitter and sweet almonds, onion, ginger, and cinnamon.

Il Libro per Cuoco and *Liber de coquina* comprised the initial forays into the creative field of the Italian *"arte della cucina,"* the art of the kitchen and the art of cooking. The manufacture of these books pointed toward the growing interest in a table covered with beautiful and properly prepared food.

Not until the latter half of the fourteenth century did anything like the cookbook as we know it today appear, and here is where we met Maestro Martino. His *Il Libro de arte coquinaria* reveals him as one of the greatest cooks of the Renaissance and one who created an elaborate and humanistic approach to the art of the kitchen.

A medieval manuscript collection of recipes generally took one of two forms: a scroll or a small handheld volume or codex. The scroll, probably the most ancient form of manuscript, was used in the original version of a French cookbook called *Le Viandier,* whereas the small codex, similar to the look of modern-day books, was used for that Venetian treatise, *Il Libro per Cuoco,* and was duplicated in the more contemporary translation edited and published by Ludovico Frati in 1899. The original codex, which lives at the Biblioteca Casentense in Rome, measures just under 5 inches by just over 3 inches. The preserved original is written in a highly legible hand, is well spaced on the page, and organizes its recipes alphabetically by title.

A fourteenth-century book called *Il Libro della Cocina,* curated and edited in Francesco Zambrini's 1863 *Il Libro della Cucina del secolo XIV* (published by Romagnoli in Bologna), contains a more continuous codex of miscellania printed on thin, translucent pages in a comprehensive notebook written in two columns.

Recipes in these early treatises are organized in one of three modes—by ingredients, by type of dish, or alphabetical by title. Alphabetical organization was not as common as the other two. Having entries categorized by ingredients—vegetables, meats, eggs, fish, etc.—allowed for a kind of culinary encyclopedia, a form used by the Tuscan *Liber de Coquina.* Having recipes organized by the type of dish—roasts, sauces, fritters, tortes—as done by Maestro Martino, emphasized the art of dining. But these last two forms were not exclusive of one another within a given manuscript; the boundary between one often blurred into another.

Many medieval documents were signed anonymously, while others bear the name of the chef of a royal or noble kitchen. But we cannot assume all of these manuscripts were meant only for a royal readership (after all, royalty never cooked). These cookbooks would need a literate reader, and by that time a growing merchant class had been educated; not only priests, queens, and princes could read. One such book written in France gives proof of this: a Parisian bourgeois getting on in years who had a young and inexperienced wife wrote a book of advice for her, a guide to morality, to domestic management, to cookery. He titled his book *Le Ménagier de Paris.*

Both the bourgeois author and the noble chef convey practical information in their recipes: each one sets out a method of creating a dish or a meal, a traditional format tied to the oral tradition of passing down from mother to daughter, or master to apprentice. The cookbooks written in Latin would most likely have been kept in aristocratic or monastic libraries, which would have allowed those living there to select daily or special menus based on the season and the religious calender. Books written in vernacular Italian were obviously designed to be accessible to a broader readership, especially to professional cooks like Martino. All the manuscripts include recipes that cover a wide variety of information: the cost of ingredients, fuel requirements or options, kitchen utensils and equipment, and the duration and difficulty of preparation. A book like Zambrini's translation of the Tuscan-language treatise explains simple recipes for cooking garden vegetables and wild greens alongside more complex, fabulous combinations such as a seven-story *torta parmigiana,* a stuffed calf, or a tart containing live birds.

The kitchens for which these manuscripts were written bear little resemblance to modern kitchens. Villagers and artisans—the common folk—ate and cooked in common rooms whose smoky hearth provided heat, light, and a place to prepare food. Only in aristocratic or upper middle-class houses were kitchens a separate space. Sometimes at these villas or great houses, the kitchens were even put in another building altogether.

In both situations, the fireplace stays at the heart of any culinary preparation, though the hearth is separate from the need for an oven. Ovens were owned by a lord or a professional *fornaio,* or oven keeper. In the country, ovens might be the property of the whole rural community, where they were built inside the walls of a small town at a central location accessible to all. Ovens were largely used for baking bread, but they were not imperative for pastry, which could in most cases be cooked in a special container on the floor of the fireplace.

A skilled cook knew how to control cooking paraphernalia like cauldrons, crocks, fry pans, grills, and spits, which were all exposed to the open flame. Hooks, strings, tripods, and containers with legs or feet helped maintain indirect contact with the flame. The repeated instructions in culinary manuscripts on how to overcome a strong or smoky fire that might ruin a dish indicate what a major concern the fire was for the cook of centuries past.

I can picture Maestro Martino in his kitchen. The space is deep and narrow with a long thin table that serves every need, from preparing pastry to pounding meats. A cavernous mouth large enough to frame a standing man, the hearth, black with soot, boasts a powerful blaze tended by a young boy no older than ten. Martino's team of cooks and helpers works hard: a woman with muscular arms, her sleeves rolled up, sweat dotting the blouse against her back, grinds spices with a mortar and pestle; two other women strain almond milk through a sieve; another young boy has quick, busy hands that skim foam off broth as it cooks in a pot hung from a hook in the fire. The downy hair on the boy's hands and arms is singed. Another man bastes the pig, watching it roast on the spit, his face mottled red by the heat. I see Maestro himself, famous for his sauces, first whisking, then stirring with a large, carved wooden spoon, the medieval symbol for cook. A grand cage of songbirds sits just over there, near the window, ready.

Maestro Martino, whom Caleb and I first read about under the watchful eye of the painted Joseph II, came to life for us through pages of books carefully preserved in Milan. These books contain his recipes, as well as the importance of his place in the history of the kitchens and cuisines of Europe. His technical mastery mingles with his aesthetic brilliance and clear sensitivity that not only define his national cuisine but serve as the rudiments of a sophisticated Western European cookery.

After a few years cooking for the Patriarch, Maestro Martino was recognized as the greatest cook of his time, anywhere, by the Renaissance humanist Bartolomeo Sacchi, or *il Platina*. By translating Martino's recipes into Latin and bringing them into a discussion of nutrition and medicine, *il Platina* made it possible for Martino's creations to spread like a handful of seed thrown to birds. By the sixteenth century, Martino would be translated into French, Italian, and English, among other languages, and the success of Italian cooking would be unquestionably owed to this pair, *il Platina* and Maestro Martino.

So, as Caleb and I dive into our own attempt at organizing recipes and experiences that root themselves in the world of everyday classical Italian cooking, we invoke Maestro Martino. I continue to imagine Martino, a spirit in our own kitchen now, as we try his blackberry-ginger sauce for veal or chicken, his Dover sole with bitter oranges, or his pumpkin tart. His presence grows more distinct when I discover again the recipe for a dish we will never make, one I wrote down in a tired, cramped hand while sitting at the library table in Milan, one that is an enchantment created by a true artisan:

> *Make a very large pastry casing; and at the bottom you shall make a hole big enough to pass your fist through, or larger if you wish. The sides must be a little higher than usual. You shall bake this casing in the oven, filled with flour. When it is cooked, you shall open the hole in the bottom and remove the flour. You will have already prepared another small pie full of good things, properly baked and ready to eat, made to fit the hole you made in the large casing; you shall put it through that hole. Into the remaining space surrounding the small pie, you shall put live birds, as many as will fit. These little birds should be put in at the very moment you present [the pie] at table. When it has been presented to those seated for the banquet, you shall remove the lid, and the little birds will fly—*

In Late Winter We Ate Pears

spring

the physic of spring

FIFTEEN DAYS AFTER THE FACT, the radio weather fore-
caster tells us that March fifth was really the first day of
spring, the day the earth's pattern began to change significantly. Although
we've noticed the sun rising earlier and that it's still light out when we drive
home from work at night, this is a fool's game I think: up here in northern
New England we've had more snow since the first of March than we've had
all winter. Three feet, six inches on top of the eighteen inches already on the
ground, with a prediction of two *more* feet by the end of this week, a storm
I overheard someone say began as rain in Peru. Maybe time leaped both
backward *and* forward since the last day of February. I think the leap confused the clocks, confused the spring birds whose calls have started to punc-
tuate the silence of the landscape, confused the skunk who came out and
fended off a dog the other night in front of our restaurant. The leap even
confused the porcupine who stopped to look over his shoulder at my husband Caleb when he drove home the other night, and of course our cat,
Tommasino, who sits at the door ready to go outside. How rudely surprised
he was when the door opened to be blinded by the great wall of white snow
our shovels and the plow have made, a solid barricade bordering our front
walk. Tommasino looked out in disbelief—hair on end and trembling from
the cold—and turned back inside. Maybe April Fool's Day has inverted itself,
like one of those undulating principles in physics, and this whole month of
March in Vermont will be one long, cruel joke, these thirty-one boxes on

the calendar displacing the twenty-four hours of a single day. But why am I surprised? Isn't it always like this?

We battle these late-winter days with an effort toward spring. Skiers from New York and Boston arrive each weekend, slowing the highway veins leading to our point—Woodstock, Vermont—every Friday night, clear weather or blizzard. Each weekend threatens to be their last of the ski season, and they embrace each chance to enjoy what may be their final run. At our restaurant, we feed them hints of spring: mashed fava beans with garlic, salt, and pepper served on crostini with a curl of *parmigiano,* or early asparagus, tender and thin, with two fried eggs and a grating of hard cheese from Lombardia. Or *il raviolo,* our handmade pasta, one large pillow the size of a large, flat soup bowl, stuffed with fresh ricotta, spinach, and an egg yolk served with butter and fresh sage. We've filled tall vases with pussy willows, those naked stems taunting warmer weather. And the days *are* warmer, the sun bright, and the sky blue in the face. The sap has begun to run, the signs of sugaring season dotting the edges of forest outside the village. We forgive the balance of cold nights for keeping the old tradition of maple syrup alive.

Caleb and I stave off doldrums by poring over big Michelin maps spread out on the floor in front of the fire, our well-worn Italian guidebooks, dictionaries, and wine compendiums in piles all over the living room. We're planning our spring trip—yes, another attempt to thumb our noses at the longest Vermont season. We leave in ten days for Paris, from where we'll make our way to Torino and then north to the dramatic mountains of Aosta, exploring the sights, tastes, and hospitality of the Piedmont region, where we've never been. We yearn to taste ruby wines in ancient cantinas, take baths at one of the hot springs, visit a couple of cheese farms—whose La Tur, Rocchetta, and Robiola we stock in our cheese case, creamy cheeses made from goat, cow, and sheep's milk, all with a rind blushed with white mold.

We crave an antipasti plate with raw celery and carrots, sautéed eggplant and zucchini, steamed red peppers, all served with *bagna cauda,* a traditional dip made with garlic and anchovies long simmered in butter and olive oil. Or we imagine a deep wine-red risotto made with Barolo, and beef braised in red wine too, with more carrots and celery, the meat so tender. We remember days spent north of Milan on a lake where we ate the first spring asparagus served with the surprise of fried eggs and shaved *parmigiano.*

On the first day of spring as we know it, this twentieth of March, we'll serve that asparagus with two gently fried eggs with *parmigiano,* or *tagliatelle* with shrimp, tomatoes, and black Ligurian olives, or a sauce of artichoke hearts sautéed in white wine. The past two weeks have been crazy with visitors, a strange coincidence of people who are from the Piedmont, or know people who live there. Strange because, though we know no one there, we suddenly have a wealth of names and places to visit. After long talks at our bar regarding the culture of Italian coffee and why the *zucce* (the pumpkins) in Mantova taste different from any other pumpkins in the world, one gentleman from Verona—who now lives in New York—tells us he will secure a room for us at his company's hotel in Torino. And we've met another couple from the city, a wine and food writer and his wife, a food photographer. They make us lists of places to see, eat, visit, and include names of friends in Torino or La Morra with whom we should talk. *Go see the chocolatier in Torino, or tour the Lavazza factory, or the small, artisanal pastaficcie, and meet with the winemaker in Annunziata and talk with his viticulturalist. Compare the modern wines with the classical methods. Eat at the Tre Galline, make a reservation in advance.* In exchange for an espresso, biscotti, and hot food after a ski, they offer us such gems. Then there's the guy who moved away, back in Woodstock for his fortieth birthday, who will call his friends who live outside Torino, who've also eaten at our restaurant, an older couple who have a castle, a vineyard, horses, and one floor devoted to a ballroom. "Wait until you see the ballroom!" he exclaims.

Just two days ago a woman originally from Torino came in. I'll call her Carolina (because she reminds us of Caleb's mother, Carol). She traveled to this country when she was twenty-two and hasn't been back to Italy for many years. Our white vanilla *meringhe* look just like the sweets of her childhood on the corso, and she relishes the scent of the panino Caleb makes her, prosciutto and arugula with olive oil. She and her husband chat with Caleb for over an hour. I listen as I lean into the pastry table shaping *biscotti di dina,* round orange-lemon cookies. Carolina is overcome with memories, the sharing of stories and recipes exchanged, and can hardly take all these thoughts and emotions in at once. She wants to tell us everything, and breathlessly talks of her siblings, her family, a twin sister who died not long ago, a brother who still lives in Torino with his wife and family. She tells us about her mother who's since moved to the seaside, and how she used to send dry goods like pasta, beans, and chocolate to her and her twin when they first came here, when they spoke no English, and life was hard. She asks us to go to her old street in the city where the buildings are of white marble, *yes,* white like the *meringhe,* she says, and will we come back and tell her *all* that we've seen? She'll make us lunch, or dinner, we can stay as long as we like, and she'll teach us all her mother's old recipes. We can lean over her shoulder while she cooks.

She now lives in Danville, Vermont, nearly a two-hour drive from here. We give her two loaves of bread to take with her and she takes my face between her hands and says, "Bread like this is a gift from the mouth of God. I am blessed, and He will bless you."

I feel like we are blessed in these past few weeks—even though the snow falls hard today, the electricity has gone out, and one building contractor for our house can't fit us into his schedule so we'll have to find yet another, this will be the third, and because I can't reach the plowman on the phone I will have to shovel my car out of the driveway. In these past couple of weeks, the restaurant has been filled with life-lines intersecting: each junction allows the flow to change course. We've been given a gift to include these new people whose lives and stories are now part of ours, simply because of these chance meetings, and their experiences will change us, move us forward. Days will move forward. Though time seems to keep pulling us back into winter, it only *seems* to be regressive, because eventually the electricity will return, spring will come, and we will travel to Paris and northwest Italy. Like stepping into a page of a storybook, we'll go to Carolina's childhood street. We'll eat fanciful chocolates, walk through vineyards tasting new wines, and fall asleep in featherbeds with big white goosedown comforters that look like mountains of fresh snow.

Time won't stop. A page will turn. Eventually, we'll return to Vermont. Physics will play a role here too, the lines of time, circumstance, and chance rolling and intersecting. Two places on a map, thousands of miles apart, will become one and the same. Because of our history and love for another language, food, landscape, our notions and feelings about home will somehow encompass both locations. We'll leave part of ourselves in Italy, and come back to the part of ourselves in Vermont. We will be blessed by this largess. I imagine us like Carolina, moved by the crossing of her life in Vermont with her childhood in Italy, and I know our true fortune lies in our return to a country in which we used to live, in which we learned to love, and—anyway we look at it—whether we're headed east or west, we get to come home again.

roman holiday

WE WERE TWO: Caleb and I. Usually Caleb and I work side by side, whether in the kitchen or behind the wine bar or at tableside, but that day we were in Rome. We'd returned to Italy together for food, for adventure, for an experience, for love. Traveling is like falling in love—weightless and giddy, you believe anything is possible. We'd come back after a long time away to retrieve a part of ourselves, to retrace the first year of our marriage. We'd lived in Italy then. It's a gift to experience anew a place that has grown familiar through memory, to see a place again as if for the first time.

On a Tuesday morning in April, we flew into Rome, the sun hot and high, the surf ruffling the coast as the ground rose up beneath us, the landscape so different from the place we'd just left—snow-covered hills and mudseason valleys of Vermont. The long winter had made us greedy for the shift of climate and psyche this visit would provide. My anticipation of our trip had grown out of memories I had of earlier stays in Rome, in Italy, had been fed by my nostalgia for a place that had informed my life as only unforgettable events do—like an earthquake, like a great love.

Caleb and I stood for forty minutes on the commuter train from the Leonardo da Vinci airport to the city, our car filled with other husbands and wives returning, visiting, coming home. The women in knee-length skirts and silk scarves, the men in tweeds and caps, all looking strung-out and eager, as if they all wanted a smoke but suffered the ride in the glare of a small no-smoking sign at the end of the car. A few distracted themselves with opening windows. The air rolled in as we watched black lambs romp in small track-edged gardens replete with lean-tos and grapevine pergolas. It seemed nothing could take our eyes away until we came to the Roman wall embracing the city. Tall and crumbling, it heralded our arrival.

We would have Rome for only twenty-four hours; Caleb and I would see our small window of time here like the bittersweet meter set on an illicit rendezvous. We got off the train wistful at the time already passed, expectant for the time that remained, and we walked straight into the thick chaos of Rome, our eyes raised up to the light and the baroque faces of buildings. We were dizzy. There are palm trees in Rome; I'd forgotten about the palm trees. Squadrons of vespas, small motorscooters locals use to get around, buzzed and sped up and down the streets. Women riding them were dressed in high heels, short skirts, sheer stockings. Everyone around us still wore heavy wool coats and scarves in April; we'd already stripped down to our T-shirts—crazy Americans. We sat outside the *tavola calda,* a restaurant and buffet, eating wonderfully flat, thin Roman pizza in the sun at a table covered with a red cloth, special clips fastened to its hem to reign it in when the wind blows. From the *tavola calda* I could see the windows of the Hotel Miami, where we stayed our last visit here. A pretty, chic kind of place, so different from the first hotel in Rome we'd ever stayed in, a dingy spot near the train station, the kind the guidebooks warn of prostitutes and pickpockets.

Another time, I came to Rome in order to leave. That time, Caleb and I stayed at the Hotel Suisse on the sixth floor, brocade wallpaper and sinks in every bedroom, a charming black cat who follows visitors in and out of the narrow elevator. That visit to the city was prelude to a separation: I was returning to the United States for work; Caleb was staying in Italy for his apprenticeship with a baker outside of Florence. On that night at the Hotel Suisse we went out to Tullio, the restaurant of *la dolce vita* fame, because we wanted to know something of what Fellini knew, and Giulietta Masina, and Sophia Loren, and Marcello Mastroianni. We ate a classical Roman meal of roast pork and roasted potatoes at tables pinched close alongside Japanese businessmen and older, wealthy-looking couples on honeymoons for marriages most likely not their first.

But this April our return was my fourth time in Rome, this was still my only marriage, and in many ways it felt like another stop on my first honeymoon trip.

From our lunch of pizza and reminiscence, Caleb and I took on small sections of the city, our particular locations of sentimental memory and longing, some well-traveled tourist sites, others odd corners we'd happened upon: the Spanish Steps, the Pantheon, the Trevi Fountain, the octagonal interior of St. Agnes in the Piazza Navona, then Piazza Barberini, and the haunting Crypt of the Cappuccini. The Spanish Steps were open and full of portrait artists, teenagers, and gypsies. A gypsy man stood with his son, one hand held out for change and the other being chewed on by their puppy. Across the way a small gypsy girl, a toddler, sat eating a prosciutto sandwich given to her by a group of parochial schoolgirls.

At the Trevi Fountain, designed by Nicola Salvi in the early 1700s and also of Fellini fame, we took a rest. The fountain, carved into the side of a plain white stone building with small high windows, swelled out from the building, a mass of mythical sea creatures and cascades of splashing water. A French girl traveling alone wearing dark sparkly blue pants asked Caleb to take her photograph. Then a Japanese family asked me to take theirs. Later, Caleb obliged four young German women who posed with crossed legs, lit cigarettes, and smiles for the camera. I wondered what it was about us, why we were chosen and trusted with small, new cameras shiny with first use. Were our expressions so open? Did that make us unmistakably American? (When in Italy, I shamefully admit, I no longer want to be American.)

Perhaps the Trevi Fountain had opened our faces this way. Trevi moves constantly, a blur of people and sculpture suspended in the moment before the sea horses reach their own height, when the tourists need to return to their hotels, or when the water must reach up only to fall again. I think this movement draws me back to Trevi. It somehow stops time on the wave of anticipation; offering a comforting reliability in its ebb and flow, without disappointment, hurt, or regret. Intimate and hopeful, forever on the rise, Trevi showers down on the wish for luck reflected in all those coins at the bottom of the fountain pool.

After Caleb and I checked into our *pensione,* we went out into the night in search of food. Around the corner we found a round-the-clock pastry shop, its glass cases packed with biscotti, little ricotta cakes, fried doughnuts stuffed with cream, *cornetti,* those horns of pastry filled with almond or apricot. We took away a tray full of treats carefully wrapped in pale pink paper and tied with grosgrain ribbon to tide us over until dinner. The scent of pastry sugar wrapped around the block as we did, triggering the past: Caleb and I had once lived north of here in a town with a *zuccherificio,* a beet sugar refinery, I had forgotten about the *zuccherificio.* On a Rome street at night I was reminded that for me the scent of Italy hints of something sweet and burning.

That night, we ate a traditionally Roman dinner. As soon as we were seated, plates of antipasti arrived: little white beans in garlic, olive oil, salt, and pepper. In Italian, they're called *perline,* or little pearls, only grown outside of Rome in the region of Lazio. Dried sausage, bruschetta, and a tuna-potato puree prepared with onions and capers filled our plates. A simple white wine from the owner's vinyard on a patch of land near the sea. Like a harbor dotted with boats at day's end, our table began to fill. For pasta we ate potato gnocchi, and *cacio e pepe,* guitar-string tagliatelle with young sheep's cheese and ground pepper, Roman macaroni and cheese. Veal meatballs stuffed with raisins and pine nuts, filets of beef rolled around mortadella, the Italian bologna studded with pistachios and peppercorns. Every taste a treasure. Large bowls brimming with greens and fresh tomatoes arrived, and when we could barely finish our salad course, those plates were replaced with a platter of *ciambelline,* ring-shaped anise-and-almond cookies to be dipped in a sweet red wine. All that was left of the evening was sleep.

The next morning we headed on foot to St. Peter's Cathedral. Already, the city was preparing the piazza with aisles and chairs for Easter Mass with the pope, cleaning the facade for all the Easter pilgrims. Caleb and I were dumb with amazement as we walked through the heavy bronze doors into St. Peter's. I had seen this church three times, Caleb four, and still we were stunned. There was the famous gold sculpture of Death's skeleton with scythe in hand flying above us under an impossible undulating curtain of marble. At the top of the nave beckoned the rising ebony chair of Christ, empty, aloft on a golden cloud of smoke bursting into the even golder rays of a white dove. I kept thinking of the analogy Caleb had given me: our own village of Woodstock, Vermont—all its brick and white clapboard houses and storefronts, the oval town green, the narrow covered bridge crossing the Ottaquechee River—would fit *within* this cathedral, an image I liked. "This is where High Street would be," Caleb pointed to an area of marble floor.

Twenty-four hours runs fast, and I ran fast through the Vatican Museum, my destination the Sistine Chapel. Caleb and I had parted, so I could see the restored *Last Judgment* and he could walk the streets in search of bakeries and new delicacies. At the museum, I ducked and dove through crowds of people, pushed through years of antiquity, mostly Greek and Roman sculpture; my pace slowed slightly as I walked through halls lined with red and blue tapestries so intricate they could be line drawings, and I stopped briefly in the medieval map gallery awash in blue and green wall paintings.

"This is where we're going this afternoon," I said softly to no one in particular, pointing to Lago Trasimeno and Castiglion F. No. Suddenly self-conscious, I wondered how I'd known just where to stop in this long hall, just where to point, as if everything one did here in this city was somehow divined by magic. But as magical as Italy is, this was no wizard's trick, I simply chose the place I knew best as home.

Later, having woven through and gotten lost in the Raphael rooms, I wound through the rooms another time. Then, suddenly I was there, like a surprise. *The Last Judgment.* Finally revealed after several years of restoration, a sea of blue with a miraculous tumble of bodies and muscles appeared before me. The gray skin of one of the condemned hung as if by a fingertip, a focal point in this gargantuan fresco, the eyes and mouth were most cavernous. A hungry man.

Above me, the chapel ceiling caught my eye—God creating Adam, Eve rising from Adam's rib, *The Fall of Man* panels lined by sybils and profits. There was ancient Cumaea's marvelous and haggard profile, and the broad articulated back of the Libyan Sybil as she looked over her shoulder. I saw myself making the same gesture all the way to the train station. Looking behind me, my eyes grabbing at the city, I felt both pursued by Rome herself and by my own desire to be back in this country, nearly caught by the melancholy of being one step closer to leaving again. The first day of my return had already passed.

Leaving Rome is like leaving a friend who delights but exhausts you. Caleb and I met again on the train. We sat together quietly, our knees touching, the passenger seats so close. A mix of urban and pastoral images flitted by like old-fashioned moving pictures. We took it all in with a picnic lunch of rolls with strong cheese and delicate pine nut *meringhe,* treats Caleb had found for us on his own tour of the city. A rich perfume of air blew in as the train hurtled forward, sending me back to the town in which I once lived, then back to my first stay in Italy, and in through the window came the sweet, smoky scent of sugar.

at the villa ruccellai

THE CITY OF PRATO IS ONE of the largest in Tuscany, perhaps second only to Florence. It's a working city built on woolen factories, looms, and the dexterous and calloused hands of weavers. Reaching the edges of the city is like having one foot on shore and the other in the ocean's foam: the country quickly laps at your feet. To the north and east rise the gently sleeping slopes of the *Appennini,* old villas, ancient olive groves, and vineyards washing over the hillsides.

The Villa Ruccellai is hidden in a hillside olive grove. From terraced rows of gnarled olive trees a path emerges to lead followers through a pair of iron gates into a courtyard nestled within an enclave of mature trees: larch, umbrella pine, cypress. Up from the yard, at the top of a series of wide stairs looms the old house—an odd but somehow harmonious assemblage of period styles, with a few architectural follies thrown in and patterns of rough local stone and ochre stucco absorbing the light. The courtyard surrounds a reflecting pool guarded by two white geese who wait for the pool to be drained of winter-stained water, refilled by the spring rushing and gurgling down the hillside, and reopened for summer holidays when the youngest Ruccellai children will jump, dive, and splash, drenched with the memories of all their ancestors.

If you go, arrive in the late afternoon, when the spring sun has traveled three-quarters across the sky, when the light is clear and hallowed in the new greens pushing through earth in the garden, in the deep pink buds necklacing the trees. At the entrance to the villa, two dogs might meet you, one, a chocolate and vanilla spaniel, may bark ferociously, pretending to test you, but, as you move closer, you see he is mostly blind and a little lame. At the top of the stairs, another, smaller dog sleeps on a soft cushion in a wicker chair. She is called *Trovatella,* foundling, of no specific lineage other than loyalty and good humor.

Cristina will give you your keys when you sign in, in an office filled with books and black-and-white photographs of various Ruccellai over the past hundred and some years. She'll take you to your room, one right off the main hall, or one that takes you winding back into a warren of guest quarters. A small, hand-drawn placard marks each room with a number and name—like number "Three, *Il Prete,*" The Priest, or number "Seven, *Due Corvi,*" Two Ravens. You are mesmerized by pen and ink drawings of a pair of hands making shadow puppets in the name of each room—there's the prelate in his wide-brimmed black hat, and over there two blackbirds in flight—and you feel welcomed by the whimsy at the center of each plaque, a detail resulting perhaps from a late-night dinner party followed by a game of charades or cards.

Enter your room and lie down on the antique bed, float on the faded chintz coverlet for a moment and catch your breath. Notice the old chintz-covered armchair, the majestic walnut desk, a small vase of flowers left just so. You feel as is you've come to visit a good friend in the country, and it's almost summer.

Evening in such old, gracious houses like the Villa Ruccellai call for quiet reading or thoughtful discussion in the comfortable *salotto* before going to dinner. The fire has been laid, started by invisible hands, with logs at least eight feet in length. After all, it's still spring, the night may turn cool. Over on the bar sit several bottles of Ruccellai wine, glasses, a bottle opener. Have a glass, or two, and admire the four grand portraits of the nineteenth-century Ruccellai and the eighteenth-century family tableau. Look up at that family piece over the fireplace, see the brown-and-white spaniel sitting near the mistress's chair. Have the Ruccellai had these spotted spaniels for so many hundreds of years? Do some things in this country really never change?

An entire wall of hand-painted botanicals in the *salotto* brings delight and surprise. You are told it is the work of the current mistress Giovanna's grandmother. In the breakfast room, someone has painted a series of border panels depicting the elegant, social life of Newport, Rhode Island, in summer over a century ago. Did this same grandmother stand on some sort of tall scaffolding in a brightly colored and fringed shawl with her hair tied in a loose bun and paint these scenes as well? And why Newport in this small country post in a foreign land so far away?

The Villa Ruccellai has a story. In the early 1920s, two American sisters from Newport came to the continent for their European tour. Slightly wild, they kicked up their heels across France, Spain, and Italy, dancing the Charleston in beaded flapper dresses, wearing smart cloche hats, and smoking French cigarettes in gilded cafés over coffee or champagne. One of these beauties married an Italian count, the young Signor Ruccellai. It dawns on you that two of the portraits in the *salotto,* painted in browns and blacks and stiff smiles, are of the sisters' proper Bostonian parents. In retrospect, they are unmistakably American.

After a first glass of wine, Giovanna Rucellai and her husband might take you through the gardens before they're off to the opera in Prato—*La Boheme* plays tonight. In the back garden, the ducks mate near the circular fountain in a whirlwind of noise and chasing. Through the open doors of the *limonaia,* the lemon house, you see the late-afternoon light still dappling the heavy green foliage inside. The lemon trees, three hundred years old, thick-trunked with curling tangled arms, live in five-hundred-year-old terra-cotta pots sturdy and stained with lichen. Each spring the trees long to be washed, and watered, then wheeled out to their elegant and ancient positions along the garden footpath where they await the warmer months like bright dowagers at a champagne cocktail party.

The changing light slips down into the city, leaving the country in the lavender-blue cloak of dusk. You walk out onto the road meandering through stepped olive groves and stride toward dinner, a small country restaurant nearby. The 7:30 train from Prato to Bologna whistles by, and across the way, in one of many private garden plots lining the tracks, you glimpse a figure harvesting spring lettuces for an evening meal. The flowering apple trees perfume the air, spiced now with the scent of wood smoke from the trattoria just ahead.

You arrive at eight o'clock, just as they're opening. The tables are set, the dining room empty. Your table awaits. Just outside the front door of the restaurant stands the grill, fired and ready. Two men dressed in chef's whites linger at the entrance waiting for the first order. One takes a smoke. The restaurant is built into the side of a hillock and as you go to your table you see two sides of the dining room framed by a spring-fed grotto, and you understand the establishment is aptly named *La Fontana*, the fountain. Within minutes, the dining room begins to fill with other diners, their conversation and laughter, and you imagine this trattoria has always been here, has always been like this, and that fifty years ago someone else sat in your seat and prepared to eat. Then, a *telefonino* rings: the woman with a little red cell phone sitting next to you answers her call, and you realize it hasn't always been quite like *this*. Yet, even this small interruption of contemporary life cannot take away from the deep sense of history and romance of being in this place at this time.

Eat of springtime. Order the *insalata di carciofi* made of artichoke hearts sautéed in white wine, arugula, and shaved *parmigiano*. Then have the *Bistecca Fiorentina,* quickly seared on both sides then seasoned with hot olive oil and crushed peppercorns, or dine on *pollo al mattone,* chicken pressed into the grill by large bricks, the skin infused with olive wood smoke. Always have the plate of mixed gilled vegetables: tomatoes, zucchini, onions, eggplant. Drink from a bottle of local red wine, tart and fruity on your tongue.

On the walk back to the villa, your stomach is as full as the sky, starless and moonless, as clouds roll in. The air feels brisk as you walk by cars parked along the grove road, and it takes a minute to see the fog on the windows, to understand. The grove road serves as a late-night lover's lane. It is, after all, springtime, desire is still simply desire. You laugh with your companions at the surprise and beauty of it all as you reach for your sweetheart's hand. When you return to the villa you fall into bed, cocooned by flowered linens, blanketed by a dream in which you stay at the Villa Ruccellai for another day, maybe a week, the week running into a month, the month into seasons, until a year has passed and you realize you've forgotten a reason to leave, and the Villa Ruccellai has miraculously become home.

the little world of the past

NOT SO MANY SPRINGTIMES AGO, Caleb and I had driven
through Italy to Switzerland and back again into Italy
where we arrived at a small hotel: the Stella d'Italia on the Italian edge of
the Lago di Lugano. Our winter in Vermont had been long and bleak, and
we were looking for a respite from the cold, the snow, the gray. We needed
the balm of sunshine, the color and flavors of spring to lift us from the
drowsy, stir-crazy days of our longest, most relentless season.

At the hotel, which was located in the small town of San Mamete just past
the city of Lugano, the air smelled clean and slightly salty. The old, pale yellow stucco building sat at the edge of the water. French doors and balconies
overlooked the lake and the mountains rising from its banks. Ducks swam
and flew about, and the green foothills dressed in early foliage were backed
by the snow-capped glaciers of the Alps. Though the lake in Lugano is tight
and narrow, it appeared more expansive, like how I've always imagined a
seaside resort on the French Riviera. I remembered scenes from films like
Rebecca or *To Catch a Thief* as we drove the car back and forth and up the
steep mountainside; we thought of Grace Kelly and Cary Grant in their convertible, her chic chiffon headscarf and sunglasses, his easy, witty banter of
an era gone by.

The sky was brilliant and clear there that day, the spring sun so bright it
hurt my eyes to look at the mountains. When I put my own sunglasses on,
I felt like we'd driven through some strange window of celluloid, and this

was all an intriguing, glamorous movie. Exhilarated by the light and the beauty of the water, we parked our car in a small lot overlooking the lake, even the cars had a view. As we walked down the street with our bags in hand to the entrance of the hotel we couldn't stop smiling.

Once inside the hotel's foyer, we soaked up the cool and quiet shade. Old photographs of the Stella covered the walls. Mixed in were black-and-white images of the couple who'd originally opened the hotel back at the turn of the century, when travelers would come waterside for their health. Carefully handwritten copies of poems were framed too, the work of the poet Antonio Fogazzaro who stayed there in 1910. The gentleman at the reception desk spoke five languages—French, Italian, English, Spanish, and German. *"Guten Tag,"* he said when we arrived, mistaking us for German. *"Buon Giorno,"* we answered. "Hello," he then said when he took our passports to process our reservation. Then, just like in an old-fashioned hotel in Nice or Monte Carlo, the porter, dressed in a dark red jacket and matching hat trimmed with gold braiding, showed us to our room, which itself was elegant and antiquated. I wondered, as I often do, if I wasn't born at the wrong time, feeling my senses firing as if with recognition of my surroundings, or if Caleb and I could have been here, or someplace like here, long ago, feeling that our life was somehow divided into prisms of déjà vu. Cut-glass wall sconces lighted our guest room. A small sitting area arranged at the foot of the bed consisted of two old chairs dressed in a worn, soft olive-green velvet, a coffee table, and a small writing desk beneath a gold-framed mirror on the wall. Over on the door a gold tassle hung from the knob. There was something easy about the room, in the setting, that made it all feel like home. I could imagine us setting up residence here like Signor Fogazzaro. Or maybe this was just a dream of home.

The light on the water brought us down from our room. To be in the sun, we ate lunch under the rose bower arcade outfitted with lamps ready for lighting at dusk. Our table on the terrace overlooked the water, and we could hear waves lapping as a speedboat passed by. Caleb ordered lunch: we started with two plates of spring asparagus covered with fried eggs and shaved *parmigiano—asparagi alla Milanese*—and a mixed antipasti plate served with a liver terrine. We savored each taste, the flavors like spring itself; we ate these first two plates slowly, our faces turned toward the sun, as we wanted the meal to linger. While we craved these spring flavors, we didn't want this lunch to be like spring, fleeting and all too short.

As if the waiter—dressed in his white jacket, white shirt, and black tie even at lunch—knew our thoughts, he waited until our plates were empty and our faces drowsy and then he reappeared with a plate of fresh mozzarella and basil, prosciutto and melon and a *carpaccio* of duck breast. We drank a deep ruby Barbera. Then there were *tortellone* in a sauce of butter and sage, risotto primavera, Spring's rice complimented by shrimp, and fresh papardelle with tomatoes, cream, and *funghi porcini,* and a fresh fettucine with four cheeses. As we'd hoped, our lunch was long and the sun delightfully hot. Already we began to feel a cure from our long, cold winter at home. We left our table in the sun only to go into Lugano for a walk along the lake, through flower gardens where tulips, magnolias, and begonias bloomed, where early leaves adorned the muscular, stunted branches of lime trees. Families and pairs of young lovers promenaded along the boardwalk; small groups of paddleboats drifted about sending out ripples of laughter. Again, I felt thrust back in time to those polished films of the 1940s and 1950s. The fashion of the times was different, but the social dance in the city's gardens remained the same.

The sun's warmth felt incredible, but we weren't used to the intensity. We felt too hot too soon. To cool down we headed for the one museum in Lugano, just across the street from the promenade, and found ourselves surrounded by a retrospective of Modigliani drawings, all his women long-faced and with modest awkward bodies. Looking at the last drawing of the exhibit, we realized we were hungry again (was it the thin form of the model in the frame that made us want to eat, or that we could eat just because we wanted to?). We left the museum and circled the lake again, shaded by linden trees, to find the gelato maker with the red-and-white awning-covered cart we'd passed on the boardwalk earlier. We ate our gelato quickly before it melted, Caleb's from a waffle cone, mine in a paper cup with a small plastic spoon. Caleb had three flavors: *bacio,* a kiss (chocolate hazelnut), lemon, and coffee, while I ate only one, *nocciola,* plain hazelnut. The gelato was so smooth, almost like tasting cream, different than the more milky texture of our American ice cream. As we looked out across the water back toward the hotel, the light danced on the waves as if a thousand stars had just fallen from the sky.

We drove back to San Mamete, stopping along the winding road to park across the street from the narrow cobblestone path. Leading each other by the hand we walked up to a church built on a rocky promontory. It looked as though it sat on nothing but air. Its bell tower rose above the roofs of the scabbed-together hillside houses. Inside, the chapel walls were all blue and gold, painted with lustrous faces of saints and angels barely visible in the scant light making its way in. Our eyes were hungry. For months, we'd seen nothing but fields of blank snow and the skeletal grays and browns of naked trees. We couldn't take in enough of this landscape, the slant of a roof, an arched doorway, the colors of fertile earth, moving water, sky. Of course, in sympathy, our bodies were hungry too: we bought cookies at the local grocery, *amaretti* and *lingue di gatto,* "cat's tongues" (narrow, oblong sugar cookies), to placate our expanding appetites.

Our craving to see and experience everything in this little corner of northern Italy quickly gave way to the drowsy, opiate lull of late afternoon. We returned to our room, tumbled into bed, and fell into weary sleep. After working long hard days in our kitchen at the restaurant, we were overcome by the pleasant fatigue of being on holiday, far away from the concerns of home.

Dinner in the dining room brought us around. We sat in fine, mustard-colored silk-covered chairs and the tables were laid with the smoothest of white linens. Families and couples filled the room, everyone's face lit by the warm glow of candles. I wore a dress and my grandmother's pearls. She too was a traveler, making a pilgrimage somewhere every year after my grandfather died. I remember photographs of her wearing white gloves, a pill box hat, these same pearls—in places like Dublin, Lisbon, Rome.

My inheritance from my grandmother consisted of these pearls and one other trinket, a medallion she bought in Rome that had been blessed by the pope and engraved with the date she was there in that city, "April 9, 1962, Roma." She had given the medallion to me long before she died, and as a small child I used to pretend that the medal bore the date and place of my birth—my desire for an exotic personal history having started young. Translated from the Gaelic, my name Deirdre means "one who wanders." Perhaps the pearls and medallion are not all my grandmother bequeathed to me.

I looked at Caleb across the table: he looked relaxed and sleepy, his cheeks lightly sunburned. Here we were on an April night on the Lago di Laguno. We were completely in the present eating our *risotto alla Milanese* and roasted trout. But it might have been any other time, like forty years earlier on another April evening when my grandmother could have sat down beside us.

Later that night, we went out into the small Piazza Roma across from the hotel and walked through the narrow, climbing streets to nowhere in particular, just out for a stroll, to take in the cool air and the sights of this small town. Some of the streets were lighted, some darkened with shadows. The cafe was full of music, card playing, and drinking. An elegant but faded house at the back of the piazza, one with two baroque arched balconies, had a second-story window illuminated by a grand chandelier. What could we not see—a ballroom or music room filled with dancers? We had just been talking of pianos, and I imagined there must be a piano up on that second floor. We had nowhere to go, no time to be back, so we stood in each other's arms in a quiet corner of the piazza and waited for someone to begin playing.

Easter morning, the sun brilliant again. From the balcony of our room we watched a woman walk her cat on a leash in the courtyard of the hotel. Earlier, I had touched the Easter lilies decorating the downstairs lobby to see if they were real. Their dusky scent clung to my fingertips, the smell peculiar to both life and death. I spent all morning getting ready to do nothing but sit on the balcony and look at the view. After a hot shower I dressed and walked with Caleb to the Bar Roma for a cappuccino so hot it scalded my tongue, and then we headed to the *panificio* for a small bag of pastry. The bakery made it's own *colomba*, an Easter sweet bread in the shape of a dove studded with whole almonds and crystallized sugar. We asked if we could see the kitchen and meet the baker, whose name we found out was Franco.

The view from Franco's white-tiled kitchen was better than any other. Every morning while he worked, he saw the sun rise over the lake and mountains. While Franco shaped loaves of bread, flour covering his hands and the butcher block, he treated us to cake. Franco was delighted that Caleb wanted to take his photograph next to the open window—the dough mixer, ovens, and worktables off to the side. This is how we'd remember Easter Sunday. We paused then to listen to the ducks calling and watched them flying low over the water again.

When we went back to the hotel, we saw that the cat on the leash didn't want to be pulled out of the lime tree and his quack of displeasure reminded us of the ducks. We ate breakfast under our rose bower. A boat with a quiet motor went by and the church bells rang for Easter.

I could see fish darting through the water. Were they trout? Two people rowed in a thin skull slicing the placid water. In the distance, the voices of churchgoers greeted one another, *"Auguri,"* Best wishes. We had already packed up our bags and the car, but had gone back to the terrace once more. We hung over the railing, reluctant to leave. We had found that romance like a rare souvenir that travelers hope to capture when they step off a boat or plane, a particular sort of romance sometimes found in tucked-away places: the antiquity, the beauty, the flavor, a place almost unchanged.

We drove away from the lake in the full sun and headed up into the mountains to find a village restaurant for Easter lunch. Then we continued on over to the other side where the map showed we would wind down to Lago di Como. *Auguri* to the lady and her tangled cat, *Auguri* to Franco and his sweet doves, and to each other, so that we might return.

Asparagi alla Milanese

ASPARAGUS WITH FRIED EGGS

THIS IS THE DISH to eat on a warm June day, outside in the sunshine, with a basket of crusty rolls and a glass of cold beer or crisp Lugana from the shores of Lake Garda. It is simple and satisfying, especially if you are blessed with your own asparagus patch, or a neighbor who has one, as freshly cut asparagus is worlds beyond that which must travel far to reach your local produce purveyor. This recipe is for one person, but simply multiply to suit the number dining at your table.

> 2-inch-thick bundle fresh asparagus
> 2 to 3 tablespoons butter
> Salt and freshly ground pepper
> 2 eggs
> *Parmigiano-Reggiano*

Wash and trim the asparagus of any tough, fibrous ends. If the asparagus is quite large, you can peel the bottom half of the shoots to remove the tough outer layers. In a large skillet with a lid bring ½ inch of lightly salted water to the boil and lay in the asparagus. Cover and cook until the bottoms of the shoots are just tender when poked with a fork. (Very slender asparagus will cook in 6 to 8 minutes, and fat shoots can take up to 15 minutes, but you must pay attention, as overcooked asparagus is limp and all wrong for this dish.) Using the lid to hold back the asparagus, pour off the water. Melt a little butter in the pan with the asparagus and season with salt and pepper. Remove the asparagus immediately to the serving plate(s) and quickly wipe out the skillet with a paper towel if there are bits of asparagus remaining in the pan. Restore the heat under the pan to medium low, melt a little more butter, crack the eggs into the pan, season with a little salt and pepper and gently cook them to your preferred state of doneness. (At a café, this dish would be served sunny-side up or over easy so the broken yolks provide a dressing for the asparagus.) Slide the cooked eggs directly on top of the asparagus. Top with a blanket of freshly grated *Parmigiano-Reggiano* and serve immediately.

Crostini con le Fave

CROSTINI WITH FAVA BEAN SPREAD

FRESH FAVA BEANS are a wonder to behold and they make for fabulous eating. For many Italians, favas represent one of the best things their *cucina* has to offer: fresh fava beans, pecorino, and a glass of wine. Imagine warm spring days, sunshine and the smell of the grass, the trees putting out their new growth. Imagine shelling fresh favas, finishing your meal by the open window . . .

This spread for eating atop *crostini* provides a way to increase enjoyment of favas, as fresh favas can be hard to come by. I know that if I had only a few, I would be reluctant to share. Makes about 2 cups of the spread.

> 1 cup dried fava beans, rinsed and soaked overnight in plenty
>   of cold water
> 3 garlic cloves, peeled and smashed
> Extra-virgin olive oil
> Salt and freshly ground pepper

Remove the skins from the soaked beans. Place the beans in a pot large enough to cover them with plenty of water (the water should cover the beans by about 2 inches) and cook gently with the garlic cloves until tender. Drain the beans and the garlic and allow to cool for at least 30 minutes.

Put the beans in a flat-bottomed bowl. Add a little extra-virgin olive oil and salt and pepper and mash some of the beans with a potato masher or a big wooden spoon. The consistency should be spreadable, but still chunky, even with some whole beans remaining. Taste the spread and correct the oil, salt, and pepper if necessary. Spread on thick slices of bread and serve. Don't skimp.

Insalata di Carciofi

Arugula Salad with Artichokes and Parmigiano

Fresh, cold arugula is easy to eat in quantity. If the arugula available to you comes with its dirty roots attached, cut off the roots—leaving most of the stem attached to the leaf—and submerge the arugula in a bowl of cold water and agitate it gently to clean it. You may need to do this a couple of times to remove all the dirt, but the arugula will appreciate the cold bath and become crisper if you let it rest in the water after the rinsing. Dry it well, either using a salad spinner or by gently wrapping the greens in a dish-towel, shaking them carefully, and letting the whole package rest in the fridge while you prepare the other ingredients. Serve this salad with very crusty country bread. Serves 2.

    2 to 3 tablespoons olive oil
    1 cup artichoke hearts (use *either* canned or jarred, marinated or
        in oil, drained and cut into quarters or your own prepared
        fresh artichoke hearts cut into pinky-sized slices)
    ⅓ cup white wine or water
    Fresh arugula, enough so that once tossed each plate will be filled,
        but not overflowing
    Vinaigrette (any simple bottled or homemade one will do)
    Salt and freshly ground pepper
    Parmigiano-Reggiano, a chunk for grating

Warm a skillet or saucepan over medium-low heat for about 1 minute, then add the oil and turn the pan to coat the bottom. Add the artichokes, toss them in the oil, and then add the white wine or water and let simmer.

Dress the arugula with the vinaigrette and put it on the plates.

Poke the thickest part of the artichoke slices: they should feel tender. Season with a little salt and pepper and let the liquid reduce so that the pieces can sauté briefly in the last bit of oil. Place the artichokes over the dressed arugula. Grate a light snowfall of *Parmigiano-Reggiano* over the salads and serve.

Carabaccia

POTATO AND ONION SOUP WITH FRESH PEAS

WHILE MAKING this soup with spring peas, imagine a rainy day in the fall when the days are beginning to be cold more than they are warm. You return home after a long day of work, and perhaps you are too tired and distracted to compose and prepare a whole meal for yourself or anyone else in your household. But if you're lucky, or at least foresighted enough, you can simply go to the freezer for this soup and put it on the stove to warm up while you go about all the little chores of transition and homecoming.

This is an easy soup to prepare. It is definitely a peasant soup, and very satisfying. The potatoes should be waxy potatoes (which is to say, not a mealy baking potato like a Russet or Idaho). It is not necessary to peel them. I recommend making the soup at least a day before you serve it, but you can get away with serving it fresh from the pot, as long as the soup has enough time to cook very thoroughly. This recipe makes a lot, because soup made in quantity turns out better than soup made for only a few. And it seems to me that soup should always be made to feed many. Soup for few seems so . . . paltry. If it's more than you need, call some friends up—right now!—or freeze the remainder for another day. Serves 8 to 10.

  4 cups chicken stock and/or water, plus extra water
  2 to 3 tablespoons olive oil
  2 to 3 tablespoons butter
  2 medium to large yellow onions, diced small
  8 to 9 cups diced potatoes (scrubbed well, but not peeled)

Salt and freshly ground pepper
4 cups fresh, frozen, or canned (drained and rinsed) peas
Parmigiano-Reggiano, a chunk for grating
Extra-virgin olive oil

Heat the chicken stock or fresh water in a saucepan till it is just steaming. In a large soup pot, heat the oil and butter and add the diced onions, stirring well to coat them. Let the onions soften and brown just slightly over medium heat.

Add the potatoes to the pot, along with some salt and pepper, and again stir everything around. Add enough warmed stock and/or water to cover the potatoes by about 2 inches. (If you have stock left over, keep it handy. The soup may need thinning later.) Bring the soup to a gentle simmer, cover the pot, and let cook until the potatoes are tender, about 30 to 40 minutes. (To check, use the back of a spoon to mash a piece of potato against the side of the pot. It should mash easily.)

Add the peas, bring the soup back to a simmer, and cook the soup for 8 to 10 more minutes.

This next step can be done by hand or with a blender: Either mash some of the potatoes and peas against the pot by using a wooden spoon or a potato masher, or puree about ⅓ of the soup in the blender. (*Careful:* The soup is hot. Set the blender lid on allowing a slight gap for steam to escape and cover the lid with a kitchen towel; puree small amounts at a time; and use short pulses or low speeds at first to keep the soup at bay. If you are serving the soup the next day, simply let it cool in the refrigerator before pureeing.) Return the blended portion to the pot and stir well. The soup should not be too thick. (It's not porridge.) Add some leftover stock or more water if it seems too thick. Taste the soup and correct the salt and pepper.

Ladle into bowls. Grate fresh *Parmigiano-Reggiano* onto each serving, drizzle a little extra-virgin olive oil over top, and serve.

Penne con Asparagi

PENNE WITH ASPARAGUS

THIS IS THE DISH to make when last-minute dinner guests show up or you realize that you have less asparagus than you thought. *Penne Rigate Regine* are the preferred size and shape—and one of the most versatile—so stock up when you find them. For this recipe, the asparagus cooks at the same time as the pasta, making for a brief preparation. Keep in mind: When draining the pasta, don't drain it completely, as a little water on the *penne* will help make the finished dish properly saucy. Serves 4 as a *primo*.

  1 cup freshly grated *Parmigiano-Reggiano* or *Grana Padano*, plus extra to
     pass at the table
  2-inch bundle fresh asparagus
  4½ cups *Penne Rigate Regine*
  2 to 3 tablespoons butter or extra-virgin olive oil
  Salt and freshly ground pepper
  Chicken stock or water
  Extra-virgin olive oil

Bring salted water to a boil for the pasta.
Grate the cheese and set aside.
Wash the asparagus and trim the toughest fibers from the base of the stalks. Slice the spears very thinly (as thick as a nickel) at a sharp diagonal to just below the tip, leaving the tips whole.
Pre-warm a serving bowl with a little of the boiling water.
Put the pasta into the boiling water.

Place the butter or oil in a skillet or saucepan over medium heat. Add the sliced asparagus, a few pinches of salt and pepper, and a few tablespoons of water or chicken stock to the heated oil or melted butter. Cover the pan and cook the asparagus briskly, adding a little splash of additional water to the saucepan if it starts to dry out before the asparagus is cooked.

Stir the pasta and shake the saucepan: if both are cooking briskly, the *penne* and the asparagus will be ready at the same time. Pour out the water used to warm your serving bowl. When the pasta is al dente, drain and toss it together in the serving bowl with the asparagus, the cheese, and extra-virgin olive oil if needed to keep the dish from being too dry. Adjust the seasoning and serve.

Risotto al Limone

RISOTTO WITH LEMON

ONE SPRING WE STAYED at a house on Monte Argentario. It was a modern, sprawling, 1960s-era house. Almost every room looked out over Porto Ercole and the bay beyond. It was surrounded by olive trees and gardens with lemon trees, all loaded with fruit. The perfume of the lemon blossoms was magical—*What is that? Can you smell that?*—and it took us some time to figure out where it was coming from. And then we put our noses right into the flowers. Intoxication.

This risotto is simple, bordering on the plain. It would be merely *risotto con parmigiano* (merely!), but for a brilliant fragrance of sunshine. Be sure to use a good clear chicken stock. Serves 6.

2 egg yolks
Freshly grated zest of 2 lemons
Juice of 1 lemon
3 cups clear chicken stock
1 cup dry white wine (I recommend a Trebbiano d'Abruzzo or Lugana)
4 tablespoons butter
1 medium yellow onion, diced small
2 cups Italian Arborio or Carnaroli rice
Salt and freshly ground pepper
¼ cup freshly grated *parmigiano* or *Grana Padano*

In a bowl whisk together the yolks, lemon zest, and lemon juice, and set aside.

Heat the chicken stock and wine together until hot and keep warm over low heat.

Melt the butter in your risotto pot of choice (a large saucepan will do), add the diced onion, and stir well to coat. Let the onions simmer gently over medium heat, stirring occasionally, until they just turn golden brown. (At this point, you must be prepared to attend to the dish until it is finished, about 15 to 20 minutes.)

Add the rice, several large pinches of salt and pepper, and stir well again to coat. Add ½ cup hot chicken stock wine and begin a steady stirring motion, scraping back and forth across the bottom of the pot, allowing the liquid to become absorbed by the rice, at which point add the next ½ cup of liquid. Continue stirring over a medium, yet lively heat, adding hot liquid in ½-cup increments each time it is absorbed. (If you run out of liquid you can finish with hot water.)

After 15 minutes of stirring and adding liquid, taste the rice for doneness: it should be tender, but still resist the bite, in other words, al dente. If needed, continue the cooking procedure, adding liquid if needed. As soon as the rice is ready, stir in the lemon and yolk mixture and the grated cheese. Bring the dish to the proper consistency for serving by adding liquid if necessary: It should be liquid enough so that it is not stiff and lumpy, but it must not be runny. It must be softly creamy. Correct the salt and pepper and serve immediately.

Pasta e Porri

PASTA WITH LEEKS AND PARMIGIANO

LET'S NOT PRETEND that this dish isn't really just a vehicle for the cheese. The heat of the pasta and the sweetness of the leeks seem to elevate the aroma and flavor of the *parmigiano* to the front of the dish. And that's just fine. If you don't have leeks, you can substitute yellow onions. Serves 4.

4 leeks (each about 1 inch in diameter)
4 tablespoons butter
Salt and freshly ground pepper
¾ pound pasta [I recomend *penne, orecchiete,* or
     Tajarín (p. 112)]
2 cups freshly grated *Parmigiano-Reggiano,* plus additional as needed
Olive oil

Cut off the bottoms of the leeks and wash the leaves well. Agitate the leaves in a tub of cold water and rub off any stubborn dirt with your fingers. Shake off as much water as you can. Cut the leeks crosswise into ¼-inch slices.

Melt the butter in a large saucepan over medium heat. Add the leeks and a few large pinches of salt and pepper, and stir well to coat. Cover the pot, keeping the heat medium. Stir the leeks after 6 or 8 minutes, cover again, and cook them down until they are completely softened. Taste them and correct the seasoning. Turn off the heat, but let the sauce stay warm in its pot while you cook the pasta. Cook the pasta. Once it's ready, drain the pasta but don't shake off all the water.

Add the 2 cups grated cheese to the sauce and stir. Add the pasta to the sauce and toss together thoroughly. Give the cheese a chance to melt and really bind everything together. Add a little olive oil if the dish seems too dry. Taste and adjust with salt and pepper. Serve with additional grated *Parmigiano-Reggiano* so that each diner may add cheese as desired at the table.

Costolette d'Agnello con Caprino

LAMB CHOPS WITH FRESH GOAT CHEESE

ONE DAY IN CASTIGLION FIORENTINO I was out shopping when I stopped at the butcher shop, the *Macelleria,* to pick up some sausages for grilling. Except there weren't any sausages. I could see the butcher, busy with a side of beef in the back room. He came out to lean on the counter and ask what I wanted. *"Niente salsiccie, oggi?"* No sausages today? I asked. He said he would make some as soon as he finished what he was working on and that I should return in one hour.

Everyone who regularly shops for groceries in Italy has some kind of working relationship with their local butcher. Just as it is a good idea to get along well with, and show your respect and appreciation for, your auto mechanic, so it is with the butcher. In fact, in my opinion, good butchers don't get enough attention in this country. So if you realize you have found a good butcher—and he might be in a big supermarket, not just in a specialty shop—ask if he will prepare cuts for you, such as these lamb chops. To ask these things is to show that you value his professional skills.

While you're at it, ask him if he will cut steaks to order (with enough notice, of course), such as 3-inch-thick Porterhouse or T-bones. Or a butterflied pork loin for *Arista di Maiale al' Mercato* (p. 59). And what about veal cutlets and chops? Does he have confidence in his veal supplier? A good butcher has opinions about the products he receives, because he is the one who decides how the cuts will come out of each piece. Defer to his better judgment.

Ask your butcher to cut the lamb chops only one rib thick for this recipe. (And the younger the lamb, the better.) You can pound out the meat—the eye of the chop—at home to tenderize it. This recipe is per person.

1 lamb chop
Salt and freshly ground pepper
2 tablespoons vegetable oil
2 tablespoons butter, divided
1 tablespoon chopped rosemary leaves
White wine
Fresh goat cheese

Season the chop(s) with salt and pepper on both sides. Heat the oil and 1 tablespoon butter in a heavy skillet until a haze begins to form over the pan. Lay in the chop(s) and sauté over medium heat on each side for 4 to 7 minutes, depending on their size. When done (but still pink in the middle), remove the chops to a platter.

Return the pan to the heat and add the chopped rosemary, a splash of white wine, a couple pinches of salt and pepper, and a tablespoon of butter. Raise the heat and scrape the pan with a spatula. Stir and let the sauce reduce until the butter and wine have cooked together to form a sauce. Return the chops to the pan to reheat, turning them in the glaze, and remove to serving plates. Place a spoonful of goat cheese on each chop, grind a little fresh pepper over all, and serve.

Pollo Arrosto

TUSCAN-STYLE ROASTED CHICKEN

WHEN I HAVE HAD THE CHANCE to either watch or assist a skilled Italian cook in his or her kitchen, I have been repeatedly amazed by the quantities of olive oil and salt employed, especially in Tuscany where the cuisine is very strongly seasoned. This recipe is a good example of that Tuscan style when roasting meats. You may use a whole chicken if you wish, but this recipe calls for only leg quarters (the drumstick and thigh together), which are easier to prepare and less time-consuming than roasting a whole chicken, unless you choose to quarter the chicken into serving pieces before cooking.

This dish is almost always served with roasted potatoes and either salad or a green vegetable. Ingredients are per serving. Multipy as needed.

    1 chicken leg (per person), rinsed under cold water and patted dry
    Salt and freshly ground pepper
    1 large garlic clove (per person)
    Some fresh rosemary leaves
    Extra-virgin olive oil, for drizzling on chicken
    1 large lemon, quartered (per leg)

Preheat oven to 375 degrees.

In a large roasting pan, arrange the chicken legs skin-side down, but not cramped together. Salt and pepper both sides of the chicken well, leaving the chicken skin-side up. (Don't skimp on the salt: you should be able to see it clearly on the meat but it shouldn't look like a heavy snowfall.) Smash the garlic cloves well and tuck one beneath each leg. Sprinkle the rosemary around the pan and again, don't skimp. Drizzle some olive oil over all, squeeze fresh juice from the quartered lemons over all, and tuck the lemon pieces in among the meat. If the legs are small, add a small slosh of water or wine (white or red) to the pan to maintain a little moisture until the legs begin to give up their own juices.

Place the pan in the oven and roast the legs for 50 to 60 minutes, checking the pan after 25 or 30 minutes. (If the meat is very lean you may need to add some more liquid to the pan so that the meat doesn't get dry.) The skin should be well browned and crispy; the leg joint should be loose. Test by grabbing one end of a drumstick with tongs and piercing the meat with a sharp knife: the juices should be clear, and when you cut into the meat it should fall off the bone.

Usually this chicken won't require a sauce, but if your chicken is lean, you can deglaze the pan with a little wine or water, swirl in a little butter, and pour the reduced sauce over the meat. Let the legs rest for 5 to 10 minutes before serving with your preferred vegetable *contorno* or a salad of fresh greens.

Arista di Maiale al' Mercato

Market-Style Roasted Pork

Tuscan towns enjoy a busy and varied weekly market where one can almost always find a vendor selling *porchetta*. His truck might be hidden among or beyond the sellers of cheese, *salumi*, olives, fish, poultry, fried foods (you'd better stop there, too, for some stuffed olives), but you might notice that some people are eating as they wander, and some of them are eating sandwiches wrapped in white paper spotted with oil. Once you find the right truck, just ask for a *panino con la porchetta*. Be sure to get a sandwich for each member of your party and, well, if someone doesn't want his, all the better for you.

For this preparation you can use boneless pork loin or shoulder, though it is also remarkably succulent when made with fresh belly, especially if you can buy it with the skin on, which will become deliciously crackly. You will need to cut a fissure down the center of the meat in order to season it and then tie it up again. If it's a loin, you can ask your butcher to butterfly it to 1-inch thick. Don't worry about having leftovers, just make sandwiches. (The dough for making Tuscan pizza also makes excellent rolls for just such a purpose.)

The quantities of salt employed may seem daunting, but a large roast can swallow insufficient seasonings whole, and this one should be anything but bland. Pork in the United States is generally leaner than that found in Italy, so don't skimp on the olive oil. A dominant feature of this dish in its native setting is the strength of the seasonings. If you have ever wondered when a meat thermometer would come in handy, now is the time. This recipe is for a 3- to 4-pound loin, serving 6 to 8 people.

2 tablespoons fresh rosemary leaves
8 to 10 fresh sage leaves
8 to 10 medium garlic cloves
Salt and freshly ground pepper
1 3- to 4-pound pork loin, shoulder or belly
Kosher or other large-grained salt
Extra-virgin olive oil
Wine or water

Preheat oven to 375 degrees.

Chop or process together the rosemary, sage, and garlic with several generous pinches of salt and plenty of ground pepper. Arrange your pork in its roasting pan. If using a shoulder or whole loin, make some 3-inch deep incisions in the meat with a small knife, and stuff in the seasoning mixture into the holes. If using a butterflied loin or belly, spead the mixture over the whole interior surface, roll up the meat and tie it with heavy butcher's twine. Season the exterior with salt, lightly blanketing the entire surface. Drizzle extra-virgin olive oil over all, and add some wine or water to the pan, at least a half inch deep.

Roast the pork for 2 to 2½ hours or until the internal temperature of the roast reads at least 130 degrees (medium), or you can cut into the thickest part of the roast to verify the doneness visually. As it roasts, watch the liquid in the bottom of the pan, adding more wine or water as needed to keep it moist under the meat. If the meat begins to darken too much once it has browned nicely on the outside, cover the pan with tin foil, though keep in mind that a certain degree of crustiness is desirable. Once the meat is out of the oven for good, let it rest for 15 minutes before untying and carving.

If you like you may deglaze the roasting pan on the stovetop and pour the juices over the meat, but equally typical of the Tuscan style would be to drizzle a little extra-virgin olive oil over each serving. Serve with roasted potatoes and a salad.

Sarde Fresche in Padella

SAUTÉED FRESH SARDINES

YET AGAIN, this is a dish inspired at the market when you come across fresh, beautiful sardines that glimmer like silvery jewels. Finding these treasures so fresh is rare, so when you do you must take advantage of the day's catch and abandon all other menu plans. Fresh sardines are very easy to clean yourself, but you can also politely ask the fishmonger to clean them for you while you finish your shopping, thus sparing you some mess and disposal. Serves 1. Feel free to multiply.

  2 or 3 fresh sardines, each 5 to 8 inches long
  Salt and freshly ground pepper
  Extra-virgin olive oil
  Bread crumbs
  2 tablespoons butter and/or olive oil
  White wine
  Chopped fresh parsley

If your sardines are whole, simply pinch off the heads and then run your finger through the body cavity and scoop out the interior of the fish, opening up the belly, allowing you to lay the fish out butterfly-style. Rinse the fish under cold-running water and lay them on paper towel skin-side down and pat them dry. Sprinkle the meat with a little salt and pepper, a little extra-virgin olive oil, and some of the bread crumbs.

Heat a large skillet over medium heat. Brush the pan with butter and/or olive oil and lay in the sardines, skin-side down. Add a small splash of white wine to the pan (just enough to make it steamy, not enough so that the fish are poaching in the liquid) and cover the pan. Briskly cook the sardines for 5 to 8 minutes, depending upon their size. The fish is done when you poke a knife between the thickest flakes of the flesh and the inside is cooked and pearly white throughout. Use a large spatula to remove the fish to a serving platter, garnish with parsley and serve immediately.

Piselli con Prosciutto

PEAS AND PROSCIUTTO

SOMEWHERE ON ONE of the streets behind the Mercato Centrale in Florence we had lunch at a small neighborhood restaurant on a cold spring day. It was drizzly and windy, and once we made it past the impressive display of antipasti in the front window, the warmth of the interior was a welcome retreat. There we had roasted chicken served with peas and roasted potatoes. These are the peas, a classic Florentine *contorno,* or side dish.

This is the dish to serve people who think they don't like peas. The prosciutto gives it a wonderful smokiness that somehow brings out the sweetness of the peas. If you can't locate fresh peas and you must use frozen, just be sure to choose tiny peas, as the big ones develop an unpleasant mushiness. The cooking time for frozen peas will be only a few minutes, while fresh peas can take up to 30 minutes, depending upon their size. Serves 4.

   2 to 3 tablespoons olive oil
   ½ cup diced prosciutto or *pancetta*
   2 cups shelled, rinsed peas
   Salt and freshly ground pepper
   Freshly chopped parsley

Heat the olive oil in a skillet over medium heat. Add the diced prosciutto or *pancetta* and sauté for a few minutes to brown the meat lightly. Add the peas, a little salt and pepper, and stir well. (If you are using fresh peas, add a few tablespoons of water.) Cook until the peas are just tender, correct the seasoning and stir in parsley to taste, and serve.

Spinaci Saporiti

Sautéed Spinach

Spinach is a common *contorno* in Italy, both in the home and at restaurants. You don't eat enough spinach? I understand. How often at the produce market do you see spinach so beautiful that you cannot resist it? Maybe for a few weeks in spring or fall, when the spinach really thrives in the cooler temperatures. Eating this dish, the wake-up call of spinach dishes, will help you remember to eat it more often. You will ask, How could I have forgotten you? You can even use the spinach sold in those crinkly cellophane bags. Serves 1. Multiply as needed.

    1 large handful fresh spinach
    1 small pat butter
    Salt and freshly ground pepper
    A lemon for squeezing
    2 tablespoons olive oil
    2 or 3 small garlic cloves, gently crushed

Strip out any tough stems from the spinach leaves and wash them thoroughly in cold water. Leave the spinach to soak.

Melt the butter in a sauté pan over low heat.

Drain and shake the spinach and add it to the pan with some water still clinging to it. Add 1 or 2 pinches of salt and pepper, cover the pan, and cook the spinach over medium-low heat for 12 to 15 minutes, turning it occasionally until it has cooked down completely. Remove the spinach to a warm serving dish and squeeze a little lemon juice over it.

Return the pan to the heat, add the olive oil and the garlic, and sauté for a few minutes, until the garlic just begins to brown. Turn off the heat. Lift the garlic out with a fork and discard it. Pour the oil over the spinach and toss well. Adjust the seasoning to taste and serve immediately.

Scarola con Olio e Aceto

Escarole with Oil and Vinegar

I'VE INCLUDED THIS SALAD here not because I think you really require direction in its preparation, but to remind you that it exists and of what a good cleansing salad for the palate it makes, especially when it follows a *secondo* of roasted meats. Serves 4 to 6.

    1 head escarole or endive
    1 tablespoon white wine vinegar
    3 tablespoons olive oil
    Salt and freshly ground pepper

Separate the escarole or endive leaves and wash them well, soaking them in a bowl of cold water and running the leaves under more cool water, paying particular attention to the base of the leaves. Dry the greens well.

Stack the leaves and cut them into 1-inch pieces.

In a large salad or mixing bowl whisk together the vinegar, olive oil, a few pinches of salt, and freshly ground pepper. Add the escarole and toss it well with the dressing. Let the salad rest a few minutes to give the sturdy leaves a chance to absorb some of the dressing. Toss well again and serve.

Zaletti

CRUNCHY CORNMEAL COOKIES FROM THE VENETO

THIS IS A CLASSIC *biscotto* of the Veneto and is excellent when served with fresh fruit as a simple dessert.

¾ cup dried currants
1 to 1½ cups rum
½ pound unsalted butter, softened
¾ cup sugar
3 eggs
1¾ cups plus additional cornmeal
1 tablespoon baking powder
1 teaspoon salt
2¼ cups all-purpose flour, sifted
½ cup flour for dusting currants

30 minutes (or more) ahead of time: Place the dried currants in a medium-sized bowl. Add just enough rum to cover the currants. (Keep the currants submerged; if necessary, place a smaller bowl inside the medium bowl to rest on top of the currants.) Soak the currants for at least 30 minutes. While the currants soak, proceed with the recipe.

To make the cookies: In a mixer with a paddle or in a large mixing bowl and using a fork, cream the butter and sugar together until fluffy. Add the eggs and mix well. In a separate bowl, toss the cornmeal, baking powder, and salt together. Add ⅓ of the cornmeal mixture to the butter-sugar mixture, mixing well. Repeat until cornmeal mixture and sugar-butter mixture are thoroughly combined. Add the sifted flour to the dough, mixing gently but thoroughly.

Drain the currants, reserving and storing the now-infused rum for later use (try pouring it over ice cream).

In a separate bowl, place the currants and the additional ½ cup flour and toss until currants are lightly coated. Remove the currants from the flour, add them to the dough, and mix just enough to distribute the currants evenly throughout the dough.

Divide dough into thirds. On a floured work surface, use your hands to roll each portion into a 2-inch-thick log. Wrap the logs in plastic wrap. Place in refrigerator and chill for at least 30 minutes, or until you are ready to bake. (The dough can keep for a few days in the refrigerator, but the leavening begins to tire if stored longer. Cookies will bake up lighter when the dough is fresh.)

Preheat oven to 375 degrees. Line a cookie sheet with parchment or butter it lightly and dust it with flour. Using a serrated knife, gently slice chilled-dough logs into ¼- to ⅜-inch-thick disks. Arrange disks on baking sheet about ½ inch apart. Bake for about 15 minutes, watching carefully for browning. Remove from oven when just a touch of golden brown edges the cookies.

When cool, store in a cookie tin or a plastic container with tight-fitting lid. Makes 50 to 60 cookies.

Ciambelline

ALMOND BUTTER COOKIES WITH ANISE

ROME NEVER SLEEPS. Beyond its many blocks of government ministry offices is a neighborhood complete unto itself: cheese shops; groceries and produce shops; hardware and motorcycle accessories stores; wineshops; shops selling hosiery, linens, discount clothing; and bread bakeries and pastry shops. The pastry shop on *via Barletta* is open twenty-four hours a day.

At a restaurant we found around the corner and a few blocks away we were served a ring-shaped cookie (a *ciambella*) along with a sweet red dessert wine. Unfortunately, we left without the recipe. So good was just the memory of this cookie that we were forced to reconstruct it once we had returned home.

Here is our recipe.

> 1 cup blanched almonds
> Scant cup sugar
> 1½ cups flour
> 1 teaspoon baking powder
> ¼ teaspoon salt
> 1 tablespoon whole anise seeds
> 6 tablespoons butter
> 2 eggs
> 1 teaspoon vanilla extract

Preheat oven to 350 degrees.

In a food processor, pulverize almonds with ¼ cup of the sugar until fine. Combine the almonds, flour, baking powder, salt, and anise seeds in a large bowl, mix together, and set aside.

In a separate bowl, cream together the butter and remaining sugar until fluffy. Add the eggs and vanilla extract and mix thoroughly. Add one-third of the dry mixture and mix thoroughly. Add the remaining dry mixture in two additions.

Grease a cookie sheet or line it with parchment.

Drop the batter by teaspoonfuls onto the greased cookie sheet or parchment paper. (Or you can pipe them out as 3-inch-diameter rings with a pastry bag and a plain tip. If the batter is stiff and difficult to pipe, loosen it up by adding one beaten egg white.) Bake until cookies just begin to turn golden brown at the edges, about 12 to 15 minutes, but watch carefully.

Budino di Ricotta alla Cioccolata

CHOCOLATE-RICOTTA PUDDING

THIS DESSERT ALSO DOUBLES well as a filling for a tart. And if you like, you can increase the chocolate to suit your taste. Though, if your ricotta is particularly good and fresh, I recommend that you not overwhelm it with too much chocolate. A few raspberries or cherries and a mint leaf, should you require any additional garnish, are adequate. Serves 6 to 8.

 1 pound fresh ricotta
 ½ cup grated baking chocolate (or more to taste)
 ½ cup sugar (or to taste)
 3 egg yolks
 1 tablespoon vanilla extract
 2 tablespoons rum (optional)
 8 8-ounce buttered ramekins
 Confectioner's sugar for garnish

Preheat oven to 350 degrees.

If your ricotta is particularly wet and loose, allow it to drain in a colander.

Place all the ingredients except the confectioner's sugar in a large bowl and mix together well. (The result should have the consistency of a cake batter.) Pour pudding into buttered ramekins.

Place the ramekins in a casserole dish or rectangular cake pan with space between. Place the pan of ramekins in the oven, pull the oven rack out halfway, and pour water between the ramekins until it is about halfway up the sides of the ramekins. Bake in water bath 30 to 40 minutes, or until a knife inserted into the middle comes out clean. Remove from oven. Let cool. Either serve right in the ramekins or turn the *budini* out onto plates. Decorate with a little confectioner's sugar if desired.

summer

ode

SUMMER HAS ARRIVED in all her fits and starts—sun, rain, intense heat, air thick like gauze. The mercurial sky pushes east, south, north, scrubs our small world clean, and again brings sun. The days are often brutal and hot. Just moving from the kitchen to the dining room at the restaurant makes your shirt stick to your back and the hair at the nape of your neck damp. The summer months in our Vermont valley and mountains are punctuated by spells of Delta-style heat up against a day or night so cool we burn wood in our stoves or fireplaces to dry out the damp and warm the chill from our skin.

In the mornings we open wide both doors at the restaurant, flanked by big pots of tansy, meadow sage, and lady's-mantle. The outdoor tables and chairs on our small brick terrace are protected from most of the heat with market umbrellas that reflect white under the sun or against a rain-promised horizon. People flow in and out of our town, through our doors and our summer, a constant motion, but not so harried or teeming that the locals don't feel there's room enough to walk on the sidewalk. Visitors leisurely stroll the streets. In only four months, autumn will bring so many people to our corner that the sidewalks will be impassable and there will be nowhere to park, sit, or think.

Summer. The people coming and going remind me of movie cinematography, those aerial shots of city highways, the images always taken at dusk with the traffic a blur of lights and speed, a perpetual curve of motion. The people are like those infinite streaks of light traveling from here to there, whether it's just across town or across the world. And it's for them that we open our doors, plant the terrace garden with potted herbs and roses, and set the tables for lunch and dinner. They remind me of why Caleb and I center our life around feeding people. Certainly, we do it for ourselves. We do it out of our convictions about food and culture and preservation. We try to recapture a life we lived in Italy, to give back something of the hospitality we received from the people who fed us, housed us, and apprenticed us. But even more, I think we try to bring our experience *there* to life *here* for those people we see everyday and for those who come through the door having never tasted of Italy but curious to try. We do this for the grandchild of immigrants who came to this country from Sicily or Naples, who comes into the restaurant and remembers his childhood and the biscotti his grandmother made when he was small.

Standing in front of the hot stove stirring a pot on a hazy June day, getting up at 4:00 in the morning to mix and shape bread dough, or staying up late rolling out *cornetti,* we are in love with the work and the experiences that brought us here. We think of the couple who live on High Street around the corner. What fish will we serve them Friday night? We think of friends we've met over the bar with whom we share a love of Italy; of the man who comes in regularly and finishes his meal with an espresso and bread pastry who told us he had been dead for two minutes once from a heart attack; of the woman who stood in the doorway to our kitchen after a breakfast of cappuccino and chocolate *cornetto* and cried because she was reminded of when she lived in Rome and felt like somebody real in the world.

On an evening off I drive home with dinner from the restaurant packed in a box sitting next to me on the passenger seat: roasted chicken, cold haricots verts and beets in vinaigrette, fresh bread, cheese. We don't cook so much at home anymore. Usually we bring something home from the restaurant on the nights we aren't open, but sometimes we get home early and feel compelled to cook a meal from the beginning. We'll set the table with white linens and pull out our wedding silver . . .

The car windows are open and the air smells like freshly mown hay. The light is soft as the sun recedes a little to the west. I pass the Lewis Farm, their pretty brown dairy cows grazing on hillside pastures. I see their new swimming pool behind the house, the family all gathered around it, children splashing in the water, mothers sitting beneath an umbrella staying cool. How perfect for the farmer and his wife, for their sons and daughters, and for *their* sons and daughters to have a place to swim right on the farm. Between chores on these long summer days, they can take a break waterside and survey the corn that's grown almost knee-high in the west field or the crop of beans growing luxuriant and green just next to the house.

I think about taking a dive in our neighbor's pond or stopping at the lake in the village, but I keep driving, picnic at hand, toward home, where Caleb is waiting for me to sit and look out over my own fields, see the edge of the Franconia Ridge or look out seventy miles through the saddle of hills to the north, and listen for the train a valley away or the coyotes call.

This summer night, Caleb and I sit in our garden at a small table with two chairs eating dinner, that picnic so carefully packed. The peonies have been blooming for three weeks now, the classic magenta, the blush Sarah Bernhardts, the ones that remind me of Napoleon's first wife, the Empress Josephine, who loved roses, these fragrant Festiva Maximas, white with flecks of magenta at their centers, which we gather or have delivered from the flower farm down the road so we can fill huge vases at the restaurant and at home to begin and end each day with the balm that summer continues, the sting of winter fainter but not entirely forgotten.

The garden runs ahead, the weeds starting to crowd the magenta peonies we just planted this spring. They were a gift from our friend Tommaso's own garden, an Italian man who's family came to this country from the Emilia-Romagna and settled in New York City. When he comes in to eat a plate of prosciutto and fresh mozzarella, he tells us family stories, like how every year his family has a gala in the city, at a big rented ballroom at a hotel where everyone dresses in their finest and relatives come from across the ocean to celebrate the family, eat, dance, and listen to the sixteen accordian players weave music through the night. Tommaso shares his stories with us, the bounty of his garden, because he knows our appreciation. We hope we can trigger memory for him, a doorway to the coffee bar on the street in the small town near Parma that he used to frequent with his father, uncles, and grandfather when he was a boy.

The days are longer. When we get home in the evening we take time to sit on the porch or on a bench in the grass and notice that the fields are changing, that around our house wild madder and buttercups bloom, the old Tudor roses along the stone wall have budded pink and blush, a few just opened to their yellow coronas. The catmint, *nepeta,* and sage have flowered purple in our upper garden. The wild vine that twists around our blackberry bushes shows its pink- or white-petaled trumpets.

The food has changed too, growing up fresh around us. Salad greens from the organic farm are fresh and tangy, herbs and romaine lettuces newly cut each morning. The cantaloupe we eat, not yet ripe here, arrives at the Boston market perfect and ready, the fruit fresh, sweet, and flooded with juice. I think of the Sabine *cantalupo,* "fruit of the singing wolf," those small, sweet early melons, once grown hundreds of years ago in a palace garden outside of Rome. The fresh figs have just arrived too, dark and grape-colored.

Back at the restaurant one quiet Sunday morning at the table of two friends I tell a story of the walk Caleb and I used to take in the valley out beyond the town in Italy where we lived, how we followed the Stations of the Cross threaded through the countryside for the devout who work the land. We would stop at each marker to admire its design, the work of a sculptor-slash-elementary-school-teacher who took one of the English classes we taught on Wednesday nights, and would quietly remember the man, be he fact or fiction, the stations honor.

In those days, we walked with our picnic on our backs, with two fresh rolls made with *strutto,* lard, from old Mazzino's bakery. Mazzino's small, white-tiled, street-level kitchen was open only at his whim or when he felt like singing opera, which he did in the throaty tones of a deep tenor—Caruso in a baker's apron, the tones wafting into the street like the delectable aroma of his baked goods. With our two rolls, we'd pack a hunk of sheep's cheese cut fresh from the wheel at the *alimentari* on the tree-lined boulevard just down from the old town, only a block from our apartment. We'd have fruit—pears, oranges, or apricots depending on the season—from Mariella's, the fruit vendor across from the *alimentari*. If it was late spring we'd fill a bag with fresh cherries from the neighbor's tree. We'd stride out from the town, down into the Val di Chio. Our destination was the *Madonna del Bagno*, a small jewel-like church painted yellow with white pillars whose saint lies buried up in the tall stone *campanile*, a woman nominated for beatification, a woman who could heal the sick with her hands, a woman who gave her shoes to the poor and chose to walk the long country roads barefoot. Half a century ago, you could take the waters at the *bagno*, immerse your ailing self, body and soul, in one of the baths built into the small loggia next to the *limonaia*, the winter house for the lemon trees. Now the stalls with the baths cut into the ground are gone, having been renovated into a glassed-in meeting room, but there is a shrine, a Madonna in a grotto. Holy water seeps from the stones behind her. There is a fount where you can fill a cup for drinking, or for rinsing the summer sun and dust from your face. A quartet of picnic tables waits in the shade of the neighboring, overgrown olive grove.

Before reaching the grotto and church, we'd come to an abandoned farmhouse, a small stone structure with a wood-fired oven attached and a large fig tree in front. In the spring, we'd stop to collect daffodils and pretend the house was ours, walk around it, up the stone steps, imagine the changes we'd make, and in the early summer we'd pick fresh figs and like children eat until we could eat no more, spoiling our appetites.

Another summer Sunday. Two friends come to the restaurant for brunch. We serve them the first plate of fresh figs and prosciutto of this season. One remembers a fig tree that grew in her yard in California when she was a child, how she and the neighborhood children would play, throwing handfuls of the soft, sweet, sticky fruit at each other. Now they cost more than gold, she says. I tell her I want a fig tree in my own northern garden, that I've been told certain varieties can grow here. "Bury them up to their necks for the winter," she tells me. If I dig a trench and blanket them with earth and newspapers, maybe they'll hibernate like bears and survive our most un-Mediterranean of seasons, but unfortunately with no guarantee they'll give fruit the next year.

This summer it seems like everyone is talking of figs, even the Turkish man who comes from south of Istanbul, who asks about our espresso as he wants to read his fortune in the grounds. He comes in with a woman from town whose mother is Parisian and whose father is from Provence. After we discuss green figs and black figs and white figs, she mentions the red-beaded necklace I'm wearing, so like the red beads her grandmother in Paris gave her as a gift when she was nine, when she went to Paris to meet her grand-mother for the first time. (They drove in a convertible through the city.) Yes, just like mine, she says. Her strand broke years ago but, while she's kept them, she's never had them restrung and so hasn't worn them since. Her hand moves curiously at her neck, as if her fingers rediscover each bead. She and the Turkish man and I, we talk of figs, of beads, of Venice and how they'll rent a place there in the spring for vacation. I think of the top-floor windows of a villa and how they might be able to look out across the rooftops of the city to the Doge's rose-colored palace on the lagoon. They plot to take a boat from Venice down the clear blue of the Adriatic to Turkey. "Venice is the last outpost of the Ottoman Empire," she says, while he reads their fortunes in the bottoms of their espresso cups.

The Fourth of July. We take the day off and spend the evening with friends watching the town's fireworks from a high meadow with cows grazing be-low us. It is the first time their children have stayed up this late to watch, and they laugh and exclaim when the rockets boom then explode in color and lights. Two days later, a young woman from Belarus walks through our bak-ery doors looking for work. She arrived in this country on the Fourth, and there is something patriotic and inspiring about her setting foot on American soil on our Independence Day. We hire her on the spot and she comes to work that afternoon.

Olga, with her heart-shaped face and cat-eyes, is a Checkovian beauty. A string of young men follow her around town. She is as animated as she is delighted to be in this country. We feed her every day that she works, plying her with cookies and loaves of bread, remembering what it is like to have just arrived in a foreign land. When we break for our afternoon meal, we sit and talk about her days here, or the application of a new word or phrase in English. I ask her if she's getting enough to eat. She pats her stomach and says, "I'm worried I'll get fat. Never before have I had such opportunity to eat so many different things."

The tables are set for summer dinner at the restaurant, all their lit candles flicker in the baroque mirror at the back of the dining room, patrons chatter, glasses chink in toasts and salutations, and a bossa nova plays quietly through the loudspeakers. The dining room is filled with people we know and don't know, those locals who are thankful to be able to walk on the sidewalk still, and the travelers who leisurely stroll through town. There, the doctor and his wife who just moved here; over there, the woman who once studied in Perugia and married an Italian man—an ill-fated marriage that lasted less than a year; and there are the parents of the boy who works in the kitchen with Caleb on Friday and Saturday nights. Friends of ours sit with friends of theirs drinking magenta *aperativi,* our house cocktail of bitters, orange juice, spumante, and mint, and discuss a future trip to Italy. They plot out possible itineraries.

They could go back to Tuscany, where they've gone before. If they do, we'll send them to Siena again. To the historic *centro* they'll go. We'll tell them to turn right, up toward the black-and-white-striped stone *cattedrale,* to our new acquaintance Roberto's emporio where he sells biscotti, pastries, Siennese *panforte*—that dark chocolate, almond, and raisin confection laced with cinnamon and orange peel, and they can take a coffee there at Roberto's shop, the Roberto of the Window Table who lunched just this past Monday at the restaurant on spaghetti with an artichoke sauce and a salad of arugula and *bresaola,* air-cured beef. Roberto, whose last name is so old it's still written in the Latin, with whom we shake hands and promise to see again in *his* town. Roberto who passed through our village after visiting Niagra Falls. Now, it's Saturday and Monday seems like weeks ago. The days come and go, a blur of constant motion.

At the end of each day, I think about the faces I noticed, stories I heard, stories I told. I close my eyes and see the food that came from the kitchen on large white plates or in ample bowls. I think about why I get up every morning and drive into work, why I write about what I see, taste, hear, and touch. I think about Caleb working each day on a minimum of sleep, baking, cooking, paying bills, fixing a dripping faucet in the sink or an oven that's gone on the blink. I think about how late we stay up on Thursday nights planning the new dinner menu for every Friday, and I know why we do this. We do this for Roberto of the Window Table, for Olga who is a stranger in an unfamiliar land, for the Turkish man, the French woman, and all the other faces we see and to whom we smile and say, Good day. We do this as an inverse of our experiences three thousand miles away, in honor of the Italian traveler who finds himself in Woodstock, hungry and homesick, and arrives at our threshold curious.

mythology

La pizza è una cosa seria—Pizza is a serious thing.
—a Piemontese gentleman

ABOUT TWENTY MINUTES SOUTH and a little east of Florence, a small S-curve of a town sits high above what is known as *la strada de Chianti,* the road of wine. This outpost, a collection of ochre-washed houses and lichen-covered stone buildings, is nestled against groves of olive trees gone wild, blooming rosemary, and the remains of an abandoned village surrounded by empty colonial farmhouses. The town, christened Ponte agli Stolli centuries before, is a place grown up from the broken foundations of a Roman bridge. It is also the home of a particular trattoria, a classic countryside restaurant, home to the Uffreduzi family who created it, whose hospitality and food were to shift our lives. This is a place built up from its own mythology, a Roman history, and our personal past. The place where we first tasted truth and purity, where we understood that all else is suspended when you sit down at the table.

Truth comes in many forms. For us it came and continues to come on a plate where chemistry, math, heart, and imagination are shaped into a beautiful and utter form—*la pizza Toscana.* Tuscan pizza, which is thin and crisp like the Sardinian flatbread *carta di musica,* music paper, is an elegant one-plate meal. The crust tastes of salt, grain, and the oven, of wood smoke if baked on the stone surface of a wood-fired oven. Toppings are traditional:

margherita with fresh mozzarella, basil, and tomato, or *quattro stagione* with ham, mushrooms, artichokes, and olives highlighting the four seasons. The trattoria in Ponte agli Stolli, a hidden dining room with no name to herald its existence, began its life as a pizzeria over thirty years ago and has grown to include a few fresh pasta dishes and one or two select roasted meats, along with *insalate* and wine and beer. It has a bar where the men smoke and play cards and the boys wrestle with the pinball machine or foosball table, a social room for parties, and the *ballo al liscio,* a ballroom where dancing takes place every other Saturday night. The trattoria, the *circolo ricreativo,* which provides the social circle for the town, grew up not from the foundations of an ancient bridge but from a simple plate of pizza set down before a hungry village.

The history of pizza in Italy is complicated and as varied as pizza is today from region to region. I've heard it told that the Greeks brought flat-shaped breads seasoned with herbs to the southern heart of Italy once called Magna Graecia, the land south of the Bay of Naples and the Gulf of Taranto. The bread was called *picea.* The Romans borrowed this style of baking from the Greeks. At the same time the Etruscans, a tribe who ventured from the north and settled the area we now know as Tuscany, were cooking *focacce* and *schiacciate* on their hearths. History and legend tell us that the modern pizza was born in nineteenth-century Naples, in the ovens of her narrow, baroque streets.

For this Neapolitan pizza the dough was rolled to the size of a dinner plate, then a band of thicker crust was added to the edge to give the dish a border, to contain all the added goodness. Ingredients were placed on the top of those flattened breads. If the diner could afford it, tasty ingredients like fat artichoke hearts in spring, ham or sausage, or anchovies—those little bright bits of the sea—could be included; if not, the flat dough could be painted with olive oil and sprinkled with just enough salt and herbs, like the rosemary or sage growing readily in the wild. Almost always, the dough would be rubbed with crushed tomatoes and seasoned with fresh oregano.

During the heart of this gilded age, a man named Antonio Testa was baking in his small shop in Naples, plying the citizens with pizza and *calzone,* and causing a sensation, so much so that even the crowned heads of Napoli could not resist the temptation. It is said with certainty that the Bourbon King Ferdinand I, defying all the rules of protocol, paid a visit to the bakery of Antonio Testa; he acquired a taste for the savory treat. But his wife the queen detested the rustic simplicity of a single-plate meal. In the late-night hours, after he'd sent her home following the opera, or in the quiet afternoons, when the rest of the countryside slept off lunch in the cool stone shadows of their houses, the king would disguise himself as a regular Neapolitan and dine at the city's *pizzerie* and hope to never be caught by his wife.

It wasn't until the next Bourbon monarch ruled that this round delicacy became acceptable in the aristocratic salons of Naples. Ferdinand II commissioned another famous *pizzaiolo*, Don Domenico Testa, to offer his art in honor of the ladies of the court at the magnificent garden of the royal Capodimonte estate. Brought to the king and queen by four horses in a royal carriage painted blue and gold, he served forth at the king and queen's table, and this time the new queen gave no debate. Don Domenico's pizza sent the king into such ecstasy that he bestowed the pizza maker with the title of *monzu,* an honorable designation and a corruption of the French *monsieur,* which was reserved for only the French *chefs de cuisine* who worked in wealthy Neapolitan households. Ferdinand II is said to have been so enamored of such dishes from Campania, especially the pizza, that he had wood-fired ovens built into the palace so that he and his guests could delight in this fancy whenever he chose.

After 1861 and the unification of Italy, the House of Savoy gained the throne. When in 1889 the new king, Umberto I, visited Naples with his wife and entourage, they were received with great honor. Black-shawled grandmothers in their steamy kitchens still tell the tale of the great *pizzaiolo* Don Raffaele Esposito and Queen Margherita, as do countless newspaper articles lining the walls of the *ristorante Brandi,* the very place where Raeffale Esposito toiled gracefully in the restaurant kitchen under the patronage of *la famiglia* Brandi more than a century ago. As the story goes, when the Savoy king and queen came to Napoli they were escorted one blossoming spring evening through the back streets of the city to the Salita Sant'Anna di Palazzo, where Raffaelle Esposito created a magnificent pizza for their majesties. Having accepted the challenge of representing his fellow citizens,

Signor Esposito designed a pizza decorated with the milk-white flowers of cheese known as *fior di latte mozzarella,* tomatoes, and basil pulled fresh and fragrant from the stem, all in honor of the colors of the new unified Italy. This time, the king's queen was transported, and Esposito, blushing and gratified by her pretty smile and fluttering eyelashes, bestowed upon her the only honor he could, naming the pizza of red, white, and green *Margherita* for his esteemed highness.

The roll of the train slowed as we came into Florence, rocking us back and forth, and the still hot sun began its descent, casting gold about the long, even train station. We'd gathered our baggage and stood beside our seats, an odor of piss, sweat, salame, and warm sheep's cheese acrid in our noses.

Our friend Gianfranco wildly drove us through the city, turning right then left then right through traffic, cars honking, exhaust spewing, until suddenly we were out in the open crossing the River Arno, light sinking gold and lavender behind the hills. The road jumped and dove. The air smelled like sun, everything burned clean. Quickly, Florence was long behind us: the Duomo, the Uffizi, the Tower, the train station replaced by hill and cypress, by vineyard. Road went back and forth, back and forth until we were there, pulling into a small parking lot built over a small brook, the car sidling next to a rough stone building, Gianfranco's parents' restaurant, in Ponte agli Stolli.

That first evening, Ponte shimmered, a group of ancient stone buildings hugging curves along the mountain road that brought travelers over deep ravine and river. Lichen stained terra-cotta-tiled roofs, the gray facades were dark with dampness, and Venetian shutters in browns and greens hid small windows. A few stucco houses, painted cream or yellow with fresh forest-green window trim and red clay roofs with dovecotes nestled in the hills above and below the town. To the northeast there rose a settlement of aban-doned farms, colonial houses with small chapels built between the main house and the livestock, walls dusty with disuse blending in with the dry clay-colored ground, thirsty-looking umbrella pines, and the silver leaves of hoary, gnarled olive trees. This settlement, nearly the deep center of

Tuscany, looked simultaneously arid and lush, the colors full but worn, the land combed and husbanded for hundreds, even thousands of years. Yet the landscape was not completely cultivated. Awe and surprise planted themselves in the rosemary and blooming oregano that grew wild along the roads, their perfume redolent in the air, and in the spring peach trees in the valley below would bloom, a blanket of purple and pink blossoms covering the valley floor.

We arrived on a Saturday night in Ponte where we were fed our first meal in Italy, where we'd come to find romance and history and beauty, and it came to us that first night on the dinner plates—in the taste of *la pizza Toscana*.

Revived and warmed by the food, a pitcher of local red wine, then espresso, and the hospitality of Gianfranco's family, we left the restaurant chorused by the Uffreduzi's salutations, future invitations, and a collective insistence that we promise to return.

And we have. Again and again we've gone back to Ponte agli Stolli—to have a coffee, to come in from the rain, to wait until dinner, to help roll out the dough for pizza until it's so thin, to cut ravioli circles from a wide sheet of fresh egg pasta—using only the lip of a simple juice glass—until midnight on a Thursday, to dance with shapely matrons, shuffle-footed uncles, or each other while the jazz band plays for the *ballo al liscio* every other Saturday night. Once we did this under a September moon, the wild dogs baying and singing in the abandoned villages above us in the hills.

The Uffreduzzis no longer run the restaurant and bar. They've grown older and have passed the responsibility of what they created on to another family who we've heard continues in the same tradition of excellence. Now we serve our own Tuscan pizza, along with a *menu completo*—a carefully chosen selection: *antipasti, primi, secondi, formaggi,* and *dolci.* We take what we learned in that kitchen in Ponte and try to create a similar experience for those who come through our door and sit at our tables, for whom we hope everything but truth and purity is suspended, at least for a moment.

the charcoal burner's pasta

ON A HOT, CITY MORNING we got out of bed in the narrow room we kept at a hotel near the train station, and we walked the Milan streets to the shaded corridors of the Biblioteca Nationale Braidense. We spent that morning holed up among books of heritage recipes on dark and musty shelves, thumbing through early Italian cooking manuals and popular nineteenth-century almanacs that contained recipes, astrology forecasts, and news of Italian royalty. We made notes, copied carefully antiquated Tuscan dialects, and grew hungry while sitting beneath the watchful gaze of Austrian Joseph the II, the son of Maria Theresa who once ruled northern Italy with the firm hand of the Hapsburgs, Maria Theresa who was mother to the ill-fated Marie Antoinette. We felt like we'd been in the library for days we were so hungry, even though only the morning had passed, our stomachs empty and wanting the more we read about pastas with raisins and pine nuts, or grilled, sweet toasts with an orange, rose water, and saffron tea.

We broke for lunch late, relieved to find out we could leave our selected books on our worktable. We walked out into the day, our eyes surprised by the bright sunlight. Caleb thought a picnic from a neighborhood bakery and *alimentari* would provide, but we were too famished to stop at so many shops to gather our lunch, so we stopped at the first outdoor café we came to. Everyone else had grown hungry too over the course of the morning, and the café was full. We decided to move on, but just then a table in the sun miraculously emptied. Our dull brains no longer needed to decide where to go, or where to sit. All we needed to think about was what to eat. I pounced on that empty table like a nervous cat afraid that someone else would steal my fish. We sat down, looked at the people eating next to us, saw their full bowls, and then we both ordered the same thing we saw on their table: *spaghetti alla carbonara.*

A classic dish, *spaghetti alla carbonara* has been absorbed into the whole of Italian cuisine. You can find it on a hot day in Milan (as we did after a morning spent pouring over eighteenth-century cookery manuals), at a little osteria in Rome, or at a small eatery in the Umbrian countryside. Its origins are a little vague though. The Romans claim the first bowl of *carbonara* wholeheartedly, saying it comes from their own Lazio, a dish cooked by the healthy tribe of Sabine women of the hills, those sturdy daughters who were gladly married off to Roman Centurions, until the Roman army officers became too drunk at an engagement banquet one evening and abused their hosts' maidens. From then on, history records that the Sabines broke all connection with the imperial powers of Rome. Others say *carbonara* was invented as a way to use the bacon and eggs bought on the black market from American service personnel during World War II.

Still, other sources say the *Carbonari*, the charcoal burners of Umbria who developed into a secret revolutionary society that spread to France and Spain, are the true creators. Originally known as workers who burned coal over open fire pits to smelt the silver ore in silver mining, the *Carbonari* loosely based their group on the Freemasons in the Kingdom of Naples during the reign of Joachim Murat in the early 1800s. Murat was married to Napoleon's sister Caroline. The *Carbonari* plotted to free the country from foreign rule. The society was influential in the revolt in Naples in 1820, which resulted in the granting of a constitution to the Kingdom of the Two Sicilies. Similar revolts took place in Spain and Portugal in 1820, the Piemonte in 1821, Romagna and Parma in 1831, all in turn being suppressed. The *Carbonari* movement was eventually supplanted in Italy by the more broadly based Young Italy movement. It was then absorbed by the Risorgimento, which brought about the unification of Italy.

It was our first time in Milan, it was hot, and we were dizzy with hunger. Our bowls of *spaghetti alla carbonara* were an incredible treat of fresh cheese grated over *pancetta* and egg yolk, the egg warmed by the heat of the pasta. Sitting in that outdoor café, we were mesmerized by our dishes. It wasn't until I had eaten a little and come part way back to the real world that I became aware of three women sitting at the table next to us. Two older women—one dressed richly with her hair pulled back tight in a chignon, the other more bohemian looking, her long hair cascading down her back and streaked with gray—treated a third to lunch and cooed at her like she was a young child. The younger woman seemed bored and spoiled. She was dressed in athleticware and running shoes, her face was tan and lightly freckled. Through their conversation I understood she must have been the daughter of the sophisticate and it was the daughter's birthday. The three of them seemed completely mismatched.

Caleb saw that I had become distracted by this other talk. He made a motion with his hands next to his ears like big elephant ears. "You're flapping," he said in English, our word for my eavesdropping. I put my finger to my lips and replied, "Shhh . . ." We smiled at each other.

Evidently, the two women were sisters who hadn't seen each other in a long time. They were somehow estranged, though they were not uncomfortable with each other; and it seemed there was no tension after what must have been a long separation. They seemed glad to be together, as if they'd been thrust back to their girlhood. The sophisticate's daughter had never met her aunt, and her aunt worked hard to catch up on lost stories. The sisters talked of the past: the house called La Margherita, or the Daisy, north of Rome in the Sabine hills where they had spent summers, a stern father, a mother who always wore clothing by Chanel. Despite their careful manners, they ate their lunch heartily (the bowls of *carbonara* we first spotted). "This tastes like those summers," the aunt said and pointed at her bowl with her fork. Her sister nodded and said, *"Ma meglio."* But better. They ate quietly.

The aunt had become a jewelry designer, creating rings like the large gold and diamond geometry on her thick finger. She made a gift to the birthday girl, who was recently engaged, and the niece became animated for the first time during the course of their luncheon, she and her aunt suddenly kissing on both cheeks as the mother shared the good news of an impending wedding. I watched as the aunt poured a fistful of baubles onto the table from a black velvet bag. The niece was offered one of the rings, tried on several of the designs—all monstrous on her thin fingers, and in the end she chose a plain gold band.

I watched the aunt smile and finger her goods during the negotiation. I could see the empty space at the side of her mouth where she had lost a tooth. She talked of having the ring size changed if her niece wanted. I found myself distracted by trying to look beyond the gold mesh band of her antique watch. There was a star tattooed on her wrist, and a matching one on her sister's wrist. Printed in blue-black ink, each was a star of David yet without the intersecting interior lines. I wondered if these were tattooes from the Second World War. The two women could have been the right age, but they seem too jovial in comparing their twin marks. Perhaps the marks were just a folly of their teenage sisterhood, or perhaps they laughed at the novelty that they were still alive? When I look back, I think of them like a series of film images: a close-up of the missing tooth, the bowl of spaghetti, ringed fingers, a star tattoo.

Since that hot day in the city of Milan, I have eaten *spaghetti alla carbonara* countless times, mostly at the restaurant, or at my own table. I have it on cold days with a glass of red wine, or when I'm tired, or when I am in want of comfort. *Carbonara* is a wholesome dish that gets you through. And whenever I eat that classic dish or our customers order it from our menu, I think of Caleb and myself in Milan and remember us leafing through the thin pages of old cookery books until we were ravenous. I remember the outdoor café that served *caffè Diemme* (we have two small espresso cups in our kitchen cupboard that Caleb negotiated that same day). I think of how I'm always looking at and listening to things in this country I've grown to love, and even though I'll never be Italian and I eavesdrop on unsuspecting families, I like to wonder, or imagine, because I'm curious about who and how these people are.

So, I think of the sisters, and I imagine them at their summer house in the Sabine hills so many years ago. Were they the descendents of strong Sabine matrons who tossed their pasta in a bowl with fresh eggs, pungent sheep's cheese, and salt-cured pork? Or were they born from a line of charcoal burn-ers, their great-great-grandfathers meeting in secret around a long wooden table, a kitchen at the back of the room, and the men rotating their cooking duties, not only a revolutionary society, but a cooking society, where they mixed their secret dish to provide them with consolation and courage?

bon viso

EARLY ONE SUMMER NIGHT, after circling the Piemonte, riding with the car windows down, the haze of the valley having lifted to show us the horizon's alpine necklace, Caleb and I arrived in Monforte d'Alba. We had been driving all day, stopping in a field to picnic on foods gathered from the market in Carrú: *lo toast,* grilled ham and cheese on *pane in cassetta,* that bread baked in a long, rectangular pan with a lid—and small sweet strawberries, so juicy they stained our fingertips. We had come to this northwest corner of Italy once again to feast our eyes on the early-summer countryside, to eat its fruits, and to gather inspiration after a long hard winter in Vermont.

By the time we reached the steep, narrow streets of Monforte it was early evening. We found our resting place off the main piazza, *Il Giardino da Felicin,* a little hotel and restaurant named after the family who had owned it for generations. *Felice* meaning "happiness," we could only deduce they had been once named for their joviality. Sure enough, our host, the son of the son of the son, had a wit to match a dry white wine that could have been grown somewhere on the hills outside the village.

Our room was elegantly dressed with heavy brocade and striped curtains that matched the bed linens. A door opened out onto our balcony with a view of the garden, and in it a chicken coop where we could see our host collecting eggs for that evening's pasta. Nearby, the roosters scratched at the few stray seeds in the dirt. We looked across the valley and realized we could see the *castello* in Novello where we had just stayed for several nights. What a strange sensation it was to look out and know the family there would be preparing for the wedding staged at the castle for the weekend, to know also the layout of the rooms in the *castello;* the winding stairs with the niche statues—one missing her two arms; the old dog going in and out of the motion-sensored door at the entrance; and Diego, the *patrone,* waiting up however late by the heater in the hallway, a surrogate father, until guests like us returned from dinners out.

We had come to Monforte via Bra, the industrial and slightly worn city of the Cuneo province. The two recommended hotels were on one of the prettiest squares in town, but that week a children's carnival was playing late into the nights with the excitement of merry-go-round rides, candies, and games. We escaped the fate of staying in a room overlooking the square and hearing shouts and laughter until early morning with the decision to drive to the town of Cherasco, a Roman village with streets laid out in perfect symmetry. After a walk through her gridded streets, a gelato, and some provisioning, we pushed on to Monforte d'Alba where we drove up, up, up to a tiny outpost in the fields above the town to a little pizzeria whose menu looked enticing. Where we took one of our favorite photographs: a small dog sunning himself on the back of a long-haired goat.

Once settled into our room, we walked up through the narrow streets weaving through town. Wisteria and bougainvillea bloomed, and the evening sun still felt hot on our backs. At the top of the town, where the sacred fort loomed, we spied on what looked to be an old, abandoned villa encircled by a high stone wall and locked away behind a tall gate made of wooden doors, once painted green, but now faded and dusty with disuse. The only signs of life were the two potted palms on the steps to the front door, visible only when we stood on higher ground next to the fortress and peered over the wall.

We had thought to eat a light meal, having gorged our way through the countryside all day. We felt tired and a little used, like most happily weary travelers, so we had planned to walk up out of the town to the pizzeria once we'd rested and washed up a bit, but then we discovered that *da Felicin* serves its guests. For the price of your room, your dinner and breakfast are included, so our host prepared us a meal from a smaller menu, and we ate delicately of three antipasti: raw tuna with a tomato and olive salsa, a terrine of *galletto,* or rooster livers, served with carmelized onions, and a vegetable puree stuffed in a cabbage leaf with a funghi porcini sauce. For pasta our host brought us the famed Piemontese *tajarin* (dialect for fresh, hand-cut tagliarini), with the lightest zucchini and tomato sauce. We talked of the Piemontese dialect and how it has slipped through the generations. We learned that our host teaches his sons how to speak in the words of their grandfathers, those old Roman words shared and still spoken in isolated villages in Provençe to the north and west of Monforte d'Alba.

We were brought ravioli stuffed with meat and cheese flavored with rosemary and butter, and we tried the *castelmagno* for our cheese course, the same cheese we had eaten in the mornings across the valley at the castle. We tasted its sharp, dry flavor, perfected over the centuries and served with chestnut honey, walnut, and *prugnolo,* a sweet-sour jam often served with cheese in this region. We drank *Arneis,* that dry and perfumey noble white of the Piemonte. We watched the other diners, a German couple with a small dog who stayed in the room next to us and a young Italian couple from Monforte, the husband a marketing man for a local vineyard. They hosted another couple, a Japanese woman and her American husband, who imported Italian wines into Tokyo. They talked of Barolo and Barbaresco late into the night. Though our stomachs were full and we could barely keep our eyes open, we finished, at our host's insistence, with their version of traditional *gianduiotto,* the Piemontese chocolate and hazelnut dessert layered with *fior di latte gelato,* this delicacy an antique recipe handed down from our host's father, and his father's father, and the father before that.

"Mangato bene?" Have you eaten well? his mother asked as we climbed the stairs to our room, the black-and-white photos of the family smiling through the years and looking out at us as we walked past. *"Si, mangato bene, Signora."*

We woke to the rooster's cry, to brilliant sun on pearl-capped mountains, to a sky long, clear, and blue. A simple breakfast arrived: horn-shaped *cornetti,* cheese, cappuccino, and juice. We ate in the conservatory, a glassed-in room that in winter was the greenhouse. Two women wheeled large-potted lemon trees into the front courtyard now that the heat and sun were here to stay, and we watched our host in the garden as he fed chickens and picked young greens for lunch.

We spoke with the woman who served us coffee, talking about the mountain range out the window, pointing toward Monte Cervino, Monte Bianco, and was that the Matterhorn? *"Un bon viso,"* we thought we heard her say. The Italian so peppered with French in this region, we translated this to mean "a good look." Only later, after having driven a hundred miles away from there to a place the neighboring French had once called *la terre rouge,* Terrugia, the red earth, did we wonder if we had mistaken *bon viso* for the name of a mountain, *Monviso.* Or had we heard exactly what she meant to say?

rock of ages

ABOUT TWENTY MINUTES beyond the sprawl outside the small, provincial city of Asti, in the cradle of the Piemontese wine hills, a collection of villages threads through high green mountain roads, open to the wide sky: Castello di Annone, Mombercelli, and Montegrosso. Before the winding descent into the broad, flat valley that makes up the city limits, you finally reach the town of Rocca d'Arazzo. Rocca d'Arazzo, the Rock of Arazzo, looks out over the great river Tanaro. A quiet hill town whose houses are painted inexplicably in the whitewashed colors of the seaside, pale blue and pink, an occasional coral red, even though the sea lives at least an hour and half away, Rocca d'Arazzo folds over two gentle slopes that melt into each other, the buildings spread like richly patterned fabric thrown over the hip and rib of a woman reclining on her side.

At the top of the town sits an old Victorian hotel where, over a century ago, the residents in Asti came for summer cures and respites. Flat-roofed, topped with a cupola, and painted white and trimmed like a wedding cake, the hotel boasts a grand entrance. In front of the marble staircase at the center of the driving circle stands an ancient umbrella pine, a tree that drops cones shaped like roses in bloom. (I collect a handful to bring home to a friend.) The hotel is named Il Conte, after the count, Il Conte Giovanni Riccardi, who once owned it in the 1920s. In early summer it is quiet and sleepy, like the town. Only one or two other guests are staying here, travelers searching, like us, for rejuvenation at the edges of real Italian town life.

We suspect it remains the rendezvous for inhabitants of Asti, and that in low season this is a place where the local rogues bring their paramours, to an unsuspecting and elegant assignation in the country. We arrive at this guess in the silence of our own room, after we've gone to bed, our ears witnessing the hearty yelps of someone down the hall rhythmically shouting God's name late into the night, and this no house of the Lord.

At the beginning of summer, the pool isn't open yet, and the season hasn't fully begun: tourists from Germany and Switzerland haven't closed up their town houses, the Tuscans haven't yet traveled north to take their holidays. But we imagine children splashing and diving come August, husbands and wives playing tennis on the shaded clay courts, teenagers dancing in the ballroom, new lovers on wedding journeys holding hands in the salon, or older married couples away from their children and grandchildren, walking through the front gates and down into the village for a stroll, time receding, and they are young again, courting each other, before the war, and the old women laugh like schoolgirls, their arms linked, while their husbands point and gesture to the horizon, their futures before them.

This is how we find Rocca d'Arazzo after our long journey through steep hillside vineyards and open valleys dotted with old acquafirs where vacationers used to take the baths: she lies resplendent in the striking horizontal of evening light.

She is the same in the morning. Not a soul about, her streets are empty, the houses' shutters all closed. The gardens are quiet, but in bloom. I wonder if we've landed in the town of a fairy tale? Will its inhabitants sleep for months until the earth begins to wake up, until the summer people arrive and take up the streets with laughter, shouts, and the ease of those on holiday? Only the dogs behind courtyard fences belie my fantasy. They bark, or growl, or wag their tails and lie in the sun, while a pair of donkeys pasturing in the courtyard of an old, empty farmhouse brays and nips at each other's heels.

In the town's heart is a small piazza with a bakery and café leading the way out. The bakery is small, but its glass cases are loaded with confections, *cannoncini,* baked spirals of pastry dough filled with butter-yellow pastry cream, *meringhe* of every kind, and small delicacies shaped like swans. This cornucopia suggests that Rocca d'Arazzo doesn't sleep for long; so many sweets and breads point to full meals, family banquets, lunch every day when the clock strikes noon, all this feasting behind the closed shutters and in the open courtyards where we can't see.

The woman behind the counter puts two smooth rolls in a bag for us. She moves deftly, like an expert ballerina rehearsing the same choreography she's danced for years. An old gentleman walks in with a cane. Wearing a tweed coat to keep out any summer chill, he is the oldest man in the village, so the woman behind the counter tells us, and he terrorizes the town with his ninety-five years. He laughs and looks at us through watered eyes opaque with age, though I think he sees past us, but he shakes our hands, smiles, and says *pleased to meet you* in a low, rough voice. His hands are thick and calloused, and he smells of smoke.

Our old gentleman begins to talk of the town, and of his pleasure at being the eldest of the elders; he flirts and jokes with the woman behind the counter. But then, like some grand actor on stage, another look crosses over his face. He is transported. It takes us a minute to travel with him. We go nearly a thousand miles from this quiet bakery to the dusty villages of Africa. The war is on and he's stationed in the city of Nairobi in Kenya. The fields are green and yellow, he says. Hungry lions look melancholy in the tall grass. People are starving, the children are but sacks of bones. The swaggering, proud man who came in the door seems suddenly broken.

Another customer comes in to break his spell. She quiets him, she will walk him home, perhaps he'd like some chamomile tea? After they leave, the woman behind the counter describes how he is sometimes lost in the past, and how, although he can't remember the way home, he can vividly remember both wars, his great-grandmother, his first kiss. Like this town, I think. For both it seems the past is more tangible than the present.

A doorway behind the counter opens down a few stairs into the kitchen, when we see two young men piping dough from pastry bags and another man, with wrinkles like fissures in a canyon floor, lines trays with frilly papers to hold individual pastries. We are curious.

Caleb asks to see the kitchen. His simple request gets us passage. We explain that we too had owned a bakery in our small town in America, an Italian bakery.

We explain that the bakery is now a restaurant, an Italian restaurant. The woman behind the counter is curious. The two young men piping out pastry dough are curious. The man with deep wrinkles is curious.

It turns out that the two young men, Claudio and Daniele, brothers who look so alike they might be twins, own this bakery, *Antico Forno*. It was once owned by the man with the wrinkles. Many years ago, he baked only bread, when another bakery a few doors down specialized in pastry. The brothers bought this bakery a few years ago, and when the *pasticceria* closed down because that baker got old and weary and dreamed of playing cards all day and of drinking coffee laced with whiskey with his comrades, they took over the pastry for the town. Ever since they have been creating cakes, cream puffs, and *uove*, the traditional handmade giant Easter eggs made of chocolate and filled with surprises for the children.

We take some photos and ask about the sugary sauces simmering on the camp-style gas burner. The old baker winks at me, entices me to eat a chocolate and cream pastry (my fourth of the morning), and giggles, saying it will improve my fertility. Claudio and Daniele roll their eyes at the old man's jokes while they create trays and trays of different-flavored *bignet*, chocolate, cream, hazelnut, some covered in *zucchero in granella*, that white crystallized sugar the size of small hail. We exchange stories, they show us their photo portfolio of birthday and wedding cakes, flat canvases filled with intricate pictures, some supporting towering baroque extravaganzas. We exchange recipes, talk of bread crust. We exchange addresses and numbers.

We leave the bakery and walk down a few doors to a small coffee bar where we drink espresso while chatting with the proprietress. We think of exchanging ourselves for a few days, a week, two, maybe a month, renting a room at Il Conte, or a small apartment, maybe something owned by the baker's cousin as surely he owns an apartment or two in town, and every day we would come to the bakery to work side by side with the brothers and the old bread baker, so pleased to be free from baking bread that his old, bent body skips and spins like a young child's. We could trade in our American lives, like we once did years ago, and balance for a spell on this precipice, this rock that does not seem to change, that seems to hold on to what once was. Perhaps this is a fairy-tale town after all, and, like the sailors in Greek mythology who once landed on an island in the Mediterranean, we too have eaten lotus flowers and are falling into a deep, narcotic dream. Perhaps next spring, or the summer after that, or two autumns from now when the white truffles will be harvested and sold for more money than gold at the market, we'll come again.

Pomodori Tonnati

Fresh Tomatoes in Tuna Mayonnaise

SOMETIMES IN THE SUMMER it's just too hot to stand over a stove. This dish is often part of our cold meal plans, especially when the local tomatoes come in, even if they are still a little green.

The sauce is the same as that used for *Vitello Tonnato*, veal in tuna mayonnaise, a classic dish served at sidewalk tables from Torino to Venezia.

Quite simply, *pomodori tonnati* are slices of fresh tomato served in a sauce based on a simple mayonnaise. This recipe makes about 1 cup mayonnaise, enough to dress tomatoes for 4 to 6 people.

    3 egg yolks
    Juice of 1 lemon
    2 or 3 pinches salt
    ½ cup plus additional olive oil
    4 ounces canned Italian tuna packed in oil, squeezed
    1 tablespoon capers
    1 anchovy fillet
    6 to 8 fresh tomatoes, cut into ¼-inch-thick slices

In a food processor (or in a medium-sized bowl and using a whisk), beat the yolks, lemon juice, and salt together. Slowly beat in the olive oil, a few drops at a time if you are working by hand, or gradually by a thin drizzle with the blade running if you are working with the food processor, until the desired texture is achieved. (Start with ½ cup olive oil in a steady stream and stop the blade as soon as the oil is finished.) If the mayonnaise is not thick enough, drizzle in a little more, taking care not to overmix: If overmixed, the emulsion may break apart and no longer suspend the oil.

Pour two-thirds of this simple mayonnaise into a separate bowl and set aside. Add the tuna, capers, and anchovy to the mayonnaise in the food processor. Process together until smooth, then fold in reserved mayonnaise until a saucy texture is reached, neither stiff nor runny. Taste and correct the salt and pepper. Spoon the mayonnaise over tomato slices and serve.

Any remaining mayonnaise can be stored in an air-tight container in the refrigerator for up to 10 days.

Fichi Freschi con Aceto Balsamico

FRESH FIGS WITH BALSAMIC VINEGAR AND MINT

THE REVELATION of a fresh fig can be addictive. Look for plump figs that aren't too firm, just a little bit soft. Either black or green figs are fine. Use a condiment-quality *balsamico* (those labeled *tradizionale* are best) and, if possible, pick your mint just before it's needed.

For each person, halve 3 or 4 figs and display fig halves cut-side up on a serving plate. Drizzle a little balsamic vinegar over the figs.

Stack mint leaves on a small plate or cutting board and cut through the pile to make fine slivers. Sprinkle slivered mint over figs and serve.

Melanzana con la Ricotta

EGGPLANT WITH RICOTTA

WE SERVE THIS ANTIPASTO at Pane e Salute and find its clean flavors are a very good way to focus the diner's attention on the meal to follow. It is quick to prepare and can be either served warm or at room temperature.

Here the ricotta is just as important as the eggplant. (The same can be said of the extra-virgin olive oil). Ricotta can vary widely depending upon the style preferred by the maker. For this dish I prefer a soft, loose-curd ricotta. The cheese should have a markedly fresh taste of grass and milk and it should taste good all on its own, so be particular. While cow's-milk ricotta is the most commonly available in this country, if you should find a source for fresh sheep's-milk ricotta, this would be a perfect venue for it.

    1 medium eggplant, thinly sliced
    Ricotta
    Extra-virgin olive oil
    Freshly ground pepper for garnish
    Fresh chopped parsley for garnish

Prepare the eggplant according to the procedure on page 183 (*Melanzana e Zucchine in Padella*). Lay the slices of cooked eggplant on serving plates and place a large dollop of fresh ricotta on the base of the slices. Make a depression in the cheese and fill it with extra-virgin olive oil. Grind a little pepper over the cheese and sprinkle the freshly chopped parsley over all and serve.

Pasta con Peperoni Gialli

PASTA WITH YELLOW PEPPER SAUCE

OUR FRIEND ROSA used to cook for the foreign studies institute at Castiglion Fiorentino, where she would turn out incredible meals for between 80 and 120 students. In the summer she would serve this pasta dish. Its aroma was sweet and heady and, while once I had never been able to eat peppers in quantity by themselves, I can now never get enough of this dish. It still takes me back to that huge dining room with the slightly damp odor of old masonry, the smoke of burning, pruned olive and vine clippings wafting through the windows, and the perfume of roasted meat that was to follow. A complete Pavlovian experience. Serves 6 as a *primo*.

  3 medium yellow peppers
  ¼ cup plus additional extra-virgin olive oil
  2 small garlic cloves, gently crushed
  Salt and freshly ground pepper
  1 pound short pasta (such as *penne, gemelli,* or *lumache*)
  1 cup plus additional freshly grated *Parmigiano-Reggiano* or *Grana Padano*

Split the peppers. Remove the core, seeds, and loose membrane and discard. Cut the peppers lengthwise into ¼-inch strips.

Heat the ¼ cup oil in a saucepan. Add the peppers, the garlic, a few pinches of salt and freshly ground pepper and stir well. Cover the pan and govern the heat to maintain a gentle simmer. (While they simmer, bring a large pot of salted water to the boil for pasta.) Cook for 12 to 15 minutes, until the peppers are well softened.

When the peppers are soft, remove the cover and let simmer for another 8 to 10 minutes to let the water cook off. You should be left with a thick sauce of just peppers and olive oil. Keep the sauce warm while pasta cooks.

Drain the cooked pasta and pour it into a large bowl. Add the pepper sauce with the freshly grated cheese and toss it all together. Taste the sauced pasta and correct the salt and pepper. If the pasta seems too dry, drizzle in some more extra-virgin olive oil. Serve with more grated cheese alongside.

Risotto della Contadina

FRESH GARDEN RISOTTO

WHILE THIS DISH features the best your garden has to offer, you will need only a few vegetables. A good theory to remember about risotto is that the vegetables should be prepared so that their size allows them to be incorporated into the texture of the rice. In this case the result has a colorful, almost confetti-like appearance. Vary the vegetables according to your taste and availability. Serves 6.

1 medium zucchini
1 small summer squash
4 cups clear chicken stock, heated
4 tablespoons butter
1 small yellow onion, diced small
2 tablespoons finely chopped marrow* or *pancetta* (optional)
1 medium carrot, cut into matchsticks and diced small
1 dark stalk celery, cut into matchsticks and diced small
2 cups Arborio or Carnaroli rice
Salt and freshly ground pepper
Freshly grated *Parmigiano-Reggiano* or *Grana Padano*

To prepare the zucchini and squash, trim off the outer skin in ¼-inch-thick strips and cut these strips into small dice to match the other diced vegetables. (You can discard the interior of the squashes or save it for later use to be diced for soup or sliced and grilled as a *contorno*.)

Heat the chicken stock in a small saucepan and keep warm.

Melt the butter in your risotto pot of choice. Add the onion and the marrow or *pancetta* and cook over medium heat until the onion is completely soft and just begins to brown. Add the diced zucchini, squash, carrot, and celery and stir well to coat with butter. (At this point you must be prepared to attend to the dish until it is finished.)

Add the rice and several large pinches of salt and pepper to the diced vegetables and stir well to coat. Add ½ cup of the heated stock and begin a steady stirring motion, scraping back and forth across the bottom of the pot, allowing the liquid to become absorbed by the rice, at which point add the next ½ cup of liquid. Continue stirring and adding liquid in ½-cup increments, always maintaining a medium, yet lively, heat.

After 15 minutes of this process, taste the rice for doneness: it should be tender, but still resist the bite. In other words, al dente. If needed, continue cooking and stirring, adding liquid as necessary. If you run out of stock, continue with water. As soon as the rice is ready, stir in the grated *parmigiano* and bring the dish to the proper consistency for serving by adding liquid if necessary: It must be liquid enough so that it is not stiff and lumpy, but it must not be runny. It must be softly creamy. Taste again for salt and pepper, correct as needed, and serve immediately.

Note: Marrow may occasionally be found in the meat section of your grocery. A good butcher should have some available either fresh or frozen.

Tajarín

I HIGHLY RECOMMEND the purchase of a hand-cranked pasta rolling and cutting machine for making fresh pasta. They are easy to come by and not very expensive. Besides, it takes a long time to become adept at rolling out fresh pasta dough by hand with a rolling pin, and there is no shame in employing the same tool as millions of Italians.

Like any part of their very particular and involved cuisine, *tajarín* is very dear to the Piemontese and held in high esteem. On paper it may look like a richer, heavier pasta, but in truth it is a lighter and more delicate pasta, suitable to sauces having light or refined flavors and textures such as the zucchini sauce that follows *(Sugo di Verde di Zucchine)*. Serves 6.

4 cups flour
5 eggs
3 egg yolks
2 tablespoons water

If you are accustomed to making pasta right on the countertop using the mound method, please do. If not, put the flour in a large mixing bowl and add the eggs and yolks. Use a stiff wooden spoon to combine the ingredients until you can use your hands to knead all the ingredients together into a somewhat shaggy mass.

Turn the dough out onto a clean countertop and work it together, compressing it into a single rectangle about 1 inch thick. Wrap it in plastic or a damp, wrung-out dishtowel and let it rest for about 15 minutes at room temperature.

Cut the dough into 3 or 4 pieces. Press or roll each piece out with a rolling pin until they are just thin enough to be put through the rollers on the pasta machine. If the dough becomes sticky, dust each piece with a little flour as you go along. Using the roller on the pasta machine, roll each piece out to the ultimate or penultimate thinness setting on the machine, according to whether you want a fine, delicate pasta or a pasta with a little more body and bite to it. Cut each sheet into pieces of the desired length and put these cut pieces through the cutters. Toss the cut pasta on the counter with a little flour to keep the strands separated while you cut the remaining sheets.

Just before cooking, gently shake excess flour off pasta. Cook the pasta in abundant salted water. *Please note:* This pasta will cook very quickly—in only 2 or 3 minutes—so pay careful attention once it is in the water and be ready to drain it quickly.

A note on storage: Any unrolled dough may be stored for several days, tightly wrapped, in the refrigerator. Once it has been cut into noodles, it must be cooked immediately or allowed to dry at room temperature for storage.

Sugo di Verde di Zucchine

GREEN ZUCCHINI SAUCE

THIS PASTA SAUCE is really intended for *Tajarín*, the Piemontese fresh egg pasta (p. 112), but it is also excellent with a good-quality dry pasta. I recommend a thin linguine or tagliatelle for this sauce. Serves 4.

When ready to serve, toss with pasta, a little olive oil, and ½ cup or more of freshly grated *Parmigiano-Reggiano* or *Grana Padano*.

 1 tablespoon olive oil
 1 tablespoon butter
 1 medium yellow onion, quartered and slivered
 Salt and freshly ground pepper
 3 small zucchini (about 5 or 6 inches long)
 1 to 2 tablespoons tomato paste
 Water or chicken stock, optional, for thinning sauce

Heat the olive oil and butter in a saucepan Add the slivered onion and a little salt and pepper and stir well to coat the onion with the fats. While the onion cooks gently over medium-low heat, trim the tops and bottoms off the zucchini. Hold a zucchini with its base on the counter so that it is standing up. Cutting from top to bottom, shave a ¼-inch-thick slice off the squash and continue slicing off similar slices all the way around the zucchini. Do the same to the other zucchini, then slice these thick peels crosswise into ¼-inch-thick slivers and add them to the onions. Stir in the tomato paste. (If the sauce seems dry at this point, add a few tablespoons of water or chicken stock.) Lower the heat and let the sauce simmer for 12 to 15 minutes. Taste the sauce and correct the seasoning.

Spaghetti alla Carbonara

SPAGHETTI WITH PANCETTA, EGG, AND CHEESE

WHEN DONE RIGHT, this ranks among the all-time comfort dishes. It can be eaten in any kind of weather, in any season. It can be lunch or dinner, is exceptional as a late-night snack after a long drive home, and makes for a serious breakfast. It is rich in flavor and texture and satisfies your most desperate protein cravings. Eat it while wearing pajamas or formal wear, and serve it with a glass of your finest red wine.

The following recipe is for two people, and the steps require that once the pasta is under water you not step away. It is crucial that the pasta portions be kept small, so that the gusto of the flavors not be spread too thinly or lost altogether—a common error, in my opinion, that ruins many pasta dishes for the sake of bulking out the size of the serving. I recommend regular spaghetti, rather than thin spaghetti, for the sake of texture. And know in advance that allowing a little water to cling to the cooked pasta will help the other ingredients blend into a sauce—so don't be too eager to shake the pasta completely dry when you drain it.

Using only the yolks for this dish gives it a more concentrated flavor and elevates it into the realm of the inspired. This was how it was prepared when we ate it under a café umbrella in Milan. If you have had *carbonara* made with the whole egg, I commend to you this new practice of omitting the whites. (If you wish, you can store the whites in the refrigerator for use in another recipe, such as a meringue-based cookie or dessert.) Serves 2.

4 egg yolks (see paragraph above)

3 to 4 tablespoons extra-virgin olive oil or melted butter (or a mixture of the two)

½ cup freshly grated *Parmigiano-Reggiano* or *Grana Padano*

2 portions spaghetti (2 nickel-thick bundles)

Salt and freshly ground black pepper

⅓ cup diced *pancetta*

2 tablespoons chopped fresh parsley, optional

Set a large pot of salted water over high heat for the pasta. While the pasta water comes to a boil, select a bowl large enough in which to toss the pasta once it's ready. In this bowl place the the egg yolks, olive oil or butter, and grated cheese.

When the pasta water boils, put a touch of water—about ⅛ inch deep—in a small skillet over medium heat. Once the skillet begins to steam well, put the spaghetti into the large pot of boiling water and stir until it is submerged.

At this point, add the *pancetta* to the steaming skillet and blanch it for about 3 minutes. Stir the pasta again. (In a perfect world, your *pancetta* water will be gone after a few minutes and the *pancetta* will sauté just a little, and this will improve its flavor, adding a touch of smokiness to the dish.)

Without adding any water to your mixing bowl, and using the grated cheese as a barrier between the hot *pancetta* and the egg yolks, add the blanched *pancetta* to the mixing bowl. Add the parsley, if using.

Test the pasta. When it is al dente, drain it (but don't shake it completely dry), and add it to the other ingredients in the mixing bowl. Immediately stir everything together and mix thoroughly so that the cheese, yolks, and water form a creamy sauce. Taste the sauce and add extra-virgin olive oil, salt, and pepper as needed. Don't skimp on the pepper. Serve immediately.

La Pizza Toscana

Tuscan Pizza

LA PIZZA TOSCANA, when done right, can change the way one thinks about pizza. In my opinion Tuscan pizza is an exercise in balance among ingredients, flavors, and textures; and restraint must be applied in order to achieve that balance. This pizza requires a thin crust, its thinness has the unusual effect of elevating the crust to prominence among all the components, rather than diminishing it. Another thing to remember about making your own pizza is that it (and the crust in particular) will improve with regular practice. But if it meant eating the best pizza available to you once a week in the comfort of your own home, wouldn't you be willing to invest a little time? Using a baking stone in your oven and prebaking the crust for only 2 minutes improves the crispiness of the crust, which is an important feature of Tuscan pizza. Prebaking makes a crust easier to handle so that more than one pizza at a time can be dressed and loaded easily into the oven. A stone also helps even out the heat of the oven, allowing the oven to perform better. (We keep our stones in the oven all the time.) The procedure following is for a basic pizza with sauce and cheese, and to this you can add the vegetables and meats you like on your pizza.

For this recipe the instructions are to mix the dough by hand. I prefer making dough by hand and recommend it for two good reasons: you can feel the change as rough ingredients transform into soft, silky dough, which tells you when the dough is well kneaded; kneading dough by hand is a pleasant, tactile experience; and comparing the final texture of the dough with its performance as a crust will help you determine if you need to make your dough a little wetter or dryer in the future. Keep in mind that every batch of dough will be a little different, if only because of variations in your kitchen's humidity. This just means you have to pay attention to the dough as it is kneaded. (Note that ¼ cup flour is set aside at the beginning, so that it can be added after the dough is mixed, as you cut and roll out each portion. It is always easier to dry out a dough with flour as you proceed than to make a dry dough wetter and thus softer and easier to handle, so err on the safe side by starting out with a wetter dough.) Making the dough by hand takes about 12 to 15 minutes. Yields about 6 pizza shells.

  2 tablespoons dry instant yeast or fresh compressed yeast
  1 ¼ cups warm water
  3 ¼ cups plus additional ¼ cup flour
  1 teaspoon salt
  ¾ cup extra-virgin (or other) olive oil (The better the olive oil,
      the better-tasting the crust; this is one place where your best
      olive oil is definitely not wasted.)
  2 cups pizza sauce (*Sugo per la Pizza*, p. 121)
  1 pound mozzarella cheese, coarsely grated

In a small bowl gently stir the yeast into the water and set aside for a few minutes to dissolve.

Set aside the additional ¼ cup flour.

In a large mixing bowl, mix together the remaining 3 ¼ cups flour and the salt, and make a large well in the middle of it. Scrape the yeast and water mixture into the well and pour in the olive oil. Use a heavy wooden spoon to stir the wet ingredients into the dry ingredients. Continue until all the liquid has been absorbed into some of the flour. At this point, abandon the spoon and work the dough together in the bowl with your hands until you can lift it out onto your floured countertop.

With the dough on the counter and using the heel of your hand, mash the dough out in one stroke. Then, using your other hand, fold it back upon itself. Rotate the dough slightly, mash it out again, and fold it back. Rotate slightly again, and continue to mash, fold, rotate. The dough will gradually become softer and silkier. When there are no more lumps or irregularities, the dough is ready. Shape it into a ball and place it in a large bowl, cover it with a towel, and let it rest and rise until it is soft and about double in size. Preheat the oven to 400 degrees while the dough rises.

Once the dough has risen, dust it lightly with flour and cut it into pieces about the size of a tennis ball. Roll a piece out into a circle to a thickness of ⅛ inch or thinner, dusting regularly with flour and turning the dough over several times as you roll it out. (Too thick and the crust will come out doughy, and Tuscan pizza is anything but doughy. But be careful: too thin, and you risk tearing the dough.) Transfer the crust to your baking stone or onto a baking pan and bake in the oven until well set, but not browned, about 2 to 4 minutes. [If you don't have a stone, prebake the crust 1 or 2 minutes longer (up to about 4 minutes total).]

Remove the crust from the oven. Spread ⅓ cup pizza sauce on each crust to within ½ inch of the edge. Add toppings, if desired, but don't overload the pizza (see variations on toppings listed below). Distribute grated mozzarella over the sauced area, transfer the pizza to the oven, and bake for 8 to 12 minutes, until the cheese has browned lightly. Serve pizza Italian-style: whole on the plate, drizzled with a little extra-virgin olive oil, with knife and fork. (If you want to eat easily with your hands, cut the pizza on the counter when it comes out of the oven.)

In Tuscany, beer is typically taken outside mealtime, wine and water being the most common beverages during mealtime, but pizza is one of the few meals with which beer might be consumed. Try a pilsener, the Tuscan favorite, or, if you prefer wine, select a good Chianti or Sangiovese.

Note: If you think you are capable of eating this pizza two or even three times a week, portion, roll, and prebake all of the crusts. They may dry out over a couple of days, but can be softened in the hot oven for about 1 minute, then dressed. Storing the prebaked crusts will give better results than storing the dough.

I've listed below a selection of topping combinations traditionally used on *pizze* found throughout Tuscany, though endless variations are enjoyed from place to place. Most call for sauce and mozzarella cheese, except where noted.

Margherita—Fresh mozzarella, tomatoes, and basil.

alla Napoletana—Fresh tomatoes, capers, garlic, and oregano.

alla Marinara—Tomatoes, garlic, and anchovies.

Funghi trifolati—Sautéed white mushrooms with olive oil, garlic, and parsley (see *La Pizza: Funghi Trifolati*, p. 122).

Carciofi—Artichoke hearts. (Season canned hearts with olive oil, salt, pepper, and garlic, and marinate in the seasoning for at least 1 hour.)

Salamino piccante—Pepperoni.

Prosciutto *cotto*—Cooked (usually plain, boiled) ham.

Prosciutto *crudo*—Cured ham.

Salsiccia—Sausage. (Pinch off nickel-size pieces of fresh Italian sausage and distribute over the pizza. Pre-cooking is not necessary.)

Wurstel—Frankfurter (sliced thinly like pepperoni).

Crostone—Fresh tomato, arugula, olive oil without any sauce. (The pizza is baked with only the tomatoes on it. When it comes out of the oven, pile the arugula on one half of the pizza, season with olive oil, and fold the crust over the arugula, making essentially a big sandwich. The heat of the pizza will wilt the arugula just enough.)

Quattro Formaggi—*Caprino fresco* (fresh goat cheese), fontina cheese, mozzarella, *Parmigiano-Reggiano*. (This "four cheese" pizza has no sauce.)

Quattro Stagioni—Ham, artichokes, mushrooms, and olives.

al Formaggio—Mozzarella and olive oil only, no sauce.

Calzone farcito bene—Mozzarella, sausage, ham, and artichokes (see page 123 for instructions on making this stuffed pizza "turnover").

Sugo per la Pizza

PIZZA SAUCE

IF THIS SAUCE weren't so good, I'd be embarrassed to confess it isn't made from scratch. But it is good, and blessedly simple and quick to make, so that you can throw it together while your pizza dough is rising. (You can even run to the store for the ingredients, run back, make the sauce, grate your cheese, and prepare your toppings—all while the dough is rising.) Makes enough sauce for at least 6 individual *pizze*.

    1 15-ounce can crushed, concentrated plum tomatoes
    2 or 3 garlic cloves, finely chopped
    1 tablespoon dried oregano
    2 pinches crushed red pepper flakes
    ¼ cup olive oil (extra-virgin or regular)
    Salt and freshly ground pepper

Place all the ingredients in a mixing bowl and mix well. Gradually add cold water to thin the sauce to a soupy (though not watery) consistency (about 1 to 1½ cups water), and mix well again. Taste the sauce and correct the salt and pepper.

La Pizza: Funghi Trifolati

MUSHROOM PIZZA WITH GARLIC AND PARSLEY

IN THIS CASE, mushrooms are cooked with chopped garlic and parsley, which is just what *"trifolati"* means. These are the mushrooms we put on our regular mushroom pizza, and you should—in my humble opinion—never settle for raw mushrooms on pizza.

    2 tablespoons extra-virgin olive oil
    2 cups small white or portobello mushrooms, rubbed clean
        and quartered
    Salt and freshly ground pepper
    2 to 3 cloves garlic, smashed and chopped
    3 to 4 tablespoons chopped fresh parley

Heat the olive oil in a skillet over medium-high heat. Just as the oil begins to smoke, toss in the mushrooms and a large pinch of salt and pepper. Shake the pan to coat the mushrooms with the oil. After 1 or 2 minutes, add the chopped garlic, lower the heat, and continue to shake or stir the mushrooms every minute or so as they cook gently for another 8 to 10 minutes, until they are browned all over. Add the parsley and shake or stir well to combine and coat the mushrooms again. Turn of the heat, but let the contents of the pan rest together for a few minutes before removing from the pan. Taste a mushroom, and correct the seasoning if necessary.

Calzone Farcito Bene

A WELL-STUFFED CALZONE

A CALZONE CAN BE a little tricky, as the crust is dressed without prebaking it, making the transfer into the oven a more delicate operation. You may choose to start with the rolled-out crust placed on your peel or sheet pan so that you don't have to move the filled calzone. While you can vary your fillings to your taste, note that—as in this recipe—wet ingredients are generally not used *inside* the crust to avoid a soggy calzone.

> 1 rolled-out raw crust (*La Pizza Toscana*, p. 117)
> 1 cup grated mozzarella
> Fresh sweet sausage, sliced or pinched into small pieces
> 4 to 5 slices artichoke hearts
> 2 thin slices cooked, plain ham
> ¼ cup pizza sauce, for garnishing (*Sugo per la Pizza*, p. 121)
> Extra-virgin olive oil, for drizzling

Preheat oven to 400 degrees.

To just one side of the centerline of your rolled-out raw crust place the grated mozzarella in a mound and set the small pieces of sausage around the base of the cheese. Place the artichoke pieces over the cheese and the ham on top of the artichokes. Close the other half of the crust over the filling and pound the edges closed with the side of your fist. Trim off some of the outer part of the sealed dough with a knife or pizza wheel, and make sure the remaining edge is well sealed all the way around.

Slide the calzone onto a peel or baking sheet and then into the oven. Bake for 10 to 15 minutes, or until the crust is crispy overall. Remove to a serving plate and spoon a little sauce and drizzle a little extra-virgin olive oil on top. Serve immediately and beware the scalding temperature of the steam inside!

Spigola al Forno con Rosmarino

Oven-Roasted Bass with Rosemary

BASS HAS A BEAUTIFUL and delicious flesh, be it Sea Bass from Chilean waters, Wild Striped Bass from the coast of Nantucket, or other ocean bass. In its raw state, fresh bass should glisten and it should feel firmly plump. If you're someone who has even the slightest trepidation about how to handle and cook fish in general, don't worry. This treatment is simple. Bass is an elegant fish, and it deserves being paired with an elegant white wine having a touch of body—perhaps a *Roero Arneis* or a *Tocai*. Serves 4.

> 1 fresh bass fillet (1½ to 2 pounds)
> 2 tablespoons plus 1 additional tablespoon extra-virgin olive oil
> Salt and freshly ground pepper
> Juice of 1 lemon
> 4 small sprigs rosemary
> Splash dry white wine
> 1 tablespoon butter

Preheat oven to 375 degrees.

Cutting perpendicular to the length of the fish, slice the bass fillet into 4 short "steaks." Put the 2 tablespoons olive oil, 2 tablespoons of the lemon juice, a few pinches of salt, and freshly ground pepper in a shallow bowl and whisk briefly to combine. Roll each steak in the mixture to coat well. Set the steaks on a plate and season the flesh again with a little salt and pepper. Insert a sprig of rosemary into the natural cleft in the meat of each portion.

Warm 1 tablespoon olive oil in a skillet large enough to hold all the steaks without cramping them. Lay the steaks in the skillet skin-side down and put the pan in the hot oven. Roast the steaks for 8 to 12 minutes until done: The fish is ready when a gentle prod with a finger on the plumpest part of the fish springs back, or when a knife inserted into the thickest part of the meat shows the inside to be uniformly opaque throughout. Remove the fish to a platter or to individual plates and return the pan to the burner over medium-high heat. Add the remaining lemon juice, a small splash of white wine, the butter, and a pinch of salt and pepper to the pan, and stir it all together, letting the liquid reduce and thicken just a little. Pour the sauce over the fish and serve.

Petto di Pollo in Padella

Sautéed Chicken Breast

Chicken breast prepared in this way can be wonderfully versatile, not to mention delicious. It can be sliced to serve alongside a salad for a picnic, be dressed in a variety of sauces, or used in sandwiches. The recipe for *Salsa Verde* (immediately following) can serve as an excellent dressing for this chicken, especially if it is to be served cold alongside a salad. This recipe is per person.

1 half boneless, skinless chicken breast
Salt and freshly ground pepper
1 tablespoon plus additional butter
1 tablespoon olive oil
Splash white wine

Place the half chicken breast flat on your cutting surface and place one hand flat on top of the breast. Using your best and longest straight-bladed knife, carefully slice the breast horizontally into 3 thin slices. Season both sides of the slices with a little salt and pepper.

Heat the fats in a medium skillet until a haze forms over the pan and lay in as many slices as will fit comfortably. Sauté the slices just 2 to 3 minutes per side, until golden brown. Remove to a platter as they cook. Add a splash of wine to the pan and a little more butter and salt and pepper, scrape the pan and let the liquid reduce to a sauce. Pour over the chicken and serve.

Salsa Verde

Green Sauce (for Chicken, Meat, or Fish)

Typically this Piemontese sauce is used with boiled meats and fish, though I have been known to put it on my own poached eggs in the morning. Adjust the proportions to suit both the meat you choose to dress with it as well as your own taste. This recipe makes perhaps more sauce than you might use in one meal. Store the rest in the refrigerator for up to a week. Mixed with an egg yolk and some *Parmigiano-Reggiano,* it also makes an excellent improvised pasta sauce.

¼ cup chopped fresh parsley
⅛ cup capers
4 to 6 anchovy fillets
1 large clove garlic, smashed
2 tablespoons lemon juice
½ to ¾ cup olive oil
Salt

In a food processor, chop or process together the parsley, capers, anchovies, and garlic. Add the lemon juice and combine, then add the oil and beat or process to mix completely. Taste the sauce and correct the seasoning with salt and more olive oil as necessary.

Fagiolini Verdi

GREEN BEANS IN OLIVE OIL AND LEMON

THESE BEANS can be served still warm from the stove or at room temperature. They are delicious as an accompaniment to almost any meat dish or with a green salad and fresh bread for a simple lunch. Just be sure the beans are tender but still have a touch of crunch to them. Adjust the quantity of beans to suit your situation, and the dressing to suit the quantity of beans.

Green beans
Salt and freshly ground pepper
Olive oil
Lemon juice

Place the beans in a large pot and cover with plenty of salted water. Bring to a boil over medium-high heat and cook until just tender. Drain immediately and rinse with cold water to stop the beans from cooking. Dress the beans with salt and pepper, olive oil, and lemon juice to taste. Toss gently to coat the beans and let them rest in the dressing a few minutes before tasting. Taste, correct the seasoning, toss again, and serve.

Zucca Gialla in Saor

YELLOW SQUASH IN RED WINE AND MINT SAUCE

THIS IS A SIMPLE yet flavorful way to prepare yellow summer squash or zucchini quickly, something to be done in the last few minutes before dinner is served. If you cook the red wine sauce in advance, it will keep for a couple of weeks in the refrigerator. The mint may be added at your choosing as the sauce is excellent without. Serves 4 to 6.

1 cup red wine
⅛ cup sugar
10 to 12 fresh mint leaves, optional
3 or 4 small (about 2 inches thick, 5 to 6 inches long)
    yellow summer squash
Olive oil
Salt and freshly ground pepper

To make the sauce: In a saucepan, combine the red wine and the sugar and bring to a gentle boil until it begins to become syrupy, anywhere from 15 to 30 minutes depending upon the wine. To test, stir it with a spoon and then observe how the liquid runs off the spoon. As it thickens it will leave behind a heavier and heavier film on the spoon. (Be careful that you don't reduce the wine to nothing but a hard glaze in the pan.) When it turns into a light syrup, gently crush 10 to 12 mint leaves to release their flavor and stir them into the wine, if desired, turn off the heat, and let the sauce cool. (Store in a well-sealed container and refrigerate if using it another day.)

To prepare the squash: Trim the ends off the squash and cut them lengthwise into quarters. Cut the quarters into 1-inch pieces. Heat the oil in a skillet until a haze forms over the pan and add the squash and a few pinches of salt and pepper. Toss the contents to coat well with the oil and seasoning. Govern the heat at medium-high to maintain a brisk cooking pace and let the pieces sear for about 1 minute, stirring or tossing to cook evenly. Lower the heat to medium and cook for 3 to 4 minutes. Carefully add about 3 tablespoons of the wine sauce and stir to coat the squash. Cook for 1 minute longer to give the squash a chance to absorb some of the sauce, remove any mint leaves, and serve.

Tartina di Frutta

FRESH BERRY AND PEACH TART

TO MY EYES, this combination makes one of the prettiest tarts one can bring to the table. Celebrate the glory of a perfect summer day with a little cold *Moscato d'Asti* in a tall flute alongside. The quantities below are deliberately unspecified so that you can suit them to whatever size tart you choose to prepare.

    1 prebaked tart shell, according to the recipe for *Pasta Frolla* (p. 244)
    Mascarpone cheese
    2 to 4 peaches, peeled and pitted
    2 cups or more berries
    Sugar

Preheat oven to 350 degrees.

Spread a thin layer of *mascarpone* over the tart shell. Arrange the peach slices evenly on top of the cheese, leaving a little space between slices. Distribute the berries over the tart, filling in all the spaces between the peaches. Don't skimp on berries, as they will cook down quite a bit. Sprinkle a light blanket of sugar over all the fruit. Bake for 15 to 20 minutes, until the peaches are tender and the edge of the crust is lightly browned. Allow to cool before serving.

Panna Cotta con Frutti di Bosco

Cooked Creams with Fresh Berries

A GOOD FRIEND OF MINE frequently reminds me that I am "dealing with forces I just don't understand." Gelatin in *panna cotta* is one of those forces, as it is affected by variables such as temperature and quality of dairy products, which introduce vagaries into the mix. But time has tested *panna cotta*, and I've never had results that were less than delicious. Makes 4 servings.

 1 cup half-and-half
 ⅓ cup sugar
 1 teaspoon vanilla extract
 2 teaspoons unflavored gelatin
 4 tablespoons boiling water
 1 cup heavy cream
 Fresh blackberries

Place the half-and-half, sugar, and vanilla in a saucepan over medium heat, stir to combine, and heat until warm. In a separate bowl, stir the gelatin into the hot water, and then pour the gelatin-water mixture into the warm half-and-half mixture. Let this mixture cool for 15 to 20 minutes at room temperature. Whip the heavy cream and fold it gently into the half-and-half mixture until just combined.

Pour the cream into ramekins, place in the refrigerator, and chill until set. Serve the creams either in the ramekins or turned out onto plates with fresh blackberries spooned over the tops.

Pesche al Vino Rosso

PEACHES IN RED WINE

VIA TWO SISTERS OF VERONA we had the fortune of becoming acquainted with Enrico and Valeria, who have a bed-and-breakfast, *La Trebisonda,* near Valeggio sul Mincio, just north of Mantova. Valeria runs the show there, and the show includes 1,000 trees and seven varieties of peaches that must be harvested yearly according to a rigorous schedule to avoid spoilage. Peaches are big business in the Po River Valley of northern Italy, where in springtime one looks out upon miles of their pink and white blossoms.

Once harvest begins, the ripened fruit must be picked from each tree every three days over a period of eleven or twelve days. The entire harvest begins in late June and lasts for almost two months. Valeria sells as much of the crop as she can. Every year it is a race to make a complete and timely harvest and to get the crop to market as quickly as possible. Valeria always puts some peaches away for her own use throughout the year, to serve for dessert to guests, or to give as gifts.

This recipe can be prepared in advance, stored cold, and then be brought out and allowed to come to room temperature while you are preparing and enjoying your meal with friends. Or you can prepare it on the spot and serve it warm, much like the Pears in Pernod Caramel (p. 242).

The peaches you choose for this recipe should be just barely ripe and still a little bit firm. Serves 4.

1 ½ cups red wine (*Valpolicella* is a good choice)
½ cup sugar

4 peaches, peeled, halved and pitted
Fresh mint leaves for garnish

Pour about ¼ inch of wine in a skillet large enough to accommodate several peach halves at once. Place over medium heat, add the sugar, and stir to dissolve. Let the liquid simmer and cook together for a couple of minutes, then add the peaches, cut-side down. Baste the peaches with the liquid as they cook for 5 to 8 minutes, until just heated through. Remove the peaches to a platter or individual plates. Return the skillet to the burner over medium heat and let the liquid reduce to a syrupy, red caramel. Remove from heat and pour the syrup over the fruit. Garnish with a few mint leaves and serve.

autumn

return

LABOR DAY WEEKEND has come and gone. We made an escape on the Tuesday and Wednesday after, a getaway from ill-behaved dogs who trampled my newly planted asters in the garden around the restaurant terrace; from the chores of cleaning up after runny-nosed children who flung themselves against our glass pastry case straining against hope toward the vanilla *meringhe* on the other side; from the out-of-state customer who stressed, "Could you please slice that *salame Toscano* THINLY," as if I didn't know what "thin" meant or her loud enunciation might translate it for me, the same woman I smiled out the door having wrapped her cheeses, *salames,* and boxes of cookies in pale blue paper and a decorative web of strings in purple, lavender, and white. She stepped back in, her voice different then, and said, "What beautiful packages you've made, it's just like in Italy. I'll save the ribbons in my dressing table drawer!"

We take a much-needed escape from all this Labor Day purgatory to Caleb's parents' in southern Vermont for an overnight, cold and brilliantly clear as we walked to the neighbors for a dessert of truffles and peach ice cream and a lunch in the sun the next day at a picnic table draped in blue-and-white checks, laden with bowls of potato salad, chicken salad with grapes, pasta salad, and a dish of blueberry crisp with walnuts and sweet cream ice cream, all these elegant and comforting dishes made by Caleb's mother. What a joy to be on a picnic on a warm fall day, reminiscent of so many other picnics—ones in our field on a blue plaid blanket, or ones in

Italy in a roadside grove. A joy on this day to have someone cook for us. All this was much needed.

The second day of our visit, some words I had once learned roused themselves enough for my mind to be distracted by them again: remembering the Greek root, *nostos,* "to return"; I thought of words like "nostalgia"— the ache to return, to come home; "nostophobia"—the fear of returning; "nostomania"—an obsession with going back; "nostography"—writing about return. That was also the day Caleb and I drove to our old town of Middlebury. As the car climbed over the Bread Loaf Gap, the light, the colors of mown, golden hayfields and the varied greens of trees, and the scent of the air made me think of autumn in another old town of ours, one in Italy. I remembered us leaving Middlebury one September night on our way to Boston, from where we would fly to Rome. The evening sky over the Lake Champlain valley and the Adirondacks was brilliant with the variegated fire of sunset saturating so many floating and cumulus clouds.

In Middlebury, we visited with old friends, satisfying another kind of nostalgia, ate another picnic, shopped in town, drove through the country toward the lake, admiring the wide, flat farmland and the spines edging the Green and Adirondack Mountains. On the way home, we stopped at the A&W—an old-fashioned car-hop drive-in where the waitresses now wear rollerblades—for the last of Vermont roadside food as the weather has turned here, this summer—the summer we never had—now gone, the air crisp, the leaves on the trees making a slow change toward color, and places like the A&W will close, if they haven't already, after this weekend. As we approached Bread Loaf, a stately Victorian campus dedicated to the study of literature and writing, a collection of buildings that had once made an elegant mountain retreat and spa, I drove Caleb up the long drive to Robert Frost's old cabin and farm and told him about a formal picnic I'd attended here once. When we reached the top, the grounds, though empty, quiet, and pretty in the evening sun, seemed ghostlike now, missing so much of what I remembered of that meal: the grill, the clusters of people milling around or sitting on the grass. One last image of a woman with red hair and a straw hat clipping flowers next to the custodian's house still strong in my mind. Caleb and I walked up past the white farmhouse so I could show him the cabin. We sat down on the rock in front and watched as the sun began to set.

A flicker flew overhead, chattering. Walking back to the car, we stopped at the custodian's house and peered through its lace-covered windows to see the rooms, a dining room with a long table and corner cupboard, a music room with an old, small upright organ, a front parlor with a fireplace, where just beyond we could glimpse the kitchen. Leaving, we were quiet, both a little melancholy, the end of a lovely day reminding us this truly was the end of summer. This short Vermont season would drift away like my recollections of living abroad. The empty garden and farmhouse, the cabin of a dead poet, my memory of a meal shared with friends were only pieces of a livelier time like windblown ticket stubs scattered on the ground the day after the carnival leaves. Thankful for travel back and forth, between life in the present and life in the past, I began to think of a hot bath, a glass of wine, and a fire in the woodstove as we pushed homeward to our house. In the quiet comfort of Caleb asleep beside me, I let my mind drift to a million places I'd like to be at once: in Castiglione, a medieval place we once called home; with the Uffreduzi clan walking up into an abandoned village eating fresh figs and ripening grapes along the way; at our house on a dark fall day cooking an onion soup and an apple tart; with our friend Rosa at her dinner table in front of the open fire; at Silvano's eating a pizza, or a salad of white beans and onion, a plate of fresh pear and *parmigiano;* in our garden; at the seaside, anywhere, with a glass of white wine and a plate full of mussels; at our own restaurant lighting the candles for dinner; with everyone we know and love all together in a grand dining hall giddy with the evening light; or simply here, where I was, with Caleb, driving home.

From somewhere in his sleep, Caleb mumbled, "Slow down, we're in no rush," as if he didn't want the day to end, but with his eyes closed he couldn't see the sun falling fast behind our mountain.

in mantova

This is such a beautiful city that it is worth the thousand mile journey to visit her.
—Tasso, 1586

How can I describe Mantova? In Mantova, the *zucce,* the pumpkins, taste like no others. In Mantova, Veronese ladies, young and old from near and far, have always shopped for the finest shoes. It is in Mantova that Verdi's Rigoletto mocks the Duke of Gonzaga's courtiers and is then broken by their curses. In Mantova, the castle San Giorgio looms large, lit up by night, over the river Mincio—the same river that surrounded this city before Virgil was born on its banks, the same river that encircled the jeweled dominion of Mathilde de Cannosa in the eleventh century, and then the Marchioness Isabella d'Este, who ruled the city through the Renaissance after her Gonzaga husband's death.

How do I tell about the night Enrico and Valeria, our good friends who own a farm in the wide valley of Mantova, invited us over for dinner and to taste wine? Two friends of theirs had just opened a restaurant within another restaurant near the Castello di San Giorgio. These friends rented one of the large banquet rooms for their diners and shared the same kitchen as the other restaurant and named their place Saôr after the traditional Mantovana sauce used for meats. We were to meet Enrico there, but Valeria and Caleb's parents, Carol and Orion, rode with us. As we drove through the flat plains that make up the Mincio valley, Valeria spoke heatedly, sharing her concerns for this land of her childhood, the loss of the old ways of agriculture, and of respect. She grew passionate describing groups of schoolchildren on field trips she hosts ar her farm. She teaches them about their earth, their good soil. They are not yet intimate with the earth their parents once knew, the earth their parents' parents still know; they live in towns or small cities and haven't learned the names of wildflowers or why to espalier the peach, apple, quince, or kiwi trees growing in neatly cultivated rows over acres of fields that shape their landscape—to train the branches so the fruit has more room to grow and is easier to harvest. We've seen Valeria taking the students on walks through the farm, the line of children wagging like a puppy's tail. She tells them names of plants she points out or fingers, this is Lombard garlic, and this, cottony bellflower. She shows them the barn and inside the newborn foals and their still-fat mothers. She hands the teachers jars of preserved peaches and blackberry jams made in her wide, open kitchen using fruit grown on trees that mark out their land, and she carefully instructs: These jars are to be opened for the morning *merenda,* the snack, so the children can taste—the only way they will remember what she's taught them.

At dinner we will make our own memories when we taste new wines from a local winemaker named Stephano who has experimented with the vinification of the local, traditional Lambrusco Mantovano. Lambrusco is grown mostly in the neighboring Emilia-Romagna where its dry, sparkling effervescence accompanies well the richness of Emilian cuisine. (In the United States we know Lambrusco from Riunite, that sweet sparkling pink or red variety, but Lambrusco at home is very dry, unless it is to be served with dessert, then it is *amabile,* but this is rare.) Lambrusco Mantovano is dry, red, and sparkling and can match the best Lambrusco of the Emilia-Romagna.

We have four wines to taste and four courses to eat. A half dozen or so long tables for ten fill the dining room. Already, even before the wine begins to flow, the gathering is convivial. Friends shout, "Oh! Hello there!" from across a table, from across the room. Are we in the center of an opera? The voices talk and exclaim like a well-harmonized chorus, the setting of this room acts as a backdrop for this evening's grand story. Outside, the rain fills the air with cold and damp. As guests arrive they shiver and hug themselves, rubbing their hands together, but the room is warm and soon suit jackets and sweaters slip from shoulders to be draped over chairs. More warmth comes with the *aperativo,* a lambrusco, lightly sparkling as tradition defines. Then we are brought steaming bowls of *agnoletti in brodo,* small folded ravioli stuffed with meat and cooked in a translucent, deeply scented meat broth. In Mantova, *agnelotti* are part of the traditional cuisine as are *tortelli di zucca,* fresh pasta stuffed with pureed pumpkin and the crumbs of *amaretti,* sweet almond cookies. These *paste* are usually served with a simple sauce of butter and sage, or butter and oil cooked with just a touch of tomato for color and fragrance. The two dishes have cousins in neighboring Emilia-Romagna too: *agnolini di Parma in brodo* and *cappellacci con la Zucca,* two dishes that stepped right out of the Renaissance and its passion for sweet and savory flavors.

The third course, oddly an East Indian meat dish, arrived after a Mexican tortilla with chicken and black beans. Although eating of another culture is extremely rare anywhere in Italy, the owners of Saôr want to push the boundaries of their Italian diners, to raise the culinary bar. All the dishes have been excellently prepared, and I think their effort to stretch the menu is perhaps very *alla Mantovana.* The Mantovane have a long history of deep traditional dignity, in cuisine, art, and architecture, but also of one-upmanship. Our Marchessa Isabella d'Este is perhaps the best icon of this provincial pride. A Renaissance woman in every sense, the fair Isabella and her cousin Lucretia Borgia strove to outdo each other in dress, in patronage, in parties, in banquets. Renaissance gossips wrote that the two women even went so far as to send spies to each other's wardrobes so they could know what the other would wear on a certain occasion. When Lucretia was forced to stay in because she felt unwell or was too tired, Isabella made sure she herself was present, dressed in silk and pearls, and entertaining the gentlemen by playing her lute.

The talk at our table has moved to other palpalable stories, that of Rigoletto, Verdi's hunchbacked jester who played for the Gonzaga dukes in the

Castello di San Giorgio, which we see lighted dramatically from the windows of the restaurant. "Wasn't the assassin named Scarpetto?" Orion asks. Caleb's father studies and sings opera, and he seems to know more about the story than any of the Mantovane sitting at the table. Like children, we all ask to be told the tale.

In his deep baritone Orion tells us how the Duke of Gonzaga was known for deflowering the beautious and local maidens, and how the opera opens with an elegant, candlelit ball where Rigoletto mocks the courtiers cuckolded by the profligate duke. Count Monterone pleads with the duke to release his dishonored daughter. The duke refuses, and Rigoletto continues to cruelly prod the count and his courtiers. Enraged, Monterone calls down a father's curse on the terrified jester, and so the story truly begins.

Orion tells us more of this tragic drama of stolen maidenhood, mistaken identities, and true but misguided love. In a complicated turn of events, the roguish duke is lured to a remote inn by the assassin's sister Maddalena. "I do think his name is Scarpetto," Orion pauses. Enrico sends up a flare, "Oh, *ragazze*, does any one of you Mantovane know the name of the assassin in *Rigoletto*?" We hear shouts and murmurs, but no real answers. Dessert arrives, a chocolate confection, and Orion continues.

It is a wild and rainy night. In modern-day Mantova we listeners are delighted by this turn in the weather. With our own night so wild and stormy, we can imagine the operatic scene all the better:

After Rigoletto pays the assassin to kill the duke and deliver his body in a sack so that he may throw it into the Mincio, Rigoletto brings his daughter Gilda (who has already fallen prey to the duke's advances), dressed as a man, with him to spy on the inn, hoping to reinforce the notion that the duke is not a man of honor in affairs of the heart. Gilda is unimpressed. Infatuated with the duke herself, Maddalena begs her brother to spare him and to murder the jester instead. His sense of professional responsibility offended, the assassin refuses, but agrees that, should anyone else happen to show up at the inn, he will murder him instead. Gilda, returning and hearing all this, sees her chance to help the man she loves. She boldly walks up to the door of the inn and knocks. Once admitted, she is promptly stabbed and stuffed into the sack for Rigoletto. Her father is just about to throw the sack in the river when he hears the duke singing in the inn. Wildly, he opens the sack to find his dying daughter, who with her last breath assures him that she will pray for him with her mother in heaven. Rigoletto recalls Monterone's curse.

Mantova's region of Lombardia has always been famous for this sort of blending of theater and dinner. Before La Scala opened in 1778 in Milan, operagoers attending the performances at the old Ducal Opera House brought their dinners with them. Their elegant meals were heated up in a restaurant inside the theater, whose large boxes even accommodated sitting rooms with fireplaces where theatergoers could play cards if they became bored with the performance. The Grand Duke's box even had its own bedroom. At La Canobbiana, another opera house that opened in Milan in 1779, the management served whole dinners, including steaming plates of soup and *manzo brasato all lombarda,* or thick-cut steaks seared in butter, during the performance. H. V. Morton wrote in his travel journal of the period, "Only during a popular aria was the rattle of knives and forks stilled; then a reverent silence was absolute."

And so we ate at the opera, the table at Saôr a well-choreographed theater of food, wine, and story. (Weeks later, when Orion and Carol are back in Vermont, we learn that the assassin's name isn't Scarpetto at all, but Sparafucile.) We've eaten well and too much. We clap for Orion when he finishes the story of *Rigoletto.* The wine was delicious, Stephano has given a speech, and we clap for him as well and toast all the unlabeled bottles that will soon find their way to store shelves, restaurant bars, and family tables.

Valeria will go home with Enrico, and we will drive home in the rain, just family. In the trance of the wipers on the glass, we remember poor Gilda in a sack, about to be thrown over the bridge into the Mincio, we think of Isabella d'Este ruling over this jewel of a city in the Lombardia valley, and we salute Valeria, a true daughter of Mantova, who has taught us much. In her kitchen, Caleb and I learned to create *torta allo jogurt,* a moist, lemony yogurt cake, and *sbrisolona,* a crumbly confection perfect for breakfast, lunch, or dinner, and *tortelli di zucca.* Tonight, we leave without jars of peaches and blackberry jam, but we've tasted much and, like giddy schoolchildren, we can't help but smile remembering the delicious pieces of this day.

bread and wine

OUTSIDE OF FLORENCE, near the town of San Donato in Collina, a quiet, closed-up estate sits nestled in a curve of hill and vineyard. We passed it countless times traveling by car or bus from the bakery where Caleb apprenticed into the city. This was in autumn, when the air smelled of wood smoke and chestnut, the sun grew hot during the day and then cold at night, and we lived in a little bungalow we rented on some campgrounds next to a gypsy family from Andorra. The campground owners, a father and son-in-law, used to own a fine leather boutique on the via Tornabuoni, the fancy goods street in Florence.

Those days Caleb would wake in the middle of the night and walk down to the bakery or be picked up by the baker Renato at the gates to the campgrounds in his old red *due cavalli.* Sometime later in the midmorning I would walk the ten minutes to cappuccino and pastry—my favorite the *torta di mela,* a light, buttery apple cake lifted by eggwhites—and I would sit in the kitchen and chat with Caleb and Renato and Renato's wife, Anna. Some mornings I brushed the flour from the already shaped, nearly ready-to-bake *cantucci,* those small almond biscotti that would be served with the traditional Tuscan *vin santo* after dinner.

How many times did we pass by the estate with its shuttered windows, pocked and water-damaged facade, and a chain across its driveway? The clock on its face had stopped at eight o'clock. Was it evening? Did it stop during a fancy dress ball, where something dramatic, courageous, or maybe tragic had happened, causing time to pause for this grand old house?

Years after the bungalow and Caleb's apprenticeship, we drove by the estate again on a gray and foggy afternoon and were delighted to see this monument of our nostalgia come into view. We went by slowly to look down the allée that drew a line through formal gardens to the front entrance. The chain that usually crossed the driveway was down. A small, handpainted sign hanging from the entrance gates read, *vino e olio,* wine and oil. Without saying a word we took a quick right turn and drove in.

Around the back of the villa, the cantina was open. Five men gathered around a table opening bottles of wine and pouring them into big demijohns. We stood in the large, arched doorway. *"Posso?"* Caleb asked, Can we come in?

"You're already in aren't you?" replied an older, gray-haired man.

Right away we were offered glasses of wine from the bottles being opened. A lively, rich Chianti, it was being rebottled for export to Canada. The older man explained that there had been too much sediment in the first bottling for Canadian standards, too much nature. He and the other four young men drained the bottles through a small funneled apparatus that held back the sediment while the processed wine flowed into the demijohns to be rebottled. All the men introduced themselves; their leader, the older gray-haired man, was named Giovanni Giovanno. We all shook hands in the cold, damp of the cantina, and Caleb and I sipped wine from plastic cups to stay warm.

This estate was named Torre a Cona, the tower at Cona, and Giovanni Giovanno told us it belonged to the Rossi family of Martini and Rossi. Most of the wine produced at this vineyard was used as holiday gifts for employees or clients, and an amount every year was sent to Canada. None ever made it to the States, and some was reserved for selling at the cantina when people, like us, got curious and stopped by.

The house still stood empty, except for one small apartment where Giovanni lived. The villa had three hundred and sixty-five rooms, one for each day of the year, and no one from the family had been to stay there for years. Giovanni had actually been born at the estate and had worked in the vineyard since he was thirteen. Now he was seventy-five. His father had worked the land here, as had his father's father. Like the house, Giovanni's own life played out on his face and body, in the sun-creased wrinkles around his eyes, and the intrigue of his left hand, which was missing two fingers.

Alongside the vineyard were olive groves. The estate pressed and bottled olive oil too. Giovanni motioned for us to follow him, and he took us down below the cantina into the *frantoio* where they produced and kept the oil in huge terra-cotta *orci,* urns at least three and a half feet high. Almost all the containers were stamped with dates. Giovanni rubbed the sides of the pots with his calloused and wine-stained hands, his fingers running over the dates, showing us 1940, 1920. Others, without dates, Giovanni figured were probably hundreds of years old.

The urns were covered with round wooden lids. Giovanni opened the mouth of one and told us to put our noses into the opening. *"Che profumo, eh?"* he said. What perfume. The thick, sweet olive scent, so fragrant and fresh, filled us. We would take bottles home.

The *frantoio* at Torre e Cona had been updated: no horses or oxen to turn the heavy stone disks that pressed the olives, a convenience that Giovanni seemed both saddened and relieved to face. Now the small and black or fat green and shining olives, picked in the late fall, wait in baskets to be ground and pressed by a mechanical mill. After the olives have been mashed into a thick paste, they get spread onto *fiscoli,* disks now made of plastic—another modern convenience. They were once handmade from coconut fibers reinforced with thread.

Once this paste is applied, the disks get stacked and placed on the press. Another driving machine compresses the *fiscoli* until all the oil is released. Collected in tubs, the oil is filtered through metal-screened boxes, then stored in the *orci* for natural decantation. The oil rises to the top of the urns, getting skimmed off the top usually four times in a period of two days while the sediment sinks to the bottom. After the last skimming there still remains an element of oil mixed with water that cannot be recycled. This was once used as lamp oil, but now gets carefully disposed of. But this first oil is the prize, the first pressing, named *polpa,* the pulp, what we know as extra virgin. With its heady perfume and peppery taste, this is the oil that is used to finish a dish, drizzled over everything from soups, to vegetables, to meat and pizza.

There is a second oil as well. After the fruit and pits have been ground and pressed for the *polpa,* the paste is returned to the mill for another grinding. This next pressing is named *nocciola,* nut, meaning the olive pit, which still gives up oil. The oil gleaned from this pressing is still considered extra virgin, but is used for cooking rather than as a finishing touch.

Right there in the *frantoio* Giovanni collected and poured our bottles of oil. With a special hammered-tin measuring cup with a lip, a little plate made of the same material underneath it, and a matching ladle, he scooped up the oil, the plate there to catch any drippings, and funneled the oil into several bottles that he then labeled and onto which he clamped caps.

Back upstairs, he showed us the wine. Giovanni is passionate about the wine. The young men still working at the wine table roll their eyes, shout *"Giovanni! Lavoro, eh?"* What about work? In one cantina room there were huge modern stainless steel vats that contained the basic wine, *vino da tavola,* good wine you'd drink every day, and in another corridor were the *barriques,* the wine barrels made of French oak for aging wines that showed particular promise. All this wine would mature into Chianti Colli Fiorentini, Chianti from the hills of Florence, and those in the oak might earn the name Riserva, the highest category.

Chianti, as a wine, has had a long and varied history. Imagine vineyards growing in trees. Until relatively recently Tuscans let their vines grow wild in olive groves or other available branches. The word *Chianti,* said to go back to the Etruscans, has been bandied, used, and reused over the centuries. At worst, it was taken from its original location (the area that is called Classico now), the heart of Tuscany between Florence and Siena, and given as a name essentially to all of Tuscany by a commission under Mussolini in the 1930s. Since the 1960s, when certain Chianti estates revolutionized the making of wine in Tuscany, the classification has become more specific, and many-headed, not unlike the development of the appellations of French Bordeaux.

While placing his thick, calloused hands on the bodies of the steel wine drums, Giovanni tells us a little something of native grapes. Some can be traced back to the Middle Ages, some even further than that to ancient Greece. "Sangiovese is the predominant red grape of Tuscany," he says, *sanguis Jovis,* the blood of Jupiter. But there are also the deep-colored Canaiolo, Mammolo, and Colorino, traditional blending partners with Sangiovese. It was a Ser Lapo Mazzei who first named a wine "Chianti" in a still-surviving letter written in 1398 to a merchant in the city of Prato, his lifelong friend Francesco di Marco Datini. The wine was white, the apparent preference of the Middle Ages.

It is the town of Gaiole that has perhaps played the leading historical role in the development of Chianti as the ancestral home of the Ricasoli family since the twelfth century. At the estate of Brolio, the austere Baron Bettino Ricasoli, who was later to become the first prime minister of a united Italy, spent the 1840s perfecting a model for how he believed Chianti should be made. "Chianti wine," he wrote, "draws most of its bouquet (which is what I aim for) from Sangioveto; from Canaiolo a sweetness that tempers the harshness of the latter . . . whereas Malvasia . . . makes it lighter and more suitable for everyday use at table."

In the fading afternoon light, I wonder if the baron looked anything like Giovanni.

On each of the *barriques* at Torre e Cona was a small chalkboard that showed the vintage and had a code. There was a "b" written in the lower left-hand corner of one particular board. "Do you know what this stands for?" Giovanni asked.

We shook our heads.

"*Buono,*" he said. Good. "And do you know why?" he smiled, looking mischievous.

We shook our heads again.

"Because I made it." We all laughed, and knew it was true.

He took us back to the entrance where he packed up our bottles of oil and some bottles of Chianti. We talked of food and wine, the mystery and beauty of olive oil, Caleb's apprenticeship at the bakery around the corner and down the hill. "All you need in life," Giovanni said, "is a bottle of good wine, bread, and olive oil." *E basta.* And that's enough.

in the manner of

"Y
OU CAN'T PUT SEVEN YEARS into one day, one dinner,"
Rosa chastised us.

Caleb and I had returned to the small town on the eastern edge of
Tuscany where we'd once rented two apartments, taught English, taught
dance lessons, worked as *bariste* at a friend's piano bar. We returned there to
Castiglion after having moved away, having opened the bakery and restaurant in Vermont, having bought a house elsewhere. Rosa still had not for-
given us.

We'd run into Rosa earlier in the day at the *Bar Cacciatore,* the Hunter's
Bar, which is no longer the Hunter's Bar. The name has been changed, prov-
ing that things do change even in a place like Italy, but I refuse to remember
the new name because I don't want things to change, and will only recall it
always as the way it was when I lived there, the Hunter's Bar.

Sitting in the warmth of Rosa's kitchen later, I looked around for any
changes there. Rosa's cigarettes had grown longer and thinner in the years
we'd been away, her face too. She taunted and teased, held Caleb's face in
her hands, and wagged his jaw. She is partial to thin men like Caleb. Bawdy,
she played at grabbing the seat of his pants, already dirty from sitting in the
ashes on her kitchen hearth floor. Caleb played along, told her she could pay
for the privilege of flirting. She was both delighted to see us and disap-
pointed because it had been so long. She has always been good to me too,
but she has a preference for boys and lavishes her attention on Caleb. She's

always thought I failed to understand all she said. True, I'm not as quick as Caleb in language, it's taken me longer to feel comfortable in the elastic skin of Italian, but Rosa never held it against me. She was right, I didn't always understand everything she said, the jokes, the games, her dialect and accent so dense, but now I understand so much more than I did that first year I lived in Italy.

We met Rosa years ago when we moved to Castiglion. She cooked at the American exchange program in town where we taught English classes to local schoolchildren and adults. She also owned the old building where our friend Gianfranco was opening a piano bar in the cantina. There was an old well that came up in the middle of the floor that Gianfranco planned to light from below and cover with glass, the same well, Rosa once told us, where Jews had been hidden during World War II.

We ate once or twice a week at the dining room at the exchange school. When we first moved there, the program was in the process of renovating an old convent with rooms for students, classrooms, offices, a huge—once medieval—kitchen, and a great dining room with an incredible floor of decorative tiles in bone white, pale blue, terra-cotta, and green. I remember helping to clean and scrub that floor before the dining room was opened, all of us on hands and knees. Rosa was there too.

When we'd come to eat at the school Caleb would go into the big, new, brightly lit kitchen and either watch Rosa cook or offer to help. I have a distinct image of him leaning over her shoulder, of her handing him a spoon. Rosa cooked beautifully for a hundred and more people; she cooked simple Tuscan meals comprised of a pasta first course, then meat or fish with a *contorno*—a side dish of prepared vegetables, then a plain salad. Tuscan women had been making these sorts of rustic and bold dishes for hundreds of years, pastas with meat sauces made from veal or rabbit, roasted pork loin or braised beef, vegetables sautéed in olive oil, garlic, and lemon juice, like *spinaci saporiti,* cooked spinach so bright and deep in flavor.

Rosa also had us to dinner at her house once a week on Friday or Saturday nights, nights she didn't cook at the school. She lived on the same narrow street as the converted convent in a third-floor apartment. On cold nights, she cooked for us *alla maniera di Rosa,* in her own manner. Her children

Massimo and Laura were always there, Laura's fiancé Azi, our friend Gianfranco and his business partner Paolo. Sometimes, a handsome man named Gigi would come as well and flirt with Rosa, which made her happy.

Rosa's kitchen and dining room were in one space, so she could talk and cook and drink wine while some of us sat around the long table, or some on the raised hearth of the fireplace that was always burning. In the autumn, Caleb or Gianfranco would roast chestnuts over the flame and the room would fill with the sweet, smoky scent. We'd peel and eat them, still warm in the fingers and mouth, before the pasta was passed around the table. With its yellowed walls in need of fresh paint this was a homely room made all the more beautiful by the food on the table and the people sharing it. Rosa's best room was at the front of the apartment, a sitting room she never used filled with intricate Venetian glass, a collection of dolls, and lace curtains.

Most of these meals took place in the autumn and winter when Castiglion grew cold and often heavy with fog. Our first apartment there was around the corner from Rosa's, an ancient place built into the walls of the town. Our rooms were often cold and damp, and that first year we had difficulty with the landlady getting the heat turned on. Caleb and I bought an electric space heater for our bedroom to lift some of the deep chill at night. Our apartment had only a washer, so when we did laundry we'd hang our clothes on racks to dry, and in that season dry was an impossible goal. Even after the heat got turned on, the rooms were still so damp that we would make a tent of sheets over the electric radiator to hang our clothes beneath, otherwise they would take days to dry, and still the material would feel a little moist.

At Rosa's we could sit as close to the fire as we needed. I always sat in the chair right in front of the hearth, so I would stay warm all night long, or if there was room, next to Caleb or Gianfranco on the hearth. Then the food would arrive and someone would bring a couple of nice bottles of wine, and that would further warm us.

When we returned to Rosa's after our long absence, it was almost the same. The weather was cold and damp outside, and Caleb and I shared the hearth in front of the fire. Rosa and her daughter Laura prepared dinner, Caleb moving from his perch next to me to go look over Rosa's shoulder.

She handed him a spoon, the spoon a natural extension of him now, akin to second nature. I helped set the table. Azi, Laura's husband since we last lived in Castiglion, smoked and ate quickly before the rest of us. He too teased and joked. Then Azi was gone from dinner to go play *briscola* or cards at his favorite bar. I knew nothing of his marriage to Laura, if they were in love or not, all I knew was how small Laura had become, frail like a bird. She looked like her mother.

We sat around Rosa's long dining table situated between the kitchen and the fireplace. Her youngest son Massimo had turned beautiful, truly now the golden angel his childhood face had always promised. Rosa had told us when we saw her at the Hunter's Bar that Massimo had grown up; she described him as a little *birichino,* naughty. She had said this with pride. I wasn't surprised. He'd had the look of a ruffian when he was thirteen. But at the dinner table, he did surprise me. His actions and conversation were gentle in manner, all while he stroked the big gray cat that I used to hold in my lap while sitting on the edge of the fireplace. Stylish now but out of work, Massimo's eyes lit up when he spoke of America.

He owns all the traditional beauty in this family. His chiseled, perfect face so distant from Rosa and her daughter Laura's features, their hardness, their private curses—those hard-life experiences—played out in their expressions. Massimo strikes me as gallant in manner, a gentleman, and I wonder how he got to be this way living in such a robust and ribald household. Rosa has long lived alone with her children, her husband gone for as long as we've known her, his absence a mystery to Caleb and me. We've heard stories— that he was a con artist, a thief who met an unfortunate end, and that Rosa mourned for him out of her deep and perhaps misplaced love. But this has never been confirmed, nor have I ever asked her, nor will I ever ask her. The curious air of a tragic love affair adds to her particular beauty.

To see people after so many years have passed and in a different language, to try to recapture who you were all those years ago, is difficult, like returning home. Walk through the door of your childhood home, or sit at the family table at a holiday. The clock winds backward. You are two, or eight, or seventeen, or twenty-five again. You see yourself step into the same role you've always had, when all you want to do is claim how tall you've grown, how much you've changed. We do change, and people who haven't seen us for a long time note the differences, for better or worse. Yet they also note how much we stay the same, either because it's true or because they want it to be.

The fussy cuckoo clock still hung on the wall near Rosa's front door. Listening to it, it seemed we were living just down the street, Caleb and I younger and newly wed, eating dinner every week at Rosa's. The autumn scents and the flavors were the same—pasta with the red and green pepper sauce, the risotto with calamari, the trout stuffed with rosemary and garlic, the quail and pork and sausage—the memory was the same. We had changed and yet not changed. We remembered how we were when the *Bar Cacciatore* was still the Hunter's Bar. We were children coming home.

singing carmen in the town hall

EXHAUSTION FROM FOLIAGE SEASON at the restaurant has finally set in, made a bed of my bones. I've lost my voice. For three days now I've been without sound, except the strain of whispers and an occasional rasp. I don't feel sick, no fever, just tired with a headache and an irritated body, and tired, and did I say tired? Today is our ritual day off, and a beauty it is. We woke to heat and haze in late October, sun burning down through blue sky. The trees are bare now, except for the young poplars who thread a bit of their gold through these hills where wood smoke settles thick in the tallest limbs like cloaks of iridescent muslin.

This day reminds me of the first time I saw Italy in November. The air was still warm and roses were still in bloom at the café where we'd go for our morning coffee and pull off our sweaters because it suddenly felt like summer. The world here on top of Mount Hunger, where I live (on the topographical map it sits next to Delectable Mountain—yes, really), is quiet, like a house before dawn. But not without sound. I am acutely aware of sound— crickets still hum, a light breeze rattles the leaves in the trees along the creek to the west, even fallen leaves lift off the ground for one last word. I spend the afternoon outside, sunk in an Adirondack chair stolen from our neighbor's woods. Our first winter here Caleb and I walked the perimeter of the fields and found two half-buried Adirondack chairs and a stool tossed into a stand of birch. We vowed to wait until spring, to see if our neighbor, who lives here only in the warm months, would retrieve this bounty. If not, we'd call them our own and drag them up to the house under the cover of dusk. The chairs and stool sat in the woods for most of the summer before we got the courage to claim them, but now, a little wobbly and missing a part or two, they sit in our yard or our field and call for us to come sit a while, read, or drink cocktails while playing a game of boccie.

Today, sitting close to the house, I can overlook my autumn garden, a disaster of overgrown tawny grasses and trevisana lettuces grown from seed bought two years ago in a market in Italy. Our Vermont spring was so wet and cold this year, the earth never dry enough to plow or mow, that we never had our big garden. I thumb through a garden magazine looking at glossy pictures of others' successes, and I imagine next year's garden: We'll replow the plot into one large square and divide that into eight beds with a straight path that leads from our front door to the garden shed. We'll outline the eight beds in lavender and Russian sage, and inside we'll grow a mix of vegetables and flowers, tomatoes, white Asian eggplant, Italian lettuces, edible sage, pots of rosemary, oregano, basil (did you know it's good to plant basil beneath your tomatoes so the basil gets some shade?). I'll include roses—pale creams, white, and blushes like Jaques Cartier, or Sea Foam, or New Dawn, or maybe I'll dig a root from the old Tudor roses whose bleached pink petals darken at the center. They've grown along an old stone wall here since long before we took up residence.

I lie on a picnic blanket thinking of the garden and listening to the crickets, the leaves whispering, my cat Tommasino (named after a stray who haunted our doorstep at the first apartment we rented in Italy) coming close then scuttling away like a little wind. I start to drift off in a dream where I am singing the role of Carmen in our one-hundred-year-old town hall down in Woodstock (last weekend's anniversary playing with my psyche no doubt). There I am in a red dress with bustle and a fur collar, my voice as clear and sharp as the taste of lemon in my tea. But the sun's heat on my face pulls me back to my yard, to the feel of the ground beneath me. I remember once reading something written by a woman who traveled to the coast of California. She was so moved by the cliffs and the waves at Big Sur that she felt compelled to lie down, to be a part of the ground, and I think briefly about burial, the beauty of a seed and all it promises, life beginning, but then I think about how we mark the end of life with burial of another sort, and I don't want to think about that anymore. Instead I think of this season coming to a close. Despite the teasing warmth of the sun, I know it is autumn, and winter just around the corner.

I remembered a favorite poem by Salvatore Quasimodo, and at some point I rouse myself and go inside to find a book of Italian poetry I bought years ago so Caleb and I could read aloud to each other before going to bed. (It's in Italian and translation so I can move between two worlds.) Finding the poem, I close the book on a finger to mark the page and go to find Caleb. I think, Why wait for evening?

Antico Inverno

Desiderio delle tue mani chiare
Nella penombre della fiamma:
Sapevano di rovere e di rose;
Di Morte. Antico inverno.

Cercavano il miglio gli uccelli
Ed erano subito di neve;
Cosi le parole:
Un po di sole, una raggere d'angelo,
E poi nebbia; e gli alberi,
E noi fatti d'aria al mattino.

Ancient Winter

Desire of your hands white
In the penumbra of the flame:
They had the fragrance of oak and of roses.
Of death. Ancient winter.

The birds were looking for millet
and were suddenly of snow;
So with words:
A bit of sun, an angel's halo,
And then the mist; and the trees,
And ourselves made of air in the morning.

Crostini alla Vecchia Maniera

CHICKEN LIVER CROSTINI

BEING A VERY CLASSICAL Tuscan dish, this recipe's name appropriately pronounces it to be *alla vecchia maniera,* or "in the old style." An order of assorted crostini in a Tuscan restaurant would almost certainly include some of these. A look at the ingredients might suggest that the pâté is boldly flavored, which it should be, but not so strongly as to obscure the liver itself. The flavor of this pâté pairs well with thinly sliced prosciutto and a sharp white wine like Trebbiano d'Abruzzo or a Lugana. Serves 4 to 6 people 2 to 3 crostini apiece.

1 tablespoon butter
2 cloves garlic, smashed
½ teaspoon brined green peppercorns, drained
1 cup chicken livers, rinsed well and patted dry
Salt and freshly ground pepper
½ cup chicken stock (or water or white wine)
Olive oil
¼-inch-thick slices plain, country bread (2 to 3 slices per person)

Warm a sauté pan over medium heat for about 1 minute. Add the butter and let it melt, then add the garlic, peppercorns, and chicken livers. Strew a couple pinches of salt and pepper around the pan. Sauté all this for 2 or 3 minutes longer so that the pan has time enough to get real hot again and everything is sizzling nicely. Then add the stock, bring it to a boil, and govern the heat to maintain a fast simmer. Simmer for a few more minutes until the livers feel firm all the way through: to check for firmness, press on the thickest one with your finger (it should feel firm), or feel free to cut it in half to inspect the interior.

As soon as the livers are cooked, remove livers and drippings from the pan to a bowl or plate and let them cool down for at least 10 minutes, until they reach room temperature. When cool, process it all in a food processor (or chop everything as finely as you can with a sharp chef's knife) until a granular, rough paste is achieved. A Tuscan would leave the paste like this so that is has some texture, perhaps adding just a touch of olive oil to even out the consistency. Return it to the bowl. Taste and correct seasoning. The pâté should be strong in flavor and well seasoned, as it is meant to awaken your taste buds.

Spread a skimcoat of butter on each slice of bread followed by a nice layer of pâté. Don't skimp, but don't overload the bread either. (Ideally, these crostini are served just warmed, but they are also delicious at room temperature.) Toast lightly in the oven or heat gently in a covered frying pan. When just warm and toasted, remove to a serving plate. Garnish with, at most, a touch of parsley if desired. They require nothing else. Enjoy.

Cavolo con Sugo di Acciughe

Cabbage Salad with Anchovy Dressing

Serve this salad as an appetizer. Its fresh, clean flavor and acidity are a good way to focus attention on the meal to follow. Look for bright, crisp, firm, pale green cabbage. Don't worry about having to buy a whole cabbage, the remaining cabbage can go in a soup, such as *Iota* (p. 166). Serves 4.

> 1 medium clove garlic, smashed
> 2 anchovy fillets (rinsed well and patted dry if packed in salt)
> 2 to 3 tablespoons extra-virgin olive oil
> 1 tablespoon white wine vinegar
> 1 green cabbage
> Salt and freshly ground pepper, to taste

Place the smashed garlic and anchovies on a cutting board. Using a large chef's knife, alternately mash them together with the flat of the knife and then chop with the blade. Continue mashing and chopping until the garlic and anchovies form a paste. Transfer the paste to a large salad bowl and mix in the oil and vinegar.

Cut about 1 inch off the bottom of the cabbage, and discard any browned, limp, or damaged leaves. Remove 2 or 3 leaves per person, and it doesn't matter if they tear somewhat. Clean as needed and pat dry. Open up the leaves in turn and cut out the tough rib. Stack the leaves and carefully slice the cabbage into fine slivers. Toss the cabbage very well in the dressing and then let the dish rest in the bowl for a few minutes while you do something else (finish setting the table, looking after your guests). Right before serving, toss the salad again and taste for seasoning; it may need more oil and vinegar, and some anchovies are not as salty as others, so your salad may in fact need a little extra salt and pepper. Toss again and serve immediately.

Peperoni con Bagna Cauda
PEPPERS WITH GARLIC-ANCHOVY SAUCE

BAGNA CAUDA is a classic condiment of northwestern Italy. In its traditional presentation—alongside lots of sliced raw vegetables—it can be a meal in itself. It can also dress vegetables served as antipasti, as it does the cooked peppers here. Like many classical dishes, its name simply doesn't translate sufficiently to reveal the traditions behind the dish: the words "hot bath" may not excite the palate, but that is precisely the aim of *bagna cauda*. It is a wonderful way to enjoy fresh raw vegetables in the colder months. Carrot and celery sticks, fennel, zucchini, radishes, cardoons, and peppers are typical vegetables for dipping into a central bowl.

With this recipe, you'll probably end up with more *bagna cauda* than you need. Fortunately, the sauce keeps well for a few weeks stored in a jar or tightly covered container in the refrigerator, so you can make it in advance if necessary. Serves 4 as an *antipasto*.

    1 large head garlic, cloves separated and peeled
    2 salted anchovies, or 4 to 6 small anchovy fillets in oil,
        well-rinsed
    2 tablespoons butter
    ½ cup olive oil
    ¼ cup milk
    2 small to medium bell peppers
    Salt and pepper

To make the *bagna cauda*, smash the garlic and chop and mash it together with the anchovies until they become a paste. Gently warm the butter, olive oil, and milk in a saucepan over medium-low heat, add the anchovy-garlic paste, and stir well. Reduce the heat to very low and cook 1 hour, stirring occasionally and never letting the fat begin to simmer, as you don't want the garlic to brown and become bitter. Keep the sauce warm for service.

Meanwhile, cut the peppers in half lengthwise right through the stem. Pull out and discard the stems, seeds, and any loose interior membrane. Cut the pepper lengthwise into slices about 1 inch wide. Arrange the slices in a large skillet or saucepan with a tight-fitting lid, add about ½ inch of water and a couple pinches of salt and pepper, and cover the pan. Bring it to a brisk simmer over medium-high heat and cook for 10 to 12 minutes, until tender but not mushy, adding water if needed. (To check for doneness, use a pointed knife to poke a slice of pepper.)

Remove the peppers to a serving plate and allow to cool before serving: they should be warm, not hot. Spoon the warm *bagna cauda* over them and serve, putting extra sauce in a serving bowl nearby.

Iota

Bean Soup from the Alto Adige

IOTA IS A GOOD SOUP to make during a blizzard or to have available in your freezer should a blizzard catch you by surprise. This recipe makes plenty, so either call some friends and tell them to snowshoe over while the soup is cooking or plan on storing leftovers in the freezer. Keep in mind that beans and other soup starches (like potatoes and rice) soak up incredible quantities of salt, rendering many well-intentioned soups bland and uninspiring. Do not fail to taste this, and all your soups, at the late stages of preparation and season accordingly. Serves 6 to 8.

> 1 pound dried white beans (*cannellini* or Great Northern beans)
> 2 tablespoons butter
> 2 tablespoons extra-virgin olive oil
> 1 large onion, diced small
> 3 or 4 cloves garlic, smashed
> 1 medium head savoy cabbage, core removed, leaves finely slivered
> 4 quarts water or chicken stock
> 2 bay leaves
> Salt and freshly ground black pepper
> Additional extra-virgin olive oil

One night before: Pick over the beans to remove any errant pebbles or clumps of dirt. Rinse the beans well, place them in a large container (they will swell considerably), cover them with cold water, and soak them overnight.

To make the soup: Place the butter and olive oil in a stockpot over medium heat and melt the butter. Add the onion and garlic, stir well to coat, and cook for 15 minutes over medium heat, stirring occasionally, until the onions just begin to brown. Add the slivered cabbage and stir again to coat. Cover the pot and cook for 10 minutes to wilt the cabbage. Add the water or stock.

Drain the beans and add them to the cabbage soup along with the bay leaves and some salt and pepper. Bring the pot to a slow simmer over medium heat, cover, and cook for at least 45 minutes. Test the beans for doneness: they should be very tender. Using a potato masher or wooden spoon, mash some of the beans against the side of the pot and stir it all together to thicken the soup. Taste for seasoning, add salt and pepper as needed, and stir well. Turn the burner off and let the soup rest for 10 to 15 minutes. Meanwhile, set some bowls in an oven on low to warm.

Stir the soup well again and ladle into prewarmed bowls. Drizzle a touch of extra-virgin olive oil over each serving.

Tortelli di Zucca

SQUASH RAVIOLI

AROUND THE ELEGANT northern city of Mantova these ravioli are called *Tortelli alla Mantovana*, "in the style of Mantova." Of course, in Mantova itself they are simply referred to as *Tortelli di Zucca*, "squash Tortelli." A *Tortello* is a 2-inch-square *raviolo*, also called a *Cappellaccio* in some regions. They are not difficult to make and they are worth all the time and effort.

In addition to the ingredients listed below, you will need either a pasta-rolling machine (not to be confused with a pasta-*making* machine) or (proficiency with) a rolling pin; as much open counter space as possible; a pastry brush; and a little water. *Keep in mind:* Measure the flour carefully, better to have pasta dough that requires regular dustings of flour as you work it than to have an impossibly stiff dough. And once you begin to roll out the dough you must work without interruption to avoid handling complications. Serves 4.

4 eggs
3 cups all-purpose flour, plus extra for dusting the dough
1 can (12 ounces) plain pumpkin
¼ cup crushed amaretti cookies
¼ cup plain bread crumbs
½ cup ricotta
Salt and pepper
2 to 3 tablespoons butter
Freshly grated *Parmigiano-Reggiano*

In a large bowl mix together the eggs and 3 cups flour until you can compress the mixture into one shaggy mass with your hands. Wrap this crude dough in plastic and set it aside while you prepare the filling

In a large bowl, mix together the pumpkin, cookies, bread crumbs, ricotta, and salt and pepper until well blended. Taste and correct seasoning as needed. Set filling aside while you roll out the pasta.

Cut off a piece of dough the size of a grapefruit. Set the pasta machine at its widest setting. Use a rolling pin to roll out the dough until it is just thin enough to put through the rollers of the pasta machine. Put the dough through the machine again but at the next setting down. Continue to put the pasta through the machine, each time on successively thinner settings—dusting with a little flour as necessary to keep the dough from sticking to everything in sight, except itself—until you have rolled it through the machine on the thinnest setting.

On a lightly floured work surface, lay out the sheet of pasta and cut it in half. Set aside one half. Lightly brush the remaining half sheet of dough with water. Place filling by the tablespoonful at 2-inch intervals in 2 rows down the length of the dough. Beginning at one end, carefully lay the set-aside sheet of dough over this piece, pressing it into place down the middle as you slowly lay it down to cover the dots of filling. Once in place use your hands to align and press the edges of the dough together, and to press between the dots of filling. (You must be sure to get good contact so that the ravioli don't open up when boiled.) When the dough sheets are pressed together around the filling, you are ready to cut the ravioli apart. Slice once lengthwise between the two rows and then cut crosswise between dots to free up each raviolo. Set the ravioli on a clean dishtowel where they won't be disturbed, making sure they do not touch one another. Repeat the procedure, beginning with a grapefruit-sized hunk, with the remainder of the dough until the filling is used up. (Any leftover dough can be stored or rolled and cut into another shape for use on its own.)

Fill a bowl large enough to hold the tortelli with hot water and set aside to warm.

Bring a large pot of well-salted water to a boil. Put about 10 or 12 ravioli in the boiling water and cook for 8 minutes. While they cook, gently melt the butter in a sauté pan. Empty and dry the warmed mixing bowl and transfer the melted butter to it. After about 8 minutes lift out a tortello with a slotted spoon and test one corner: it must be tender to the bite, not al dente. When tender, use the slotted spoon to remove the cooked tortelli and very carefully turn them in the melted butter. Once all the tortelli are buttered, serve immediately with a separate bowl of grated *parmigiano* alongside.

Spaghetti con Broccoletti

SPAGHETTI WITH BROCCOLI FLORETS

THIS SIMPLE DISH has more flavor than its name suggests. The broccoli is braised with garlic and olive oil, but I have found it tastes delightfully of almonds, yet without an almond in sight. If broccoli rabe is available at your market, you may want to try it in place of broccoli for its stronger yet equally delicious flavor. Serves 4 as a *primo*.

¼ cup plus additional extra-virgin olive oil
2 cups small broccoli florets
3 or 4 small cloves garlic, peeled
Salt and pepper to taste
¾ pound spaghetti
Parmigiano-Reggiano or *Grana Padano* cheese for grating

Bring a large pot of well-salted water to a boil for the pasta.

In a skillet with a tight-fitting lid, heat the ¼ cup olive oil over medium-high heat until it begins to form a haze over the pan. Add the broccoli, garlic, and a couple generous pinches of salt and pepper and toss or stir everything to coat it well with the oil. Cover the pan, lower the heat to medium-low, and let cook—stirring or tossing the ingredients once a minute for 8 to 12 minutes. The broccoli will cook down quite a bit as it wilts. To test the broccoli for doneness, spear a stem with a sharp knife or simply fork a piece and taste it: it should be nice and tender, not crunchy at all. Add salt and pepper to taste, stir again, and remove the broccoli to a large mixing or serving bowl. Remove the garlic cloves if desired.

Add the spaghetti to the boiling water and cook until al dente. Drain the pasta. Add it to the broccoli and toss. Taste and correct the seasoning. Grate just a little cheese over the pasta (this is *not* intended to be a cheesy dish), toss again, and serve. Pass extra grated cheese at the table for those who can't resist.

Risotto ai Funghi Porcini

PORCINI MUSHROOM RISOTTO

FUNGHI PORCINI are worth the trouble of finding, and trouble it can be, for in the regions of Italy where they are harvested legions of devoted forest scavengers guard the secret of their territory much like the truffle hunters. Fortunately, dried, imported *porcini* are readily available in the United States. *Porcini* do grow domestically, but their taste differs from their Italian brethren, simply because they grow in a different environment.

Once you begin to make a dish of risotto, you cannot step away from the stove and leave the dish unattended. Though this rule may make risotto appear tedious, you'll find investing in a mere 15 or 20 minutes of devotion results in something elevated far above its humble beginnings.

You will need a good large saucepan or stockpot, a sturdy wooden spatula (or one of high-heat-resistant silicon) for stirring the rice, and a quantity of chicken or vegetable stock heated and at hand. It is important to season the risotto well before it leaves the pot; the starch in this dish will absorb an amazing quantity of salt before the flavors of its elements can fully emerge. Serves 6 as a first course, or 4 as a main course.

    1 cup dried *porcini* mushrooms
    4 cups chicken stock or vegetable stock
    4 tablespoons butter (or butter and olive oil combined)
    1 medium yellow onion, diced small
    2 cups Arborio rice
    Salt and freshly ground pepper
    1 cup freshly grated *Parmigiano-Reggiano* or *Grana Padano*

Place the dried mushrooms in a medium bowl and cover with hot water. Soak for 20 to 30 minutes. Squeeze the water from the mushrooms into the bowl and reserve the liquid. Chop the soaked mushrooms into small pieces and set aside. Add the strained liquid to the 4 cups stock, but be careful to leave behind any dirt or sand. Heat the stock in a saucepan on the stove or in the microwave and keep it warm.

Heat the butter and/or oil in your risotto pot of choice, add the diced onion and stir well to coat with the fats. Simmer the onions gently over a medium heat, stirring occasionally, until they just begin to turn golden brown. (At this point you must be prepared to attend to the dish until it is finished.) Add the rice, the chopped mushrooms, and several large pinches of salt and pepper, and stir well again to coat with the fats. Add ½ cup of the warm stock and begin a steady stirring motion, scraping back and forth across the bottom of the pot, allowing the liquid to become absorbed by the rice until the rice begins to stick to the pot. Add another ½ cup of warm stock and stir and scrape until it is absorbed by the rice. Continue stirring and adding liquid in ½-cup increments, always maintaining a medium to medium-high lively heat, until all the liquid is absorbed by the rice, for about 15 minutes.

Taste the rice for doneness: it should be tender, but still resist the bite. In other words, al dente. If needed, continue the cooking procedure, adding additional stock or water. As soon as the rice is ready, stir in the grated cheese and bring the dish to the proper consistency for serving: it should be smooth and creamy, neither stiff and lumpy nor too runny. Taste, adjust seasonings, and serve immediately with extra grated cheese on the side.

La Trota all' Erbe Fresche

TROUT WITH FRESH HERBS

THIS IS THE DISH to make when you come across beautiful trout at the market. I can remember being confused by cookbooks that instructed me to look for a clear-eyed fish, until I realized this meant a fresh fish looks alive, its eyes bright and not foggy. Imagine the fish swimming along in a stream: if its eyes are dim and cloudy, move along to another stream or fishmonger until you find a fresh one.

Once you find a good-looking trout for this dish, show it the respect it deserves by presenting it whole with head and tail, surrounded by a vegetable side dish and some roasted potatoes. If you find you have squeamish dinner guests, you can always move the fish to the kitchen and cut it into portions. Serves 1. Multiply as needed.

    1 tablespoon plus additional extra-virgin olive oil
    1 whole trout (about 8 to 10 ounces, cleaned)
    Salt and freshly ground pepper
    Lemons cut for squeezing
    1 4-inch sprig rosemary
    Kosher salt
    ¼ to ⅓ cup white wine
    Lemon slices for garnishing

Preheat oven to 375 degrees.

Brush olive oil over the bottom of a roasting pan or skillet large enough to accommodate the fish. Rinse the fish inside and out under cold running water and gently shake off excess water. Place fish in the roasting pan and season it on the inside: open the fish like a book and season the inside with a little salt and pepper, a squeeze of lemon juice, and a tablespoon of extra-virgin olive oil. Lay the rosemary sprig along the inside of the backbone. Close the fish and sprinkle a light blanket of Kosher salt over the length of one side. Pour a little white wine around the fish and put the pan in the oven.

Roast the trout for 12 to 15 minutes until done. To check for doneness, carefully open up the fish near the gills so that you can poke a knife into the meat where it is plumpest. The meat should be completely opaque and be just ready to flake apart. The salt should have formed a thin crust over the outside of the fish.

With a large spatula, remove the fish to a serving plate or platter. To serve, drizzle a little extra-virgin olive oil over the fish and garnish with lemon slices.

Pagello col Sugo di Finocchio

RED SNAPPER WITH FENNEL SAUCE

FRESH FENNEL, with its gently assertive flavor, is an excellent match for several kinds of fish, including bass and trout. Here it is paired with red snapper. This sauce is easy to make, and it can be made ahead of time and simply served at room temperature. Serves 1. Multipy as needed.

1 fennel bulb
2 tablespoons butter or olive oil
Salt and freshly ground pepper
1 red snapper fillet, about 8 ounces
Additional extra-virgin olive oil

Cut the stalks and frilly leaves off the fennel bulb, quarter the bulb, and cut out the tough core. Thinly slice the quarters. Heat the butter or oil in a saucepan, add the sliced fennel, a couple pinches of salt, and freshly ground pepper, and stir well to coat with the fat. Cover the pan, lower the heat to medium-low, and let the fennel simmer gently for 12 to 15 minutes. Check the fennel: it should feel good and tender when poked with a fork. Scrape the contents of the pan into a blender or food processor and process until smooth. If the sauce seems too stiff, add a touch of water or olive oil and process again to blend. Taste the sauce and season with additional salt and pepper if needed. Set aside to serve warm (or allow to cool for storage if using later).

Rinse the fish fillet(s) under cold water, gently pat dry with a paper towel, and lay on a plate or platter. Drizzle or brush both sides of the fish with a little extra-virgin olive oil and sprinkle with salt and pepper. Heat a thin coat of oil in a skillet over medium-high heat until a haze begins to form over the pan, then lay in the fillet(s) skin-side up (if multiplying the recipe, lay in only as many fillets as the pan can comfortably accommodate). Cook for about 1 minute, then gently turn the fillet(s) over with a spatula, lower the heat to medium, and cover the pan. Cook 4 to 6 minutes longer. To test for doneness, insert a knife between the fattest flakes of the meat: it should appear uniformly white and opaque throughout. Remove the fillet(s) to a serving platter or plate. Dress with fennel sauce and an extra swirl of olive oil and serve.

Salsicce con l'Uva

SAUSAGES WITH BLACK GRAPES

WHILE THIS DISH MAKES for excellent dinner fare, I personally prefer it served on a crusty roll for lunch along with a glass of Chianti Colli Aretini. That's because we once had such sandwiches in the Piazza del Municipio in Arezzo on a brisk and bright autumn day during the monthly antiques fair. Now that I think of it, that sandwich wasn't much more than just grilled sausage and bread with a little rough local wine in a plastic cup, served in an atmosphere of shouting, joking cooks, and centuries-old sideboards, headboards, and dressers surrounded by buildings from the Renaissance—an atmosphere to elevate any meal. If you don't have good crusty bread on hand, make a few mashed potatoes while these sausages are roasting in the oven. Serves 4.

2 large yellow onions, halved and slivered
2 cups black grapes (Concord, Globe, or any other
    ripe black variety), rinsed well
Extra-virgin olive oil
Salt and pepper
4 to 8 sweet Italian sausages (1 or 2 sausages per person)

Preheat oven to 375 degrees.

In a large roasting pan or skillet mix the slivered onion and grapes together with your hands. Drizzle some oil over them and sprinkle with several generous pinches of salt and pepper. Mix again and spread out the mixture evenly. Nestle the sausages in the onion-grape layer, but don't let them be completely covered. Put the pan in the oven and roast for 30 to 40 minutes, until the onions have cooked down considerably, the grapes are soft, and the sausages are plump and browned on top, even a little bit crusty. Pierce one of the largest sausages. They are ready when the juices run clear. Spoon a bed of onions and grapes onto a serving platter or individual plates, top with the sausages, and serve.

Tacchino al Limone

Turkey Cutlets with Lemon

WHAT DO I LIKE about this dish? Its clean flavors and simple preparation. This dish can follow a rich pasta course, because it is both light and still satisfyingly meaty. It also stands up perfectly to the strong flavors of root vegetables and the weight of a good red wine. All this makes for an ideal autumn meal, but don't limit your enjoyment to one season: turkey prepared in this way is excellent when chilled to serve cold for summer picnics with Chardonnay from the Alto Adige. Serves 4.

½ skinless, boneless turkey breast, about 1½ pounds
Salt and freshly ground pepper
4 to 6 tablespoons olive oil
½ cup fresh lemon juice
2 tablespoons butter

Rinse the half turkey breast under cold water and dry it well with a paper towel. Cut the breast crosswise into slices just thicker than a pencil. Arrange the slices on a platter and sprinkle them lightly with salt and pepper.

Heat 2 to 3 tablespoons of the olive oil in a large, heavy skillet over medium-high heat. When a haze begins to show over the pan, place the turkey slices seasoned-side down in a single layer in the pan, but don't crowd the pan. Now sprinkle the top sides with salt and pepper and cook for 3 to 4 minutes, maintaining a brisk heat without letting the pan overheat. Turn the slices over, lower the heat a mere fraction, and cook for another 5 to 6 minutes. When just a little browning begins to show on each side remove the cooked slices to a warm platter and quickly wipe out the pan with a paper towel to remove any bits of meat or fat that might burn. Add 2 to 3 more tablespoons olive oil to the pan and repeat the cooking procedure with the remaining turkey slices.

Remove the last of the cooked turkey to a serving platter, return the pan to the burner over high heat (without wiping it clean), and pour in the lemon juice. Scrape the pan with a spatula to loosen all the cooked-on bits. Add the butter, a couple pinches of salt, and freshly ground pepper and continue to stir the contents of the pan, mixing the melting butter into the juice. Let the liquid reduce until it begins to thicken a little bit. Pour the sauce over the turkey and serve.

Melanzana e Zucchine in Padella

Sautéed Eggplant and Zucchini

THESE VEGETABLES are excellent alongside almost any *secondo*. They can also be served at room temperature or slightly warmed as an antipasto. Find eggplant and zucchini of the same size to make the preparation easier and the presentation easy on the eye. If you have some fresh mozzarella and good bread on hand, you can turn this dish into an exceptional sandwich. Serves 4.

1 small eggplant
1 6- to 8-inch zucchini
Salt and freshly ground pepper
Olive oil

Wash the eggplant and the zucchini and trim their ends. Cut them lengthwise into ¼- to ⅜-inch-thick slices. (Don't worry about perfectly equal slices. Varied sizes result in slight variations in texture and doneness and—on the whole—a more interesting plate.) Season the slices on each side with salt and pepper.

Coat a large skillet with olive oil, heat until a haze forms over the pan, and lay in as many slices as the pan can accommodate without crowding. Govern the heat to maintain a medium-hot pan, and cook the slices 2 to 3 minutes. Turn the slices over with tongs and cook 2 to 3 minutes longer. The slices should just be cooked through. Remove promptly to a plate and continue with the remaining slices, refreshing the olive oil in the skillet as needed between batches. Serve immediately.

Bietole in Padella

SAUTÉED BEETS

BEETS ARE AN EXCELLENT cold-weather accompaniment to roasted meats of all kinds, and here is a way to prepare them quickly. I know, I know: every other recipe I have encountered calls for roasting the beets whole first, but this method eliminates that very time-consuming step. I also recommend mixing in some carrots and parsnips, and preparing all three together. Keep in mind that the cut of the vegetables (julienne, or matchsticks) is important to their cooking time and to their final texture.

> 1 medium–small beet per person
> Butter and/or olive oil
> Salt and pepper
> Lemon for squeezing

Peel the beets and cut them into matchsticks. In a sauté pan heat a small amount of butter and/or oil, add the beets and a pinch of salt and pepper per person, and toss or stir to coat everything well with the fat. Sauté for 4 to 5 minutes over medium-high heat, shaking the pan—or stirring the contents—once every 30 seconds to keep everything cooking evenly.

Try a piece: it should have a little crisp bite to it, or rather, it should not be limp. Season with salt and pepper if needed. Squeeze in a little lemon juice and toss everything to mix well. Add a little more butter or oil if you can't see any gloss of fat on the vegetables. Serve immediately.

Le Pere con Parmigiano

PEARS AND PARMIGIANO

A RIPE PEAR is a beautiful thing. Succulent and sweet—but not overly so—a ripe pear is a perfect compliment to *Parmigiano-Reggiano* at the end of a good meal, or as an afternoon snack with a glass of red wine. If you are shopping for pears at your supermarket they will probably be quite hard and it may take up to a week, sometimes more, to ripen them at room temperature. Inside a paper bag is a good place to let this happen, especially if it is summertime. Underripe pears just do not satisfy in this situation, so if store-bought fruit is your only option, plan ahead.

If you live in an area where pears are grown, seek out a good source. It could be an operating orchard where you can pick your own, or it may be an abandoned tree: either way, the reward of a ripe pear ready to eat right off the tree is another experience all by itself. It wouldn't hurt to have some underripe pears on hand, too, so that you can prepare *Pere in Caramello al Pernod* (p. 242).

Pears and *parmigiano* require almost no preparation. Provide each person with a good knife with which to slice their pear at table, or slice the pears and display them on a plate. Break the *parmigiano* into rough pieces and provide a knife for breaking them further. Serve and let everyone help themselves.

Torta di Mele

APPLE CAKE

THIS IS ONE of those recipes that seem so unassuming, perhaps even inno-
cent, but the results far exceed the humble beginnings. Note that once you
begin to whip the egg whites you cannot step away from the recipe until the
cake goes in the oven, so good organization is essential. This recipe makes
at least one 10-inch cake, so you may need a second, smaller pan on hand to
handle extra batter.

> 4 or 5 crisp apples
> Juice of 1 lemon
> 5 eggs, separated
> 1½ cups sugar
> ½ pound butter, melted, plus additional melted butter for brushing
> 2 tablespoons baking powder
> 1 teaspoon salt
> 2 cups flour, sifted (pastry flour is preferable, but not essential)

Preheat oven to 350 degrees.

Butter and flour your cake pan(s), being careful that the coverage on the
sides of the pan is also complete.

Peel, quarter, and core the apples. Slice the apples very thinly and toss them
in the lemon juice, and let them rest in the juice while you mix the cake.

Beat together the egg yolks and sugar until fluffy. Add the ½ pound melted
butter and mix thoroughly. Mix the baking powder and salt into the flour,
then add half this mixture and combine, and then add the remaining flour
and mix together gently until just uniform.

Whip the egg whites until stiff but not dry. Add one-third of the whites to the first mixture and mix well to loosen up the batter. Gently fold in another one-third of the whites. Add the final third of the whites, but leave some streaks of white showing in the batter. Pour the batter into the cake pan(s) and spread it out to a depth of ½ inch. Immediately begin placing the apple slices on top of the batter in long rows, or, if using round pans, concentric circles, letting one slice of apple slightly overlap the previous slice, and leaving about ¼ inch between rows of apple. Very gently brush the apples with melted butter and put the cake(s) into the oven. Bake 20 to 30 minutes until a thin knife inserted into the thickest puff of batter comes out clean. (Ideally, the cake should be pulling away from the sides of the pan, too.)

Brush the top of the cake with a little melted butter. Let the cake cool for 10 to 15 minutes. Invert the cake onto an intermediate surface, then invert again onto a serving tray. (But whom are we kidding? Cut the cake right in the pan, and lift the slices out with a large spatula. Your guests don't need to see the cake presented to them whole. By now the smell will be torture. Just deliver the cake into their hands and get out of the way.)

This cake tastes even better the morning after it is baked.

Sbrisolona da Valeria

VALERIA'S CRUMB CAKE

A FEW WEEKS AGO I CALLED our friend Valeria at her farmhouse bed-and-breakfast near Valeggio sul Mincio, just south of Lago di Garda. She must have been in her kitchen at the time, because when I asked if I could use her recipe for *Sbrisolona* she asked, "Are you ready?" Of course, Valeria is so together, she may have memorized it.

When making this cake, just as you are getting ready to put the mixture into the baking pan, you might be inclined to say to yourself, "Well, this can't be right." But you must trust that the cake will perform as intended. It's a humble and delicious cake, appropriate with morning cappuccino, afternoon espresso, or after-dinner Vin Santo. Its somewhat disorganized appearance is part of what makes it so appealing. A 10-inch tart pan with a removable bottom is the ideal baking pan for this cake, making removal, slicing, and service much easier. If you only have a cake pan or other high-sided pan, just cut the cake in the pan and remove the slices with a spatula. I have seen both flat and thick versions of this cake, so the dimensions of your pan are not so important. This recipe makes 2 cakes: one to impress your guests with and one to eat over the following week.

1½ cups sugar
2 eggs
2¼ cups whole almonds, skins on, lightly chopped
2¾ sticks butter, cut into 1-inch cubes
4¼ cups flour

Preheat oven to 250 degrees.

In a large mixing bowl, cream together the sugar and eggs. Add the chopped almonds, cut-up butter, and flour and work the mixture by hand until roughly mixed. Distribute the mixture into your baking pans (no need to butter them) by crumbling it through your fingers, but don't compress the dough into the pan. Ideally, it should be ¾ to 1 inch thick.

Bake for 50 minutes and cut the cakes into slices, then bake for another 50 minutes. If you wish, leave the cakes uncut and simply break off pieces once they have cooled.

This cake keeps very well and actually improves as it dries out.

winter

our ancient winter

IT'S COLD AND WINTRY up here. We had snow on Christmas Eve and we came home after a long day of packing up orders of three-pound round loaves of bread, almond cakes, apple and cream tarts, *panettone, bucellato siciliano* (a pastry ring filled with a fig jam made with raisins, nuts, red wine), cookies, *cornetti,* and *zucchetelli* to a light dinner with two friends, our eyes drooping over a discussion of the American opera *Amal and the Night Visitors* written for television in the fifties by an Italian composer, all of which we listened to on our old record player.

It snowed again on Christmas morning with coffee, clementines, and stockings in bed. We prepared a French tea for our Christmas meal: lobster salad, pâté, tea sandwiches, and tiny cheese souffles to be tasted with a glass of sherry. I've taken to drinking sherry since Christmas afternoon, only three days ago now, having received my first bottle of sherry as a gift for Christmas along with four sherry glasses handblown with a whisper of aqua blue. Looking through the glass you can imagine you might be in Jerez, Spain, where sherry is produced, the word "sherry" a bastard delivered from English mouths trying to pronounce the Spanish *Jerez.*

We've taken three days off from work, closed the restaurant out of exhaustion. This third day has been the best, a day spent reading—everything from fashion magazines to house magazines (Look! They've put the bathroom sink right into a beautiful chest of drawers and the mistress of the house, her skin pink and her hair damp and curling around her face as if she's just stepped out of the bath to file that nail that keeps catching sits on a stool next to a claw-footed tub with at least three different types of feet), to Charles Baxter and Chekhov and finally, in my own bath with a glass of that sherry, *Paris to the Moon*. Earlier, we took a long walk up to the summit of the mountain behind us to see the view, which was far and wide, and later enjoyed a midafternoon meal of nuts, cheese, smoked salmon, and hot buttered rum.

We have grown even more sentimental during this holiday up in our little house high in this mountain field at the edge of the Chateauguay, a wild forest founded by an ever-searching Frenchman back when this Vermont land lay largely unclaimed. The Chateauguay grows thick with pine, fir, cherry, and maple and is alive with black bear, deer, coyote, racoon, the fearsome fisher cat, a long weasel-like animal with fat paws and gruesome ebony claws, and maybe even the some-say-mythical catamount, a panther who once roamed these northern mountains before his coat and his pride became lucrative for the taking.

We are sentimental about our cold New England winter, this white Christmas, the tall, straight balsam standing in our living room, the old-fashioned tin and colored-glass ornaments, the white and subtly colored lights, the gift of beeswax candles tied up in a wrapping paper of birch and bailing twine, the vases of pine boughs I cut two weeks ago on a foray into the woods. We are also pining for someplace else. On Christmas Eve, I wept although the snow fell lightly, and good friends were coming for a warm dinner, because I would not be going to Midnight Mass at Santa Chiara in Castiglion Fiorentino, in Italy, where the scene is like the painting of the Accademia by Raphael. On Christmas Eve at the cathedral, tall and pillared both inside and out, a Palladian, or Greek notion, the women dress in their finest and furs, the men in their suits or English wool blazers, teenage boys in jeans and padded jackets, farmers' daughters in taffeta sheathes, and no one listens to the old prelate as he goes on in Latin, no one but the old ladies in their woolen shawls and fine hats kneeling in the pews toward the front while altar boys swing lanterns smoking with sweet incense. Children run back and forth across the marble floor, and the women whisper to each other about who is wearing this year's newest design, or last year's fashionable failure. The men talk soccer or politics openly. I will miss this.

This morning, Caleb has found *Radio Cortina* from northern Italy on the computer and popular European dance music seeps through the speakers. We're listening to this instead of our local public radio or a handful of other Italian stations he's found on the internet because, he says, "I thought it would be fun to hear the ski reports: 'Today, there's skiing at 9,000 feet on Mount ——.'" Without him saying anything more I know what he means: we have snow, they have snow, and if you squint your eyes just a little and take a bite of *panettone*, that light and airy Christmas bread flecked with raisins and candied citron, you can imagine you're someplace in between.

farewell to the flesh

As from the stroke of an enchanter's wand:
The revel of the earth, the masque of Italy!
—Lord Byron

Go to Carnevale in Venice," they said, they being friends who knew. So we went; Caleb and I took the long, slow train from Florence. We stood most of the way because there was nowhere to sit; everyone was going to Carnevale, a celebration in Venice that had been abandoned for years but had been returned. Winter rains pelted our train car through the smoky landscape, and my body ached: ankles, knees, wrists, and shoulders. I traveled with a fever, a shiny heat that had started to take hold of me about an hour after we boarded the train.

Venice is a mysterious and surreal city on any day, a city of the unusual, of the exquisite, of extraordinary beauty; a city of complex gastronomy, and during Carnevale, mixed with fever, that wild *festa* celebrated in the weeks approaching the aestetic Lenten season was for me like strange, exotic magic. This merriment culminates in the Tuesday night before Ash Wednesday, the first day of Lent. Fat Tuesday, the French call it, the last hurrah of desire, of appetite. *Carnevale,* they say in Italian, farewell to the flesh.

Arriving in Venice on a cold February afternoon, one of us feverish, the pair of us wide-eyed, sent us back through the tricky definition of time, hurtled toward something not yet defined, like when you fall in a dream and before you hit the ground, your body turns and you land on your feet, a veritable cat with infinite lives. In that dreamlike falling, as the train swayed us over the lagoon from the mainland city of Mestre, its wheels sung low and haunting as we pulled into the station. Smoky mist wreathed about the gray and pale-colored buildings, and at the end of the platform stood a solitary figure, a man dressed in some sort of eighteenth-century garb: knickers, white silk stockings and buckled shoes, an elegant brocade redingote beneath a voluminous black cape. Under his black tri-corner hat he wore a powdered wig, and the traditional mask of *Il Dottore,* a stock character out of the Commedia dell'Arte. This is the doctor's face—a mask that hangs like a stiff piece of cloth with openings only for the eyes, no holes for the nose or mouth. The silent doctor, a figure originating in Venice during the 1600s, when a black plague webbed itself through the narrow streets and alleyways and across the canals with respect for no one. Doctors trying to help suffering patients disguised themselves with these masks, both to hide their identities and to protect them from the vapors of the deadly disease using something not unlike our modern-day dust mask. No one wanted contact with a man who'd had a hand on the plague.

So there we were, Caleb and I, on a Tuesday afternoon in winter as time slipped in different directions, and *Il Dottore* made a deep bow as we descended from the train. We'd landed on our feet; welcome to another world.

Since our decision to come to Venice had been last minute, we hadn't secured a room. We knew the chances were slim in finding accommodations in the city, and figured on a train ride as far back as Padova for the night. But we thought we'd try our luck at the hotel service at the train station. And luck took a deep bow as well. We got the last room available in the city.

The vaporetto took us down the Canale Grande. Since this was my first time in Venice, I was awed and delighted by the exotic and grand faces of the buildings, the water sluicing along the side of the boat, just the idea that we could travel by water taxi. Wrapped in warm coats, *gondolieri* brought their stately Norse-like boats to the docks along the canal. Our stop was the last stop on the Canale Grande route at the Salute, or the Santa Maria della Salute, an arabesque of white marble filagree and bald dome. The Salute had been built in the early 1600s to fulfill a senate decree that a new church would be dedicated to the Virgin Mary if the city was delivered from the plague that ravaged it, an outbreak that eventually killed roughly one-third of the people. Ever since, the Signoria head a procession on November 22 from San Marco to Salute over a specially constructed pontoon bridge, to give thanks for the city's good health and salvation, her *salute.*

This ride in Venice was long before our own Pane e Salute, a name inspired by a favorite bakery in the small city of Arezzo in Tuscany, a bakery that made crusty *pane toscano* and such delicacies as *pane al cotone,* a bread made with cottonseed flour imported all the way from Egypt. A bakery far from the labyrinthine canals and alleyways of Venice. But we have a photo of the Santa Maria della Salute on our wall at home and have returned there many times since that first visit. A grand building in all her early baroque architecture, she has somehow been an inspiration too.

Caleb had directions to our hotel and led me winding through the narrow, quiet streets to a place called Albergo di Ceci, a hotel we've never been able to find again on numerous returns, further conformation for me that Venice may really exist in a watery, yet collective dream, where time and possibility meet, and that surely on that occasion of Carnevale, Caleb and I had long ago left any semblance of the twentieth century behind.

My fever had left me dizzy and shivery, so once we were settled in our room we rested for a bit before going out again into the city. A cozy room and a hot shower comforted and revived us. Bundled in warm, woolen sweaters, scarves, and gloves, we walked outside and lost ourselves.

The whole map of the city was like a large, Gothic house or an old opera theater. The party seemed to be in the streets, in small piazze, where outdoor vendors sold costumes, intricate and plain-faced masks, and confections. Partygoers, some in costume, some dressed like us, milled about. But these areas were just the dressing rooms. When we arrived at the Piazza San Marco, we understood why Napoleon once called this space the world's drawing room.

The piazza opened like a grand stage and was filled with players, macabre, strange, beautiful. Here, almost everyone was dressed in costume, elaborate dresses and headpieces, masks, gentlemen's coats, velvet and bejeweled capes. Colors exploded against the gray of the sky and buildings. Those who were not in masquerade dressed the part of history, wearing seventeenth- and eighteenth-century bustiers and white, curled wigs, a painted mole on a high cheekbone or above a breast. You could imagine the traveling trunks needed to transport these costumes, for though many were Venetians, many others were Germans, Austrians, and French who'd come from afar.

This was a true masked ball, the piazza that grand salon, both strange and wonderful. Those in costume did not speak, but moved through the crowd in graceful poses, bowing for a photograph. String quartets played in cul de sacs outside the square, and you could hear their music wind its way through the square. A commedia play performed on an outdoor stage provided some laughter, though the sound was muted against all the whispering of so much costume fabric. We fell silent too, taking photographs, nodding our heads in recognition when a character bowed in greeting. We broke for tea at Florian, the grand, old baroque coffeehouse on the piazza.

We sat in the second dining room with its mirrored walls and painted ceilings, amid costumed princes, mistresses, ladies, and czars. Our hot chocolate came in silver pots to be mixed with warm cream in silver pitchers and poured into our cups, which were rimmed in gold. Another *Il Dottore* character stopped outside the arcade and looked in our window, even pressed himself against the glass, his arms and hands flat against the window. We felt he looked straight at us. Next to him was a short, round man dressed like a medieval beggar. We paused to see his filthy face looking in at us all with our chocolates and coffees and pastries and creams. Caleb and I both shivered, but not from cold or fever.

In the spirit of Carnivale, we donned new faces. On a side street off the piazza, Caleb bought a doctor's mask, half black velvet, half gold brocade, and a tri-corner hat. I chose a fox mask painted blue, green, and gold. Away from the piazza, meeting those in full masquerade spooked us, for they would stop and follow us with only their eyes. We crossed small footpaths over the canals where gondolas dressed in black and purple glided, a few with seventeenth-century lovers sharing a candlelit picnic. We came across one of the string quartets and listened a while, Bach and Vivaldi.

We walked until we found ourselves hungry again. We were cold and the streets and canals were empty. Darkness had set in, our way lighted only by the streetlamps. We came across a small restaurant and inn with a small, inviting dining room. Locanda Montin. Later we realized it had some fame, a watering hole for the art set of the teens and twenties, Hemingway, Pound, Guggenheim, Visconti. The walls were lined with bold efforts at painting, and little lamps lighted our tables.

Venice was an early testing ground (and kitchen pantry) for the development of fine European cooking. Her table depended on the generosity of the sea, the plenty of the market gardens and farms on the outlying islands and on the Veneto's mainland, and tasty curiosities brought to Venetian kitchens from around the expanding world. Here, polenta is colored with saffron and risotto is tinged with squid ink. Flower blossoms are fried or candied as much for their visual delight as for their taste, and the scent of ginger, nutmeg, mace, licorice, and tarragon perfume many dishes. Venetian food is elegant and colorful, yet light and balanced; it is flavored, ever so subtly, by Byzantium, Turkey, the Dalmation coast, Persia, Spain, Austria, Africa, and China.

Fish is the heart of the Venetian table; little birds are considered little gems. Meat comes rosy and translucent—prosciutto, carpaccio of beef, of tuna—or slivered and sauced, like the classic dish of *fegato alla Veneziana.* Bitter greens of radicchio di Treviso, sweet and sour marinades, olives, and anchovies all grace the Venetian table. But Venetian food is essentially simple food, frugal food even, and her cooks, as in other parts of Italy, depend on the quality and freshness of the ingredients. Once a dish is completed, and if worthy, it can be presented in the luxury of the Venetian tabletop, amid the display of spun glass, intricate lace, silver, and linen.

We bade our last hurrah to appetite at Locanda Montin. We ate traditional Venetian food, things like *fritti misti,* small fried calamari, shrimps, sardines. Caleb ate *seppioline nere,* baby cuttlefish cooked in their own ink, and *baccalá,* salt cod. I ate risotto cooked in fish sauce and roast guinea hen. Salad made with radicchio di Treviso, long maroon, bitter greens followed and then Venetian trifle, *tira mi su,* the ultimate pick-me-up. We drank the house red wine, which warmed us. Other diners left their tables to go upstairs, obviously also staying at the inn, and returned to the foyer in elaborate costumes. They wrapped themselves in mantles with fur collars and pulled on long white gloves before going out into the mist. We'd forgotten all sense of time. Our meal was long, we might have been there for two hours, maybe four.

We walked back to our hotel, sleepy and satisfied, bypassing the nighttime revelry going on at San Marco. We fell into our bed, and in the turnings of my ongoing fever, I dreamed of orphans in silk wedding dresses, shipwrecked women washed up on the Lido, and an ugly, old cook who played cards with the gold-toothed, swarthy sailors down near the docks.

In the morning, my fever broke and the city buzzed with its usual commerce. We ate in the breakfast room among the dark red velvet curtains and white linen tablecloths. Warm rolls with butter and jam, and hot coffee served in those silver pots that I will always associate with the elegance of Venice. We went out into another foggy, chill day to see the city bare of her costume, yet still mysterious, still magical, always in masquerade.

in late winter we ate pears

IT WAS LATE WINTER the first year after we had opened the bakery when Caleb and I decided to get away for a few days. This was before the bakery transformed into the restaurant. Locking up, we packed our bags and our tired bodies into the car, and we escaped to Quebec. Driving us that far north was a desire to see the city in snow, and to have a glass of champagne at the Château Frontenac, a grand old hotel on the St. Lawrence River.

We had never been to Quebec City before that, had only heard how romantic and French it was from friends who'd visited. My grandmother, the traveler, had gone once and returned home with a box of handmade table laces that I remember being so intricate they resembled the networks of frost etched on January windows. In an article about Carnivale in Quebec that I'd been saving for a couple of years, the writer had highlighted the city during the February holiday. Who wouldn't be enchanted? He wrote of candlelight parades, iceskating on the river, women dressed in thick furs, stores full of laces and linens, French and Quebecois food. He'd included a list of places to stay, places to eat, places to see. A friend recommended to us a little *auberge,* or bed-and-breakfast, near the Frontenac, and we took the article's suggestions for restaurants. In my purse, I carried a slim guidebook.

We arrived at the end of the afternoon only to get hopelessly lost and drive around in circles looking for our street. Was it outside the old fortified walls of the city, or inside? A complicated crossing and continuation of streets from the old town to the newer section outside the historic district confused us, and evening arrived before we came to our destination.

The *auberge* was intimate with narrow rooms. The common spaces, a dining area and a sitting room, were painted a dark olive green, and the staircase was carved and grand, curving up to each floor. A gold-framed portrait of a very pretty woman dated 18— hung above a console table in the foyer. Our room was snug with a slender French window and balcony. We had a television and shared a bath with the room next door.

That first night, weary from driving and in search of a simple meal, we stumbled out the hotel door and down the street looking for the first restaurant that caught our attention. We passed by a place called Le Continentale, an elegant establishment with large plate glass windows and heavy silk curtains of pale blue framing the view inside. We made a note, and thought to try it another night as it looked to be a restaurant requiring an investment of time and senses.

By our second night, after discovering that both the guidebook and my handy article had described it as an old, venerated French-Italian restaurant well worth the effort and expense, we were ready to try Le Continentale. We strolled from the *auberge,* cold and bundled up in our wool coats and wool scarves to the edge of the Place de Cartier. We wanted a walk to increase our appetites. The Place contains a small square lined with *caleche,* horse-drawn sleighs that will take you for a ride for fifty Canadian dollars through the city's park on the edge of the St. Lawrence River, a wide expanse called the Plains of Abraham. The sky was dark but clear, and the horses pawed at the cobblestones and snorted clouds of steam. The snow on the ground sparkled in the streetlight. The horses and the cold brought back memories of Central Park, reminding me of a similarly cold night in New York when we strolled before going out to eat, the very first time we ate elegantly on our own dimes.

We had been living in New York and we had just decided to move up to Vermont for the spring and summer before making a larger move to Italy. It was another late-winter evening. We had walked around New York savoring the sights and had decided to treat ourselves to a meal in a grand tradition as a send off. (Over the past couple of years together, we'd learned to love good food, and Caleb was becoming an excellent cook in our own tiny kitchen, which in New York fashion had once been a ladies' closet. We had never splurged on a meal in this way on our streamlined salaries.) We chose a place we'd heard a lot about, where waiters looked like actors yet made seventy thousand dollars a year, and the walls were painted with murals depicting eighteenth-century nudes in the fête gallant style of Boucher and Watteau. We chose Café des Artistes because it sounded like one of those restaurants you'd find tucked into a graceful corner in the city of Paris, and at the time we were mad for going to Paris. We ordered the salmon, the duck, and a white Bordeaux with the help of our server. We ate with pleasure, but also with awareness, our senses buzzing with flavor.

As we took our turn around the Place in Quebec we reminisced about that night in New York, our first gastronomic splurge, then found our way back to Le Continentale. Once we were inside, it didn't take long for the chill to recede as we took in the *dolce vita* style of the dining room. Le Continentale is owned by Romans who came to Quebec in the 1940s. Taking in the pale blue tufted chairs, crisp white linens on the table, black accents, and dark wood, we thought we spotted a young Sophia Loren dining with Fellini from the corner of our eyes. All the waiters are Italian or Quebecois. They've been trained in hotelier schools in Paris, Rome, and Milan. Dressed in formal wear, they glide between tables and are silent: Plates appear and disappear, wineglasses never empty, as if they conjure at tableside, bringing sleight of hand from the kitchen to the dining room. Consumate professionals.

Le Continentale is where we learned how to make a classic vinaigrette, how to flambé ripe fruit (just like they used to in old French restaurants, where the waiter would perform at a sleek trolley with a free-standing oil burner, a stash of ingredients below). Jean was our waiter that night, a genial and graceful Quebecois man in his late thirties. He'd been trained in France and had worked at Le Continentale for fifteen years, nothing, he said, compared to a few others who'd been there for thirty.

We ordered from the menu. I chose the grilled salmon with peppercorns and haricôts verts and Caleb ordered the duck with prunes stewed in Armagnac, two gestures to the memory of our meal at Café des Artistes.

Salad would follow, and we chose a demi of white Bordeaux to accompany my fish and hold up to Caleb's meal. Loving salmon, I had smoked salmon even to start and Caleb ate oysters.

The salmon and duck surpassed expectation. Jean then prepared the salads at our table; we watched him intently. In a large bowl he rubbed a clove of garlic on the bottom and sides, then left the clove in the bowl. Next a teaspoon of Dijon mustard, a dash of Worcestershire. From spouted bottles he then poured olive oil and red wine vinegar, fast. Salt and pepper to taste. Whisked until the vinaigrette combined. The greens, and only greens, were added to the bowl, tossed, and served, a perfect relief from the richness of our previous plates.

Next came magic, that subtle alchemy of just the right ingredients, the right amounts, the right pan, the right heat. Jean prepared the pears in Pernod over his heating plate, chatting with us all the while, his movements natural and relaxed, without the least sign of hurry. We told him of our time living in Italy, our love of food, our desire to bring some of that back to the States by opening the bakery, and how we hoped one day to have a restaurant. He spoke of his years of training in France, talked of how so few keep the old service traditions alive now. Then he placed on our table three beautifully presented halves of ripe, peeled pears sautéed in Pernod, butter, sugar, and cream—a thick caramel bathing the fruit. The flavor of sweet, anise, butter, and pear felt luxurious, but not too heavy on the tongue, the chemistry of the dish somehow blending yet bringing forth those individual tastes.

Giovanni from Rome, one of the oldest waiters there, came to the table with glasses of vin santo and cantuccini—a classic Tuscan dessert wine and the tiny almond biscotti that traditionally accompany it. He and Jean hoped we had enjoyed the pears and, with the caramel still in our mouths, we thanked them. Caleb asked about the dessert recipe, if Jean would outline it for us as we wanted to offer the same dish on our developing dinner menu. Jean obliged.

Afterward, we all toasted each other's health, the meal, the pears perfected in Pernod. We toasted the great meals of our futures.

come lo sento io

IMAGINE OPEN, ROLLING hills blanketing a valley, those hills covered with vines and the elegant spindled branches of hazelnut trees. On a clear day, the valley is surrounded by a collar of Alps, snowy and spiked, and you wonder if that peak is Mont Blanc, or if that slightly hidden one is Monte Cervino. But many days of the year are heavy with mist, a good climate for the grapes, especially those named *nebbiolo,* those Barolo grapes that thrive in *nebbia,* the fog. Picture small towns in Italy, with stone buildings, terra-cotta roofs, walled fortresses, imposing and ruined churches.

Find yourself down a main street, off the piazza where there's a *belvedere,* a good view of the whole valley—there are the shops, the wineshop, the cheese shop, the little restaurant where you can get a sandwhich made with a local cheese called *sola* (because it is flat like the sole of a shoe), or you can order a pasta dish, lasagna today, and the *barista,* the only man working, will run back to the kitchen and warm the baked pasta while making the sandwhich and pouring two glasses of wine he'll carry on a lace-covered tray out to you on the balcony, where it is surprisingly warm in the still-winter sun. Later, back inside, when he is behind the bar making your coffee, notice how hard he's working, see the sweat moistening his upper lip and forehead.

Afterward, as you wander around the restaurant, you see how it also serves as a wineshop and you look at label after label of Barolo, Barbaresco,

Barbera, Dolcetto. You look for names you might know and see names you've never known. Smile at the man sitting alone eating a dish of pasta at a long wooden table who is intently studying the wine list too.

Around the corner from this street, you run across two pastry shops. In one, you decide to buy a trayful of cookies, *baci di dama,* little chocolate and hazelnut ladies' kisses, *meringhe,* and *brutti ma buoni,* or *brutti buoni* as they say in this region, ugly but good confections made from yet more hazelnuts. At the other pastry shop you'll buy cake, *torta di mela,* so light and sweet and tasting strangely of roses.

Thus girded, you drive down the hill out of town into a collection of buildings known as another town, though there is no grocery or coffee bar here. Only houses with outbuildings, some with signs that say *cantina.* You've been told to visit a particular vineyard, to ask for the son of the man, long dead, who planted the vines and developed their recipes for wine and, if you're lucky, speak with the winemaker, for he is real and clever and performs miracles out of fruit and juice. Driving past this vineyard several times, not sure if it is the one, you stop finally and ask a woman planting winter greens if she knows where you are to go. She does, and points you in the right direction.

Pietro, the son, is not there; he's out driving around with a journalist, talking about the hopes for this year's wine. But you meet his cousin, Massimo, an older, gentle man with salt and pepper hair, a brushy mustache, and glasses. He wears blue jeans with a pair of pruners sticking out the back pocket.

Massimo gives you a tour of the cantina, which is small, a boutique operation really, the storage and processing room a garage. Three men are corking bottles, and there are cages and bins full of unlabeled wine. Boxes of labels, elegant and slightly baroque, sit in a far corner. The room is terrifically clean. Massimo tells you about this site where the family house and the vineyard offices are, and the adjacent old abbey where they run a wine museum that's open to tours. This piece of land is called *La Conca,* the dell, because of its curved, hollowed-out shape. This area is coveted in the Piemonte where several vineyards will own tracts of acreage or hillsides jointly. *La Conca* is tended by three different vineyards.

Massimo takes you into the tasting room adjacent to the offices; he must take a call. The tasting room is a library of wine with a long banquet table and one round table. You wait for Pietro here, or Massimo, depending on who returns first, and you run your fingers down the spines of old and new books, catalogs of information about wine, histories of Barolo, notebooks on land qualities and appellations. You sit for a while, suddenly tired after lunch an hour ago in town. As in many Italian social calls, you get used to the waiting—waiting for the person to get off the phone, waiting for someone to return, waiting for the next meal.

It is Massimo who returns first. He has just received word that a busload of Belgians are on their way for a tour of the wine museum. You can come too. Then you wait for the Belgians, and talk, talk about the food of the Piemonte, the wine, and the tongue, both in relation to taste and to language. Massimo talks about dialect, as many proud Piemontese do, how he loves his antiquated Roman vocabulary, a linguistic music that he and his regional family share with parts of France.

The Belgians arrive. The tour begins in the courtyard of the abbey, which is quite small. The paint on the abbey building is peeling and the roof sags. You can smell wood smoke in the air. Massimo speaks to the Belgians in French, which you perhaps studied for years but understand only with some difficulty because of his Piemontese accent, and the Belgian's tour guide translates the French into Flemish, which you don't understand at all, and you turn what you can into English. You tune in and out of the words, there are so many to catch, and you don't want to miss the curiosities themselves in the museum.

The tour enters on the ground floor, into a musty cantina with old Roman wine jugs, a wine barrel from the 1600s, a tub from the 1800s used for the *vendemmia,* the harvest when the contadine still crushed the grapes with their bare feet. There are curling and faded maps, diagrams showing the spread of phylloxera, that dreaded blight when plant lice once took out whole vineyards. A pair of ancient wooden snowshoes, shaped not unlike Japanese sandals, hangs from a post.

Upstairs in the abbey kitchen an engraving of the Marchesa Giulia Colbert de Maulevrier hangs above the fireplace. She was the last of the line of

Falletti di Barolo, the family who at the beginning of the nineteenth century created the wine we know today as Barolo. Her ancestral home was eventually bought by a man named Pietro Emilio Abonna, who, through his tenacity and pioneering efforts, became the patriarch of Barolo. At this winery, under Abonna's guidance, Barolo took its first historic steps. Abonna inherited his casks from the Marchesa Guilia, along with her sense of tradition and strong commitment to the vineyards, the winery, and the wine itself.

On the wall opposite is a letter about Barolo written by Napoleon. You cannot read its antiquated French, but you admire the shape of ink and the imperial seal. The kitchen itself is a curiosity with a wall brazier built into one windowsill and a sink in the other.

Off the kitchen is what once must have been a dining room, its walls lined with sealed cases and cupboards showcasing the evolution of the wineglass. There were small, narrow glasses with lips that grew wider than the base, then glasses that eventually ballooned at the top of the stem, then narrowed, then opened again, a curl of the lip, womanly. Another exhibit reveals how cork was harvested and used for stopping the bottles. In another room, a display of glass containers and carafes from the 1600s on, and their labels. The barolo bottle used to have a wide, irregularly blown shape, and only in the past century has it become lean and uniform. In the past hundred years, the labels have changed dramatically from just a beautifully handwritten name and date of vintage to graphic explosions that rely on the appeal of the design in an attempt to sell the wine once it has become a marketable commodity.

Massimo brings the Belgians and you back to the tasting room. A field of glasses and two bottles for tasting stand in formation on the banquet table. Four-year-old Barolos from two different areas, all across the Piemonte they are opening bottles from four years ago and declaring it a spectacular year. Massimo pours the first, and it swivels in your glass, orange and ruby, sharp in your nose when you raise your glass, dry at first, then like fruit on your tongue. You think you can taste orange flowers. The second wine has an orange cast too, and this washes over your mouth like a handful of dusty and ripened berries. Maracenesco, grown from *La Conca*. You'll take home bottles of this wine, carefully wrapped in a cardboard box packed on top of the suitcase you'll wheel across the *giardino* in front of the train station in Turin, passing the lunchtime drunkards cradling their liter bottles of wine.

The afternoon sun slants through the hazy, nearly overcast sky as you walk through rows of vines then and sit for a spell to survey the land, the earth damp and cold beneath you. You meet a man tending to the vines, clipping, securing, handling. You ask questions; he is a willing teacher. He shows you how to plant the rootstock into the ground, and gives you a lesson on grafting a fine vine onto a hardy root. Perhaps you think about your own hillside thousands of miles away, the kinds of grapes you might be able to graft onto the hardy, wild grape vines hugging your own stone walls and garden gates. We have fog, we have sun, you think, could I too grow grapes like *nebbiolo?* You imagine making wine the old way, crushing the grapes in October with your own bare feet, the dye finally fading from your arches and soles by the time of warmer weather. A bird flits by, startling you from your reverie. You realize you've been digging your fingers into this rich Piemontese earth, and you've gotten your hands dirty.

When you return to the cantina, Pietro is back. He is dressed smartly in a tweed jacket, and his dark hair is cut fashionably away from his face. He is happy to meet you, but *in fretta,* in a hurry, another place to be, he has to pack to leave tonight for an exposition. He strides back and forth between the offices, talking to the men in the garage, then his cousin, then you. Then he is gone again, and you are left to shake Massimo's hand.

It is not until you return home to three feet of thick, wet-packed snow, your field and garden and young fruit trees, your hopeful vineyard somewhere beneath the blanket of white, that you realize you forgot to ask to meet the man who made the wine. Yet you still feel lucky you met whom you met, and this is why you forgot in the first place. On these winter nights, you thumb through your wine books in front of the fire, and then you are surprised by what you read, and pleased: You remember the clippers in Massimo's back pocket. You did meet the winemaker after all.

if you look on a map

I F YOU LOOK ON A MAP of Italy, plate 78 of *The Times World Atlas,* which I often like to do, and find a small village named Vallombrosa, you'll see it's almost on the same latitude line as Woodstock, Vermont. A strange and fateful connection considering that Woodstock's most favored and troubled son, George Perkins Marsh, died at Vallombrosa in 1882 after a multifaceted career as a lawyer, scholar, linguist, conservationist, and diplomat—a career that ultimately led him to this forest haven in the Italian Appenines.

I came across this history at a visit to our local Marsh-Billings farm, now a national park and museum, a place I'd been wanting to visit since my childhood when I spent a few summers in Woodstock, years after which Caleb and I moved here. Late last fall we got our tour of the facilities and main house. Our friend Rolf, who is also the park director, graciously took us around the central grounds giving us a sense of the families who've lived there. We talked of George Perkins Marsh, his book *Man and Nature,* and that book's effect on the conservation movement in the United States. Well acquainted with our appreciation for good food and for Italy, Rolf asked, "Did you know Marsh loved a fine meal? Did you know he lived and died in Italy?"

This sparked a curiosity, and over the following months, planning our itinerary for travel back to Italy in late winter, we decided we would travel to the place where Marsh spent his last days. Worn and dog-eared Italian road maps first purchased eleven years ago guided the way. Italy is a large part of our life, ever since that day after our wedding when we flew on one-way tickets, landed south of Florence, went to live and work in a small Tuscan town. Italy laid claim to us then and has called us back, but now Woodstock has become the place we live. Somehow, Woodstock reminds us of the open fields and thick forested hillsides that shape the Italian landscape. I found myself asking over our long, snowy season if George Perkins Marsh—a man long dead who had lived both here and there, as we have—felt the same way?

II

When I arrive in a place, when I live in a place, I grab on to the history. I look for odd curiosities, stories that can follow the way back a hundred to two hundred to three hundred years ago. George Perkins Marsh became one of my tethers. I suppose I envy him his death in Vallombrosa, his funeral pallet covered in flowers and walked down a mountain by Italian forestry students to a train that carried him to Rome where he's buried.

I've grown fond of George Perkins Marsh, in part because he loved books so much. As a child he would hide under the library table to read the encyclopedia, which was too heavy for him to carry upstairs. I like that his desire for book learning was so great that it damaged his eyes, which had to be covered with folds of black silk to keep out the sun. For four years he was sworn off books, forced out of doors to see nature before returning to words. I like that he loved to feel rain on his head. As an old gentleman in a rainstorm he would remove his silk top hat and let the storm overtake him.

I like his passion for living. After his first wife died, along with one of his children, he fell in love again with a dark-haired beauty, Caroline Crane, who taught at her brother Silas's school for young ladies. I like that Caroline Crane was a poet who published a book titled *Wolfe of the Knoll* and that Marsh chose her, an invalid often unable to walk for most of her married life, to share his life with. He knew she was not without adventure: she traveled with him to Syria where she was borne on a litter, rode a camel in Egypt, and was driven in a wheelbarrow over Alpine snow.

I like knowing that when he was a baby Marsh's mother gave him a small ivory horse with a gilded mane, tail, and hooves, and because of all that white and gold and form he began to fall in love with beauty. I like that Marsh's father taught him the names of trees and that on any walk through any forest he could identify them. I especially love the story of Marsh and Caroline traveling to Paris on their way to Turkey, when Marsh convinced the officials of the museum to open the doors of the closed Louvre to his party and, holding her in his arms, he carried Caroline up innumerable flights of stairs to take her by wheelchair through the empty galleries to see the world.

III

The day was wet and gray with rain, the air full of mist shaped like spirits when we went to Vallombrosa. The winter wind felt bitter on our faces, the air so quiet, even with the muffled sounds of men working on a restored hotel. At the nearby abbey, church bells rang the hour, stirred the mist. Trees and bushes surrounded us. A flock of sparrows rustled and murmured. This is what I noticed most: box, oak, lichen-covered beech, gigantic spruce, short shaggy pines. Lavender crocus and cobalt blue scylla flowered the skirt of a sycamore.

Marsh had lived in Italy for the last twenty years of his life. Eleven days after the outbreak of the Civil War, on April 27, 1861, Marsh sailed from the United States to take up his post as Minister to the Kingdom of Italy, which had just fought its own civil war. Beginning at the age of sixty-three, he would live out the rest of his days there, never to return to Woodstock. It was from this vantage point abroad that Marsh would write his book about the losses of Vermont nature and the dangers that its landscape faced.

At the outset, he and his wife Caroline were stationed at Turin, the ancestral seat of the Duke of Savoie and Sardegnia. But Marsh had always had difficulty with finances, and while the U.S. government paid well for such posts, it did not take into account the cost of being a foreign diplomat, and how a foreign diplomat might need to entertain kings, queens, princes, and noble aristocracy in order to maintain friendly relations. Marsh and Caroline paid out of their pockets for elaborate dinners and teas. They were constantly called upon to look after wayward and hysterical Americans who'd lost they're way. Eventually, these expensive kindnesses took their toll and the Marshes, who could not afford their rent increase, were evicted from their apartment in Turin. They moved to a small hotel near Genova.

By 1865, life improved and Marsh and Caroline moved to the tawny Renaissance city of Florence, then the new capital of the Kingdom. They rented a floor in the Villa Forini that had a view of the Ponte Vecchio, of its elegant clients and savvy merchants. The terra-cotta cap of the Duomo could be seen behind the bridge and across the river. Florence was full of British and American expatriates at that time in its history, and the Marshes moved about that circle. Matthew Arnold, the Brownings, Anthony Trollope, and George Eliot (pseudonym of Marian Evans) were frequent visitors; everyone would sit under the broad loggia of the Marsh apartments and take in the view of the river Arno.

A lot changed for the Marshes in Florence. Caroline, having suffered for some time from uterine tumors, had them removed during their time in that city; and their son George, whose eyesight had been failing since before their move from the United States, got a new pair of glasses, which improved life immensely. The greatest blight was the death of George, who died from complications from a recurring bout of typhoid fever and too much drink. But shortly after George's death, he and Caroline adopted a Swedish boy whom they rescued from an unfit American foster mother. Karl, or Carlo as he came to be called, benefited a great deal, and perhaps too much, from Marsh's second youth. It was as if, so much later in life, Marsh and Caroline were starting over again—a new country, new lifestyle, new circumstances, new family. Marsh had his sizeable library shipped from Vermont.

When Lincoln was re-elected, Marsh feared he might be asked to relinquish his post. In the end, he had his choice. If he wanted to return to the States, he could, but George had died and the Woodstock property had sold to the Billings; there was no reason to come back. They had made a good life in Italy and he would not have been able to afford to re-pack and ship the library that had been so carefully sent to him. Almost as if this was the most prevailing reason to stay, Marsh was re-appointed to his post, and they moved to Rome in 1879. Shortly after, he wrote, "I have such a passion for the nature of Italy that I do not see how I can ever live under another sky."

IV

In Rome, the Marshes lived in the Rospigliosi Palace where they rented a floor with a view of the Coliseum. Their apartment was at the top of 126 stairs and needed three additional stoves, highly impractical for a family of lean means and Marsh in ailing health. But he was seduced by the palatial rooms and elegant furniture, a private gallery, and fine library. He loved the view and fancied that the Coliseum looked much the same as it had eighteen centuries before. On the days he could not climb the many, steep stairs, he was carried in a sedan chair, his large frame hoisted uneasily up and down the narrow staircase.

Living in Italy brought Marsh to his vocation, his writings and thought about the conservation and husbandry of the natural world. Italy also seasoned Marsh's taste for another kind of nature, that of food and drink. A boy grown up on traditional and rather plain New England fare, Marsh may have made his way to the table as I did. I grew up in southern Indiana where we ate simple food—fried chicken, fried catfish, barbecue, and cheeseburgers. Ours was not a food-oriented household. Both my parents grew up in the Depression, where food meant you got to go on to the next day. We ate our meat, starch, and vegetables, dishes like Irish Stew—boiled mutton with boiled carrots and onions—or calf's liver with mashed potatoes. Occasionally, we would have something more exotic like red beans and rice or a fish gumbo, remnants of the years my parents lived in New Orleans. My mother wasn't bad at cooking, but neither did she feel passionate about it. None of us spent a lot of time over the stove or looking into an oven. With their knives and implements, scalding water and hot surfaces, hidden pantries and cupboards, kitchens always seemed to me rather dark and brooding.

As we negotiated our life together, Caleb became the cook between us. He could do well the things I found daunting, like fry an egg, roast a chicken, and bake an apple pie. I would learn to do these things eventually, but my route to both cooking and eating was circuitous. As perhaps it was for George Perkins Marsh, it was Italy that helped me arrive.

In Italy, Marsh became something of a bon vivant. He praised bread made from *grana di Santa Severa,* a white wheat, shaped and fired by Viennese bakers in Rome. He preferred "that of Andalucia" and wrote of it as "the finest bread in Europe, remarkable for its light and spongy crumb and great thickness of a brown but still soft crust." He became familiar with *risotto alla Milanese,* and Roman punch. "Add rum or whiskey," he said, "to any common icecream."

Marsh and Caroline loved life in Florence and Rome, but summers in both cities were hot and unbearable. They often escaped during these months into the country, the mountains. Marsh had a love of the northern Italian Alps, the *Dolomiti,* and for the *Casentino,* the high mountain reaches of the Appenines above Tuscany. In the summer of 1882, the Marshes packed up for Vallombrosa, the forest village near Florence. Alfredo di Berenger, a good friend, had established a School of Forestry there that operated out of the small, summer resort town. Marsh would spend his days walking about the hills, and talking with the students at the school.

v

My own effort on that winter trip to Vallombrosa had been to follow Marsh's path for a day, to shuttle myself back over a hundred years. I ate risotto for lunch and thought of him at diplomatic banquets and teas, sometimes his only enjoyment found in his delight in the food. One hundred and eighteen years before me, Marsh walked the same road at Vallombrosa. Did he lean on this same larch? Did he recognize the cedar of Lebanon? In the middle of the summer of 1882, he took his morning walk, the air cool and the clouds banked and fat in their summer blue sky, then returned to the hotel to entertain his group of young nieces and nephews with stories of how the clouds were named—*cumulus, nimbus, mare's tail.* I've heard that in those clouds he saw the moving, shifting bodies of imaginary animals in flight. Later that same day, he died.

VI

On my return to Woodstock, Mr. Perkins Marsh haunts me. When I drive to work, I pass by his old house, the deep green thickness of the forest above covering the top of Mount Tom. I walk up the Carriage Road one afternoon and recite the names of trees—white pine, birch, maple. I travel from Vermont to Italy and back again. I eat well, taste wine, and have my own favorite dishes. In Rome the streets all lead to the Coliseum, and the cats bathing themselves in the monument's crumbling stone portals will remind me Marsh had this view from his window. (If I am ever in the cemetery in Rome where he's buried, I'll nod my head in greeting. Perhaps, George Perkins Marsh and I will have become old friends.) And on a summer day, probably in July, I'll sit on my terrace in Vermont looking out over the forested green hills. The thick, water-heavy clouds will roll across the sky and their full shapes will move like a dragon, a camel, the last wisp of a mare's tail as she gallops over the mountains.

When I look at map 78, I trace my finger along the contours and roads. This is where I used to live. I can do the same on map 104 of the U.S.A., North-East. Woodstock is located at N and 3, halfway between 43 and 44 degrees. This is where I live now, but every day I taste memories of our life in Italy right here at our restaurant. This is the nature of hunger: I am hungry for Italy; I am hungry for Vermont. I realize I don't want to completely resolve my desire to be in both places—I'm not sure I could—but I do feel compelled to peek at others who have gone before me, those who've taken related paths or embarked on roads I'd like to travel. Their lives are like maps. Will they help me find my way? I don't know; I don't know that I'd want to follow their exact course. But, like the stories of a life, maps are inherently beautiful, made up of blue lines, red lines, yellow lines, blue puddles of water denoting the grandeur of a lake, spiny ridges supporting the names of the towns that ride them. For Caleb and me, these maps we lay out on our dining room table so we can see better where we want to go always lead us to the same place, and here in this one instance Italy and Vermont feel almost one and the same. We two, in our hunger and love, step out on the road, always moving toward the table.

Cannellini alla Salvia

CANNELLINI SALAD WITH FRESH SAGE

THE INGREDIENTS for this salad are so few, they must be of excellent quality. This is also a perfect venue for showing off your best extra-virgin olive oil, so don't skimp. Serve these beans either as an appetizer in the evening or as a side dish for lunch.

2 cups dry Cannellini
1 shallot or 2 large garlic cloves, slivered
10 to 12 fresh sage leaves
¼ cup (or to taste) extra-virgin olive oil
Salt and freshly ground pepper

The night before: Rinse and pick over the Cannellini, then soak them overnight in a large container covered with a few inches of water.

The next day: Rinse the beans again, put them in a saucepan, and cover them with fresh water. Cook them at a gentle simmer until they are just tender, not mushy. (This may take anywhere from 45 minutes to 1½ hours. But don't let them slip out of your attention. Mushy beans make this salad a lot less fun.)

As soon as the beans are cooked, run the pot under cold water just long enough to stop the cooking process but not long enough to chill the beans. Drain the beans completely and pour them into a mixing bowl.

Add the slivered shallot (or garlic). Crush the sage leaves under a rolling pin or a bottle and toss them in, too. Douse everything with olive oil and season liberally with salt and pepper. Gently mix all the ingredients very well. Taste and correct the seasoning and serve. (*Note:* If you are serving these beans a few hours later or the next day, taste and correct the seasoning at that time, as the beans will probably have absorbed the salt, and the salad may taste bland.) Serve this salad as is, or on a small layer of chopped arugula. Give each serving a final shot of extra-virgin olive oil, or have some oil available at the table.

Bocconcini con Speck

MOZZARELLA WITH SPECK

SPECK is essentially smoked prosciutto, and a product of the northern Alpine regions of Italy, where cultural influences of German and Swiss origin continue to define a way of life. You will need to seek out a good cold-cuts vendor in order to find *Speck*, but it's worth the trouble.

Bocconcino means "mouthful," and refers to a small, walnut-size piece or ball of mozzarella. You may use either Water Buffalo *(Bufala)* or cow's-milk mozzarella *(Fior di Latte)*. Let your hunger and protein cravings determine the serving size.

> Fresh mozzarella *Bocconcini*
> *Speck*, thinly sliced and again cut into long strips
> Extra-virgin olive oil
> Freshly ground pepper

Wrap up each *Bocconcino* with a piece of the *Speck*, and arrange the pieces on serving plates or a platter. Drizzle a little extra-virgin olive oil over the *Bocconcini* and sprinkle with freshly ground black pepper. Serve.

Zuppa Valdostana

Soup of the Valle d'Aosta

THIS BEAUTIFUL soup is a traditional dish of the Valle d'Aosta, simple to make, and honest in its flavors. As suggested here, it typically incorporates Fontina, the region's local cheese. If all goes well, you'll have some left over for either the next day or your freezer. Make the soup at least one day in advance, if not two, so that it has time to compose itself as only a soup is able. *Zuppa Valdostana* can stand alone as a meal all by itself, perhaps requesting only a glass of good Barbera or Nebbiolo for company. Serves 4 or more.

2 tablespoons butter
2 tablespoons olive oil
1 large yellow onion, diced small
1 medium–large head Napa or savoy cabbage,
    slivered (about 4 packed cups)
1 bay leaf
Salt and freshly ground pepper
2 quarts chicken or beef stock
4 to 8 finger-thick slices crusty country bread
    (from a 2-day-old loaf is ideal)
Fontina cheese (or Gruyere or Raschera), very thinly sliced
Extra-virgin olive oil

Heat the butter and oil in a stockpot. Add the diced onions to the pot and stir them well to coat them with the fats. Cover the pot and let the onions simmer gently, governing the heat and stirring every few minutes until they are just wilted. Add the cabbage and stir well. (If desired, add a little water if the onions haven't given up enough of their own to keep things juicy.) Cover the pot and cook for 10 to 15 minutes, stirring occasionally, until the cabbage is well wilted. Add the bay leaf, salt and pepper, and enough of the stock to cover everything by about 1 inch. Return the soup to a gentle simmer, cover the pot but leave the lid askew (so that the temperature inside doesn't continue to rise) and cook for 40 minutes longer. Taste and correct the seasoning.

Turn on the oven broiler. Place 1 or 2 slices of bread in individual oven-proof soup bowls. Ladle in the soup and blanket the top with a couple slices of the cheese. Place the soup bowls under the broiler for a few minutes to let the cheese form a crust over the soup, watching carefully to avoid burning. Drizzle each serving with a little extra-virgin olive oil and serve.

Pasta con Sugo all'Arista di Maiale

PASTA WITH ROASTED PORK SAUCE

By including this recipe I am not suggesting that you prepare a pork roast just for the sake of making this sauce. The idea is to use up the end of a roast when there is not enough of it left over to serve as a *secondo*. Very often the ends of a pork roast will provide large grains of meat that can be pulled off the roast, and that's just the right texture of meat for this sauce. It's a very hearty dish, suitable with a robust red wine and followed by some fresh pears and a little *parmigiano*. I recommend fettuccine, spaghetti, or *conchiglie* as pasta shapes that go well with this sauce. Serves 6.

    1 to 2 tablespoons butter or olive oil
    1 small yellow onion, diced small
    1 small carrot, diced small
    1 celery stalk, diced small
    2 cups chopped roasted pork
    12–16 ounces chopped tomatoes and their juice, fresh or canned
    Salt and pepper
    Chicken stock, white wine, red wine, water or milk
    1 pound pasta (fettucine, spaghetti, or *conchiglie*)
    Freshly grated *Grana (Padano* or *parmigiano)*

Heat the butter or oil in large saucepan. Add the diced onion, carrot, and celery, cover the pot, and cook this *battuto* over medium heat for 8 to 10 minutes.

Add the chopped pork and the tomatoes and stir everything very well. At this stage the sauce should be quite liquid, and the pork should be suspended in the sauce. If you need to, add some more liquid to the pot, be it stock, wine, or water. (I've even been known to slosh in a little beer, the darker the better. You can bet that cooks have been improvising this particular step throughout the centuries, reaching for whatever liquid is most readily at hand, even if it's the liquid they are drinking at the moment.) Cover the pot, bring it to a gentle simmer, and let it cook for 30 to 40 minutes, stirring occasionally, until the tomatoes are well broken down and all the liquids have cooked together. Taste the sauce and correct the seasoning. Let the sauce rest while you cook your pasta.

Bring a large pot of salted water to the boil. Add the pasta, cook until al dente, and drain. In a large bowl, toss the pasta and the sauce together. Add the grated cheese, toss again, and serve.

Penne con Spinaci, Pignoli ed Uvette

PENNE WITH SPINACH, PINE NUTS, AND RAISINS

THE BEAUTY of this dish lies not only within its flavors, but also in the convenience of its preparation: The sauce cooks within the time it takes to cook the pasta. Serves 2. Simply multiply to serve more.

Note: Heavy cream serves to provide an effective binding for the elements of the sauce and their flavors, because the cream thickens and is absorbed into the nuts and raisins. While the cream results in a better-tasting dish, if you wish you may substitute olive oil.

> Freshly grated *Grana Padano* or *parmigiano*
> 2 large handfuls fresh spinach leaves
> ¼ cup heavy cream (or olive oil; see note above)
> 1 garlic clove, smashed
> ¼ cup pine nuts
> ¼ cup raisins
> Salt and freshly ground pepper
> 2 cups penne
> Extra-virgin olive oil, if desired

Bring a large pot of salted water to the boil. Grate some cheese now, so it's ready when the pasta is ready.

Rinse the spinach, but don't shake off all the water. In a skillet or saucepan (with a lid) large enough to contain the spinach, heat the heavy cream and the smashed garlic over medium heat. Once the cream begins to bubble, add the pine nuts, raisins, spinach, and a couple pinches of salt and pepper to the pan. Cover the pan and reduce the heat to medium-low. Put the pasta in to cook immediately. After about 2 minutes, mix the wilted spinach down into the other ingredients of the sauce. If you think the sauce looks too dry, swirl in a little extra-virgin olive oil. Taste the liquids in the pan for salt and pepper and season as needed. Cover the pan again and reduce the heat to low.

Cook the pasta until al dente, drain it, toss it with the sauce and the freshly grated cheese, and serve immediately.

Risotto alla Milanese

RISOTTO WITH SAFFRON

MAKING *Risotto alla Milanese* is like saying the rosary. Its preparation is a ritual. Not all restaurants in Italy make *risotti*, but those that do would never dream of improvising this one. In truth, that can be said about many classic dishes in Italian cuisine. And while there are some very classic dishes that do vary in their preparation from region to region, within each region that way is The Way.

The flavors of this dish are never loud or unbalanced, but rather subtly harmonic, even symphonic in their depth. This dish asks of you only the best ingredients you have to offer, but most importantly it asks for your time and devotion. Make this dish for someone who has a long drive home in cold weather. Serves 6.

    4 cups chicken stock
    4 tablespoons butter
    1 small yellow onion, diced small
    2 tablespoons marrow or *pancetta*, chopped fine
    2 cups Arborio or Carnaroli rice
    Salt and freshly ground pepper
    1 teaspoon saffron threads
    ½ cup freshly grated *Parmigiano-Reggiano*

Heat the chicken stock until hot but not boiling, and keep warm.

Melt the butter in your risotto pot of choice over medium heat. Add the onion and the marrow or *pancetta* and cook until the onion is completely soft and just beginning to brown. (At this point you must be prepared to attend to the dish until it is finished.) Add the rice and several large pinches of salt and pepper and stir well to coat with the fats. Add ½ cup of the hot stock along with the saffron and begin a steady stirring motion, scraping back and forth across the bottom of the pot, allowing the liquid to become absorbed by the rice, at which point add another ½ cup of stock, stirring and scraping again until the rice absorbs the liquid. Continue stirring and adding liquid in ½-cup increments for about 15 minutes, always maintaining a medium, yet lively, heat.

Taste the rice for doneness: It should be tender, but still resist the bite. In other words, al dente. If needed, continue the cooking procedure, adding liquid as necessary. (If you run out of stock, continue with water.) As soon as the rice is ready, stir in the grated cheese and bring the dish to the proper consistency for serving by adding liquid if necessary: It must be liquid enough so that it is not stiff and lumpy, but it must not be runny. It must be softly creamy. Taste again for salt and pepper and correct. Serve immediately.

Pasta con Radicchio e Pancetta

PASTA WITH RADICCHIO AND PANCETTA

RADICCHIO DI TREVISO (also sometimes called "Trevisana") is shaped like a head of Romaine lettuce. A very versatile vegetable, it is very good for salads, sautéing, grilling, and for use with risotto and pasta. When you come across it in the market, the leaves should be tight and bright in color. Large heads might be just beginning to brown on the outermost leaves, but if the head feels good and firm throughout, it should be fine. Just discard the browned leaves. When cooked, radicchio loses some of its bitterness and takes on a smokiness—enhanced here by the *pancetta*—and the leaves turn almost black. A very striking presentation. Serves 4.

> ½ cup *pancetta*
> 1 small head radicchio di Treviso
> 3 tablespoons olive oil
> 2 garlic cloves, gently smashed
> Salt and pepper
> ½ cup plus additional freshly grated
>   *Parmigiano-Reggiano* or *Grana Padano*

Place a large pot of salted water over high heat. While it comes to the boil, cut the *pancetta* into small julienne (about the size of half a matchstick). Stack the leaves of radicchio and crosscut them into ¼-inch-thick pieces. Preheat a large pasta serving bowl by filling it with some hot water.

In a large sauté pan, heat the garlic in the olive oil until the garlic begins to brown, then discard the garlic and add the *pancetta* to the remaining oil and let it brown for a few minutes. Add the cut radicchio and stir it well to coat it in the fats, sprinkle in a few pinches of salt and pepper, stir again, cover the pan, and sauté the radicchio until it is quite dark and well softened, for about 5 or 6 minutes, lowering the heat as needed to keep from scorching the radicchio. Taste and correct the seasoning. Drain the water from your warm pasta bowl and then scrape the contents of the pan into the bowl.

Cook the pasta until al dente, drain it, and add it to the radicchio along with the ½ cup grated cheese. Toss it all together very well, until the cheese has melted and bound everything together nicely. If the dish seems too dry, swirl in a little more olive oil. Taste and correct the seasoning and serve with additional grated cheese.

Salmone al Pepe Verde

SALMON WITH GREEN PEPPERCORNS

THIS IS A DISH that can be done on the stovetop or on the grill. You can cut your fish into serving pieces before or after cooking. Personally, I prefer cutting them before cooking: cooking time is slightly reduced and service is much easier than cutting the fish into portions at table. Note the last item among the ingredients: here you can choose between wine and cream and thus choose the final look and taste of your dish. Serves 4.

1½ pounds salmon fillet, rinsed and patted dry with paper towel
Extra-virgin olive oil
Salt and freshly ground pepper
1 large rosemary sprig, cut into 4 pieces
3 tablespoons green peppercorns in brine, drained and slightly crushed
¼ cup white wine or heavy cream

Season the flesh of the fish well with the oil and salt and pepper.

To cook on the stovetop: In a large skillet gently heat the rosemary sprigs and the peppercorns in 2 to 3 tablespoons olive oil for 2 to 3 minutes. Remove them from the oil and set aside. Turn the heat up to medium-high and when a haze begins to form over the pan lay in the salmon, skin-side up. Sear it for about 20 seconds, then carefully turn the fish over, skin-side down. Cover the pan, lower the heat to medium-low, and cook for 7 to 10 more minutes, until white fat globules show on the outside of the flesh, signaling that the fish is perfectly cooked to medium. Transfer the fish immediately to a serving platter. Pour off almost all the fat from the pan, return the rosemary and peppercorns to the pan, and add the wine or heavy cream. Turn up the heat, scraping the pan with a spatula as the liquid reduces to a slightly thickened sauce (if you are using heavy cream, its bright whiteness should cook off to an amber color). Taste the sauce and correct the seasoning. Pour the sauce over the salmon and serve.

To roast on the grill: Place the fish in a shallow dish with the olive oil, salt and pepper, and green peppercorns and let your fish marinate briefly in the oil and seasonings.

Right before you grill the fish, cook your sauce separately on the stovetop: Heat the heavy cream or white wine in a saucepan over medium heat and pour the peppercorn-olive oil marinade off the fish and into the cream or wine. Cook for 2 or 3 minutes to bind the liquids together. Keep warm.

Preheat an oiled sheet pan right on the grill or lay down a couple layers of aluminum foil and lay in the fillet(s) skin-side down and put the lid on the grill. (The ambient heat and the smoke will do the cooking, rather than the overly harsh, direct heat of the fire.) Roast the fish until white fat globules just begin to show on the outside of the flesh. Remove immediately to a serving platter, pour the sauce over top, and serve.

Stracotto al Vino Rosso

BEEF BRAISED IN RED WINE

THE BEAUTY of this dish lies in its preparation. It will require only about 30 minutes of your attention, and the rest of the time the meat just talks to itself in the privacy of the braising pot. You will need a heavy casserole with a tight-fitting lid, or that old cast-iron Dutch oven your mother gave you (either should be suitable for the stovetop), or you can just use a roasting pan and tin foil and do the braising in the oven. Which means you can also bake a cake and roast some potatoes while the meat is cooking. Serves 4 to 6 people.

> 1 medium yellow onion, diced
> 2 medium carrots, quartered lengthwise and cut into 2-inch pieces
> 2 or 3 celery stalks, quartered lengthwise and cut into 2-inch pieces
> 3 or 4 bay leaves
> 2 or 3 sprigs thyme
> 1 top or bottom round roast (about 3 to 4 pounds)
> Olive oil
> Salt and pepper
> Red wine (choose something that you would want
>   to drink with the finished dish)

If you are braising in the oven, preheat it to 350 degrees.

Put all the cut vegetables into your braising pot or roasting pan along with the herbs and mix them together. This is the bed on which the meat will braise. Heat a little olive oil in a skillet until a haze forms over the pan, put in the meat, and brown it well over high heat for about 3 or 4 minutes on each side. Keep the heat high. Use tongs or a pair of forks to turn the meat and get all its surfaces browned.

Remove the meat and transfer it to the braising pan, resting it on the vegetables, and season it all over with large pinches of salt and pepper. Add the wine to the pan, enough to cover the vegetables and some of the meat. Nestle the meat down into the vegetables and cover the pot.

If you are braising on the stovetop, bring the covered pot to a very gentle simmer and keep it there. If you are braising in the oven, cover the dish with aluminum foil, pushing the foil down around the inside of the pan so that as the juices steam onto the foil they end up dripping back down into the pan and not outside.

Braise the meat for 2½ hours. Remove the lid and replace it askew (or loosen an edge of the tin foil if using the oven) so that the juices can reduce and thicken a little bit, and cook for 30 minutes longer. Remove the meat from the pot to a cutting board and let it rest. Remove the bay leaves from the dish. Transfer all the braising liquid and vegetables to a blender or food processor and blend until smooth. Taste the sauce and correct for salt and pepper. Slice the meat across the grain and arrange it on a serving platter. Pour over the sauce and serve.

Petto di Pollo Farcito alla Valdostana

SAUTÉED CHICKEN BREAST STUFFED WITH FONTINA

BREADED AND SAUTÉED dishes are both common and a highly respected practice in the Italian kitchen. The breading is important because it gives the meat (usually a delicate cut) time to cook through while protecting it from scorching and drying out. This is the kind of dish you might come across on the menus of small city neighborhood cafés where you can eavesdrop on the conversations taking place around you. What could be better? This recipe is written per person; multiply as needed.

1 boneless, skinless half chicken breast
Salt and freshly ground pepper
2 or 3 paper-thin slices fontina cheese
1 egg, beaten
Bread crumbs
2 tablespoons vegetable oil
1 tablespoons butter

Place the half chicken breast flat on your cutting surface and one hand flat on top of the breast. Using your best and longest straight-bladed knife, carefully slice the breast horizontally through the middle starting at the outside edge and slicing toward the center edge, where the breast used to be attached to the breastbone. Don't slice all the way through. Leave a hinge about ¼ inch thick joining the two halves. Open up the breast and gently pound it out between two sheets of parchment, waxed paper, or plastic wrap to a thickness no greater than ¼ inch. Season the interior of the open breast with a little salt and pepper and lay in the slices of *Fontina* on one half of the breast, leaving a border about ½ inch wide. Close the other half over the cheese and gently pound the edges together to seal them. Season the outside of the meat with a little more salt and pepper.

Carefully turn the stuffed breast in the beaten egg, allowing the excess to drip off, then turn it in the bread crumbs. Press the meat into the crumbs to get good adherence and a thorough coating.

Heat the oil and butter in a skillet over medium-high heat. (The fats must sizzle when one corner of the meat touches the pan.) Lay in the stuffed breast and sauté until just golden brown, turn the chicken over and brown the other side. (The meat should be firm, but still tender and not dry.) Serve immediately.

Polpettine al Arancio e Menta

MEATBALLS WITH ORANGE AND MINT

TOSSED WITH SPAGHETTI or fettuccini and a little freshly grated *parmigiano*, these meatballs will serve 6 as a *primo*. They can also be served barely warm, by themselves, as part of a course of *antipasti*. You can also form the meat into large patties to grill or sauté as a *secondo*. Ground pork makes an excellent substitution for the beef.

    1 pound ground beef (or ground pork)
    ½ cup bread crumbs
    ¼ cup freshly grated orange zest
    2 eggs
    2 tablespoons minced parsley
    ¼ cup minced mint leaves
    Salt and pepper
    Olive oil, for browning
    Orange juice

In a large mixing bowl and using your hands, combine the beef, bread crumbs, orange zest, eggs, herbs, and salt and pepper, and mix well. (I recommend using your hands for this step: Touch provides a better sense of when all the ingredients have been uniformly mixed. At any rate, the following step requires use of the hands as well.)

Form the mixture into small meatballs about as big around as the diameter of a nickel, but no larger, and set them aside on a baking tray or plates.

Heat 2 tablsepoons of the olive oil in a large skillet until a haze just begins to form over the pan, put in some of the meatballs, but don't overcrowd the pan, and lower the heat to medium. Cook the meatballs, turning them gently with a spatula or by shaking the pan, until lightly browned. Test one of the plumper meatballs for doneness by cutting it in half: no pink meat should remain in the middle. Raise the heat to high and add just a little orange juice, tilting the pan carefully to glaze all the meatballs. Remove the cooked meatballs onto paper towels to drain, and then repeat the cooking process with any remaining meatballs, wiping out the pan between batches with a paper towel.

Patate Arroste al Forno

Oven-Roasted Potatoes

ROASTED POTATOES are one of the great side dishes of all time and can be served along with almost any *secondo* or salad or even by themselves. They can roast in the oven at the same time as your featured meat dish. [Use red potatoes, Yukon gold, all-purpose, or new potatoes. Don't use a Russet potato (sometimes labeled Idaho).] Serves 4.

> 4 medium potatoes
> Olive oil
> Salt and freshly ground pepper
> Rosemary leaves, to taste

Preheat oven to 375 degrees. (Time the potatoes to come out of the oven at the same time as the rest of your meal.)

Scrub the potatoes well. Do not peel them. Cut into 1-inch cubes and put them in a baking pan. Season well with the oil, salt and pepper, and rosemary. Toss or mix to coat the potatoes thoroughly. Roast the potatoes for 40 minutes to 1 hour, turning 2 or 3 times with a spatula, until tender when pierced with a fork. They should have a nice brown crust. Taste one and correct the seasoning if necessary. Serve immediately in a warmed serving dish or arranged around the *secondo*.

Radicchio di Treviso in Padella

SAUTÉED RADICCHIO

A VERSATILE DISH, suitable as an *antipasto,* or as a *contorno* alongside roasted chicken or sausages. Serves 4.

    1 large head (or 2 small heads) radicchio
    2 tablespoons olive oil
    Salt and freshly ground black pepper

Wash the radicchio head whole, but don't shake off all the water. Without removing the core, cut the radicchio lengthwise into quarters for 1 large head, or in half for 2 small heads, so that each piece is held together at its base. In a skillet heat the olive oil until a haze begins to form over the pan and put the radicchio in, cut-side down. Drizzle a touch more oil over the radicchio and sprinkle 1 or 2 pinches salt over all. Lower the heat a fraction, and cover the pan. Cook for about 5 minutes, watching the heat so that the radicchio doesn't burn, until the outermost leaves are wilted. Turn the pieces gently in the oil and seasoning and remove from the pan. The interior leaves should be gently browned. Serve.

Cavolo in Padella

PAN-BRAISED CABBAGE

CABBAGE PREPARED in this way provides an excellent accompaniment to fish prepared on the grill or stovetop or in the oven. You can use red, green, savoy, or Napa cabbage, just note that the latter two will take less time to cook. A cabbage may look like a lot, but it will cook down to a fraction of its size. Serves 4 to 6 as a *contorno*.

    1 medium head cabbage
    3 tablespoons butter and olive oil
    Salt and pepper
    Chicken stock, wine, or water (or even beer)
    Additional extra-virgin olive oil

Remove any tough, damaged, or unsightly outer leaves. (If you can see dirt within the head, remove leaves until you can't see anymore dirt and just wash the dirty leaves and proceed with the recipe.) Cut the cabbage into quarters, cut out the core from each quarter, and then slice the cabbage into slivers about ¼ inch wide.

Heat the butter and oil in a large skillet, add the cabbage, and turn it to coat it with the fats. Season with a few pinches salt and pepper. Add about ½ inch of your preferred braising liquid to the pan, cover it, and cook at a brisk simmer for 5 or 6 minutes. Turn the cabbage again and add more liquid if needed to maintain the steamy atmosphere. Continue cooking the cabbage down until it is tender and the liquid has cooked away. Taste and correct the seasoning, adding a little extra-virgin olive oil if needed, and serve.

Pere in Caramello al Pernod

PEARS IN PERNOD CARAMEL

THIS DESSERT is a regular feature at Pane e Salute and, while Pernod is a French liquor, this recipe represents a common phenomenon in northern parts of Italy where foods and ingredients from across the border have become part of the cuisine, sometimes out of longstanding practices, sometimes because in fact the borders were at one time (or at several times) quite different, or because there is something good to come out of such an adoption.

In the final step, the Pernod is lit afire, allowing all the alcohol to burn off and caramelizing the sugar. Don't worry, the flames will be contained within the pan, but *prepare yourself:* they may reach as much as a foot in height. Serves 2.

1 tablespoon butter
¼ cup heavy cream
⅛ cup sugar
3 ripe, still-firm Bartlett pears, peeled, cored, and halved
¼ cup Pernod
Mint leaves, for garnish, if available

In a large sauté pan, melt the butter over medium heat. Add the cream and sugar, stir to combine, and cook this mixture briskly for 2 minutes to bind the fats and sugar together. Add the pear halves cut-side down and poach for 2 to 3 minutes to heat them through. With a slotted spoon remove the pears to dessert plates.

Add the Pernod to the pan and raise the heat to high. Hold the pan at arm's length and step back as you prepare to ignite the liquor, being cautious as the ignition can take you by surprise. If you have a gas stove, *carefully* tilt the pan, bringing the liquids closer to the pan edge and thus the flame, until the liquor ignites. (If you have an electric stove, use a match to light the Pernod.) Set the pan down level on the burner again. As it burns, gently swirl the pan to mix the contents together. The flame will go out, but continue cooking the caramel until it thickens up a little bit, just beginning to become syrupy, then pour the caramel over the pears and serve.

Tartine con Frangipane e Prugne Fresche

FRANGIPANE AND PLUM TART

THE CRUST for this tart is quite rich, or "short," and does all a tart crust should: its strength prevents slices from disintegrating when served and its crunchy texture perfectly complements the fruity custard filling. Quite versatile, the dough, called *Pasta Frolla,* can be used to make jam-filled cookies, such as simple open rings or folded pockets called *fazzoletti.*

Likewise, frangipane is also quite versatile and goes well with other fresh fruits, such as peaches, pears, and apples. Makes at least 1 9-inch tart.

For the **Pasta Frolla** *crust:*
12 tablespoons butter (1½ sticks)
½ cup sugar
¼ teaspoon salt
1 egg
1 egg yolk
2 teaspoons vanilla extract
1 teaspoon lemon juice
2¼ cups flour

To make the crust: In a large mixing bowl, cream together the butter and the sugar. Add the salt, egg, egg yolk, vanilla, and lemon juice and mix well. Add the flour and mix completely. Chill the dough for 40 minutes or longer. (Chilling the dough before rolling it out makes it easier to handle and then transfer from countertop to pan.)

Dust a clean work surface and the dough well with flour to prevent sticking. Roll out the dough to a thickness of ¼ to ⅜ inch and line your tart pan. (If your tart pan is large, fold the rolled-out dough in half to move it to the pan and then unfold it.) Patch any tears or gaps in the dough with scraps of extra dough. (*Pasta Frolla* is very tolerant of this kind of remedial addition). With the tart pan lined, pinch the dough to a thin taper against the edge of the tart pan, turning the pan as you go, to give the crust a delicate edge.

For tarts filled with frangipane it is not necessary to prebake the crust, but for fruit-and-custard-filled tarts, prebaking will prevent the crust from becoming soggy in the end. To prebake, preheat oven to 350 degrees. Prick the uncooked crust 12 or 14 times with a fork (to keep it from puffing wildly in the oven) and bake for 12 to 15 minutes, or until the crust's surface is dry and set. Remove from the oven and let the prebaked crust cool before filling.

For the filling:
2 cups blanched almonds
1 cup sugar
1 cup plain cake and/or cookie crumbs
3 eggs
¼ to ⅔ cup milk

To make the filling: In a blender or food processor, process the blanched almonds together with the sugar and cake or cookie crumbs into a fine powder. Add the eggs and combine, then slowly add the milk, pulsing and blending until the mixture has a lava-like consistency, neither stiff nor runny.

The frangipane can be used immediately or stored in the refrigerator for up to a week.

For the Frangipane and Plum Tart:
4 to 6 plums, washed, halved, pits removed
Prebaked *Pasta Frolla* tart crust (see above)
Frangipane filling (see above)
Confectioner's sugar or apricot jam to finish

To assemble the tart: Preheat oven to 350 degrees.

Slice the plum halves into inch-thick wedges.

Using your hands, fill the prebaked tart shell with a ¾-inch layer of frangipane. Press the fruit into the frangipane, leaving about ¼ inch between slices, so that the frangipane has room to puff up around the fruit while baking. Bake for 30 to 40 minutes or until the frangipane at the center of the tart is dry on the surface and nicely browned overall. Remove and let cool.

Sprinkle a blanket of confectioner's sugar over top or coat with a thin glaze of heated apricot jam thinned with water.

Tiramisú, o Semifreddo al Caffé

ESPRESSO AND MASCARPONE TRIFLE

FIRSTLY, this version is not intended to be the sugar-and-liquor bomb so often encountered when ordering *tiramisú* afield.

Herein you will find also a recipe for making your own ladyfingers. To make ladyfingers for the sole purpose of then making *Tiramisú*, I advise spreading the ladyfinger batter in a large cake pan or on a cookie sheet in a single layer and then baking it. This will make assembling the *Tiramisú* simpler and take less time.

Tiramisù calls for good-quality espresso, brewed either on a pump-driven espresso maker or in a stovetop Moka pot. It must be espresso good enough to drink straight. (If you don't have either of these apparati, perhaps this is the time to finally get one.)

Lastly, note that the Marsala, rather than a stronger liquor like rum or Kahlúa, provides the only alcohol in the recipe, resulting in a balanced harmony of flavors and aromas when combined with the *mascarpone*, espresso, and fresh cream.

For the ladyfingers:
4 eggs, separated
½ cup sugar
1 teaspoon vanilla extract
½ cup flour, sifted
¼ teaspoon salt

Preheat oven to 350 degrees.

Butter and flour the bottom and sides of a four-sided cookie sheet or other baking pan of a similar size.

In a medium mixing bowl, beat the yolks and sugar together until light and foamy. Add the vanilla and combine, then add the flour and salt and gently mix together until smooth.

In a separate small bowl, whip the whites until stiff but not dry and fold one-third of the whites into the flour mixture. Repeat two times, until all the whites have been folded in, but not too thoroughly, so that a few streaks of white still show in the batter. Spread the batter in your pan(s) in a ¼-inch-deep layer. Bake for 12 to 15 minutes, or until the top of the batter is lightly browned, the sides are starting to pull away from the pan, and a clean knife blade inserted into the puffiest part of the batter comes out clean.

Remove from the oven and let cool before using for *Tiramisú*, below.

For the Tiramisú:
½ pound *mascarpone*
3 eggs, separated
⅛ cup Marsala
¼ cup sugar
½ cup heavy cream
1 uncut ladyfinger "cake" (see above)
1½ cups or more espresso
Powdered cocoa

In a medium bowl, beat together the *mascarpone* and egg yolks until smooth. Add the Marsala and combine, and set aside this mixture.

In a separate bowl, whip together the egg whites and the sugar to form a stiff meringue. Fold the meringue into the *mascarpone* mixture. Now whip the heavy cream until just stiff and fold that into the *mascarpone*-meringue mixture.

To assemble the *Tiramisú*, I recommend using a large loaf pan. Cut the ladyfinger cake into sheets to fit the size of your pan. You will need at least 3 layers of ladyfinger cake to complete assembly (so your pan needs to be at least 3 ladyfingers deep). Pour some of the espresso into another shallow pan for soaking the ladyfinger sheets. Spread a ¼-inch layer of the *mascar-pone* cream on the bottom of your loaf or other service pan. Briefly soak a piece of the ladyfinger in the espresso (too much espresso and the cookie will disintegrate) and press the soaked piece gently into the first layer of cream. Spread another ¼-inch layer of the *mascarpone* cream into the pan, and then repeat with two more layers of soaked ladyfinger and more cream. Finish with a smooth layer of *mascarpone* cream on top. Dust the top of the *Tiramisú* with the powdered cocoa to lightly but completely blanket the sur-face. Chill the *Tiramisú*; an overnight in the refrigerator is ideal.

Note: If you have leftover ladyfinger cake and *mascarpone* cream, impro-vise a second *Tiramisú* in another pan, bowl, or what-have-you. *Tiramisú* freezes well.

bread

bread: a season unto itself

B Y NOW, MOST PEOPLE with an abiding interest in food understand that in Italy there is a culture of bread. I am
thrilled that you are eager to undertake baking your own bread, for you are
participating in one of the most deeply revered and informative traditions
practiced by humankind.

I want to share some of my thoughts about bread baking and, in particular,
bread baking at home. First, the more regularly and frequently one bakes
bread, the simpler the process becomes and the better the results. This is a
strong argument for seeking out a skilled local baker and buying your bread.
(Besides, who has time to bake their own bread these days?) But if someone else
were baking your bread, you wouldn't be baking your own, which is a large
part of the point. Bread baking is, after all, very, very satisfying on all the physical sensory levels, and certainly some spiritual and psychological levels, too.

One reason daily bakers of artisanal breads enjoy baking success is that
yeast is alive and needs regular feedings to maintain its boosting power—just
as you and I need food—and bakers are present each day to provide the fresh
flour and water needed to maintain a strong vitality in their starters. It
sounds simple, and it is. In fact, bread baking is itself simple. Make no mis-
take: it is also work, especially when undertaken on a daily basis. Success is
a matter of persistence, of attention being paid, and of responsibility. It is a
baker's ability to respond to the needs of the dough that makes a good
bread, so you have to care enough to pay attention. I think that one of the

defining characteristics of good bread is that it is something about which one can say, "Someone cared about this." Doesn't that also imply that they care about those who consume their bread? On some level, it does.

Another advantage professional bakers enjoy is that they are practiced in the handling and shaping of their bread dough. They are familiar with its character and needs. Few people are able to shape consistently perfect loaves right off the bat. It takes practice, day after day, so that one can observe the results of one's shaping when the bread comes out of the oven, and then apply what one learns the next time, perhaps rolling the loaves a little tighter, or letting the loaves rise a little longer before baking. For this reason especially, I recommend that you begin your bread baking ventures by making just one kind of bread until you become familiar with the quirks of that bread, your ingredients and tools, your oven, and the environment at work in your kitchen. All these things affect one another, and the consistency of your practice and attention will help you overcome the inconsistencies of their effects. Your skills and knowledge will improve. So will your bread.

You must also be patient. Consider time an essential ingredient. After all, most of the time spent making bread involves waiting for the yeasts in the dough to do their job, and yeasts don't like to be rushed. So while you are waiting you can be doing other things around the house or kitchen, or—every baker's favorite—take a nap.

I believe it takes just as much time and work to make a poor bread. I also believe there is no excuse for not giving the attention necessary to make a good bread. If one is going to bother to make one's own bread, make it count.

So if you want to make your own bread, but you have never considered yourself one who bakes, consider yourself one who *can* bake, because you *can* give the attention of one who cares. Bread baking can provide such an inviting challenge, and can give such satisfaction, again and again. For me, the challenge is to make beautiful bread each day, knowing full well that today's bread will be different from yesterday's. It is perfectly conceivable that a baker's bread will be beautiful every day, yet different every day. Just as a professional dancer strives for excellence in each performance, each performance will say something different. But again let me say that bread baking is simple. It is the professional who brings complete attention to bear on the challenge at the moment of performance, who is not distracted from his or her purpose, and who keeps the greater goals of his or her pursuit in view, even as he or she attends to the details of each task.

And what is that greater goal when one is making bread? To make a thing of beauty and to share it with others.

Tools

A countertop mixer with a dough hook is ideal for making bread dough, especially when the style of bread calls for a wet dough, as these recipes do. However, a large mixing bowl, a thick-handled wooden spoon, and your hands can also do the job. You will also need to cover the dough while it rises; for this a large kitchen towel or two, or a piece of plastic sheeting, such as a plastic trash bag cut open, will do.

A few tools I strongly recommend

A wooden peel for transferring the dough into the oven and a baking stone, or even two. The stones will help provide proper crust; they will even out the heat of your ovens; and they will be ideal for baking pizza. At home we keep our stones in the oven all the time and, although they have cracked over time, they still perform perfectly after more than eight years. If I had to choose between stones and a mixer, I would take the stones.

A sharp serrated knife for slashing the dough right before it goes in the oven. (Practice slashing the dough before you shape the final loaves, so that you can get the feel of the quick, firm, yet light stroke needed to slash effectively.)

A stainless steel or hard plastic dough scraper for cutting and portioning dough.

Finally, you will need a spray bottle for misting the loaves in the oven.

Ingredients

Flour. Buy your flour from a store where you know the turnover is rapid. If this is your first bread-baking venture, try a few brands and see which flour you like. At Pane e Salute we use Sir Galahad, made by King Arthur Flour, as our white bread flour. While it is milled specifically to emulate European bread flour, we also use it as our all-purpose flour for cakes, cookies, and pasta. Finding a fresh flour you like is a priority, as old flour makes a lifeless bread because it doesn't provide enough food (proteins and sugars) for the yeast to feed on. Store your flour in a plastic bucket (with a tight-fitting lid) large enough to allow you to fluff the flour with your hand. This will remove clumps from the flour and make your dough mix more readily.

Water. Use water that tastes good to you. If your water comes from a municipal water system it is chlorinated to kill unwanted bacteria. Chlorinated water can sometimes have strong odors and flavors, but these are easy to remove either with a charcoal filter system (such as a Brita filter) or by drawing your water into an open container the night before you mix your dough, allowing the chlorine to dissipate—or "off-gas"—overnight. Usually this latter method is sufficient. If your water still tastes unpleasant after an overnight sitting out uncovered, try a filter.

Yeast. Your yeast must also be fresh, be it cake yeast or dry, instant yeast. While these recipes call for relatively small amounts of fresh yeast, you will use some of it to stimulate additional yeast growth in the starter. If your starter doesn't take off with authority, becoming bubbly and frothy, then your yeast is probably dead. At Pane e Salute we use a dry, instant baker's yeast in some of our breads to supplement the yeast in the starter and because that is the way those breads are made in Italy. (While naturally leavened breads are common in Italy, they are far from prevalent.) Yeast sold in vacuum packages should be fine, and it should be date-stamped for freshness, too. You may need to shop around a little bit to find a reliable source. If you become desperate, you can ask a bakery if they will sell you a little bit of their yeast, as their supply usually turns over more quickly than that in stores. Do not use any "Fast-Rising" or "Fast-Acting" yeast.

Salt. I recommend a good, refined sea salt for making bread. It simply tastes better and brighter than rock-derived salts. A fine, rather than coarse, salt will dissolve much more readily into your bread dough. If you are stuck with coarse salt, grind it in a pepper mill first.

a note on the bread recipes

THESE RECIPES ARE WRITTEN with this scenario in mind: I am standing at your shoulder, observing your progress throughout the mixing process, the kneading, and the shaping. I will direct your attention to certain parts of the process so that you can respond to what you *see* or *feel* is happening. Remember this: Just because you may have success one time does not mean that you can do all and only the same things the next time and be assured of success, for by then the environment in your kitchen will be different. You must be the judge of that environment, and respond accordingly as the recipe proceeds anew.

Each of the recipes calls for a *Biga*—an old Tuscan dialect word for "mother"—or the starter. The practice of using a starter comes from the time before manufactured yeast, and it provides the majority of the rising power in these doughs. The beauty of using *Biga* is that its overnight rise is the *first* rise of the bread, which means your bread gets to go in the oven sooner. The yeast added directly to the final dough serves to supplement the starter's own boosting power and reduce the rising time of the dough. In the morning the *Biga* should be frothy with lively yeast activity. If it is flat and looks like the water and flour have separated, you will have to try again. (The freshness of your yeast might be the culprit.)

If you wish, you may omit the yeast in the final dough, but then you must use more starter and allow the dough more time to rest and rise after mixing.

Pane Casareccio

HOME-STYLE BREAD

THIS IS THE BASIC COUNTRY bread found throughout much of Italy. The bread should have a thick crust and a slightly chewy interior with some irregularly sized holes. It is good plain, grilled or toasted, with anything you care to put on it. Makes 4 pounds of bread.

Make the **Biga** *the evening before the day you make the dough:*

In a 2-quart bowl or plastic container put 3 cups flour, ¼ teaspoon of yeast (or a pea-sized piece of cake yeast, crumbled), and enough water to make a slightly thick, soupy mixture. It must not be loose and splashy. Beat it well to incorporate some air into it, cover with a towel, and leave overnight in an out-of-the-way place on your countertop or in the sink (a good precaution in the event the yeast activity is extremely vigorous).

In the morning the *Biga* should be frothy with lively yeast activity. If it is flat and looks like the water and flour have separated, you will have to try again. (The freshness of your yeast might be the culprit.)

If your *Biga* looks lively pour three-fourths of it into your mixing bowl, and store the rest in the refrigerator until the night before your next batch, when it can serve to add more developed flavor to the bread.

Add to the **Biga:**
1 tablespoon yeast, dry or cake (crumbled)
2 teaspoons fine sea salt
5 cups flour
¼ cup wheat germ, optional
2 to 3 cups water at room temperature

Using the dough hook on your mixer (and the slowest speed), or a heavy wooden spoon, mix together the *Biga* and the yeast, salt, flour (and the germ, if you are using it, too), and 1 cup of the water. As the ingredients combine into a single mass, continue to add water until the mixture is no longer lumpy and tough, but has become a very soft, pliant, and resilient dough. It should clean the bowl as it mixes.

If you are using a mixer: As the dough travels around the bowl it should do so quietly and smoothly, without any bumps or clanking. If not, slowly add water in ¼-cup increments, allowing about 1 minute to assess the effect of each addition. If the dough sticks to the bowl at all, it should do so only at the very bottom of the dough, and only a little bit. If it does not move at all as a ball of dough separate from the bowl because it is too wet, then add flour in ¼-cup increments, again allowing each addition to take its effect, until it becomes a ball moving around the bowl on the hook. Let the mixer knead the dough for a total of 8 to 10 minutes, until it is silky smooth and plastic (stretchable), yet elastic.

If you are kneading by hand: Turn the dough out onto a lightly floured sur face and knead it for 13 to 15 minutes. Using the heel of one hand, mash it out in one stroke, fold it back upon itself with your other hand, rotating the dough slightly, and mash it out again, and fold it back, and so on.

Put the kneaded dough into a large mixing bowl and cover with a towel or sheet of plastic. Let the bread rest for 20 to 30 minutes.

Preheat oven to 450 degrees.

Portion the dough into 4 equal pieces.

Shape the loaves: Flour the work surface and turn a piece of dough in the flour to coat it lightly. (Throughout the shaping process the key is to use just enough flour at regular intervals to keep the dough from sticking to you or the work surface.) Let your handling of the dough be quick and assertive, so that your hands aren't touching the dough long enough for it to stick to you. If the position of your hands on the dough changes rapidly, you won't have any problems. If you are tentative and handle the dough as if it were a frag- ile and breakable thing, it will stick to you and be difficult to shape effectively.

As you shape each loaf, you will need to set them aside on a clean, lightly floured surface (a cookie sheet or counter space will be fine) for their final rise. Stretch a piece of dough out into a rough oval. If the dough is very elastic and airy, push out some of the bigger bubbles. Roll the oval up shortwise into a fat, cartoonish cigar. With one thumb tuck the ends in toward the center of the loaf and pinch the dough down over your thumb to seal the seams. Using the heel of your hand, pound the seam closed down the length of the loaf. Roll the dough under your hands against the (lightly floured) counter and shape it into a symmetrical oval shape, tapering to gentle points at the ends. Set the loaf aside for its final rise and repeat the shaping process with the remaining portions. Once all the loaves are shaped, dust them all with flour and cover them with the towel or plastic sheet.

Let them rest and rise until the touch test tells you they are ready to go in the oven: Press your finger into the middle of a loaf to a depth of ½ inch. The impression of your finger should bounce back a little bit, but the impression should remain clear. Gently lay your hand over the whole loaf and wiggle it back and forth: it should feel fluffy and, while it has relaxed somewhat, it still should have some tension and structure in it.

(At this point, take a moment to envision where the loaves must be placed in the oven, and the order in which you will place them. If you are not using a peel, you can slide the rack all the way out of the oven, place the loaves on it, and then slide it back in.)

Load the dough into the oven: Rub your peel with a little flour to thoroughly coat its surface, and rub your hands, too. Gently wiggle your fingers under a loaf from each end until your fingers touch. Move the dough onto the peel, placing it along one side of the peel, leaving room for another loaf. (A 14-inch-wide peel can load three loaves at once.) Once the loaves are on the peel, use a serrated knife to slash each one down its center: hold the knife at a 45-degree angle and slash quickly and lightly to a depth of about ¾ inch, starting 1 inch from the end of the loaf to about 1 inch from the other end. Open the oven door and place the peel so that the loaves are where you want them over the stone; imagine the sound and motion of a cracking whip: elevate the handle of the peel about 1 inch and smoothly snap the peel out from under the dough. Close the oven door and get your spray bottle, then quickly mist the loaves in the oven and close the door again. Wait 3 minutes and mist the dough again, and again after another 3 minutes. Bake for 25 minutes, then reduce the heat to 425 degrees and bake until the crust is well browned all over, perhaps as long as another 20 to 25 minutes. In the final few minutes you can spray the loaves again to help make the loaf crustier and browner.

Test for doneness: When the loaves are well browned remove a loaf with a towel and tap the bottom of the loaf: it should feel good and crusty underneath and make a slightly hollow, resonant sound. Remember, as the bread approaches doneness, the oven is getting hotter and hotter, and the bread is at increasing risk of burning. While I like my bread with a good brown crust on it, there is a point of no return. You'll know when you've passed it.

Let the loaves cool on a rack or something else that prevents their bottoms from sitting flat on the counter, otherwise condensation will form beneath them and make them soggy. Nobody likes a soggy bottom.

Pane Tipo Altamura o Materese

TRADITIONAL BREAD OF ALTAMURA OR MATERA

THIS IS A BREAD TYPICAL of the Deep South. Altamura and Matera are both small cities in the Murge, an important grain-growing area. Much *grano duro*, or "hard wheat," comes from there and is so called because of its behavior during the milling process. It is a vitreous grain, which means that instead of grinding down to a soft powder like soft wheat, it shatters when first milled. The result is semolina, a granular flour. This must be milled again in order to achieve a soft flour. Even so, when running durum flour between your fingers, you can still feel a faint granular texture.

This bread has a crisp crust, but a soft and finely textured interior. But *nota bene:* if your climate is notably humid today, either increase the proportion of white flour in the dough, or make a different bread. This dough has the ability to absorb moisture right out of the air and become heavy to the point of breaking, when its structure loses its elasticity and becomes unmanageable. Whenever this happens I swear to never attempt this bread again during the humid peaks of a Vermont summer. Then I throw the broken dough back into the *Biga* bucket, or, if I have too much, into the trash. Utter despair! Then I try again the next day.

Make the Biga *the evening before you plan to bake:*

Mix together 1 cup white flour and 2 cups durum flour. Add 2 pinches of dry yeast (or a pea-sized piece of cake yeast, crumbled) and enough cool water to make a slightly thick, soupy mixture. It must not be loose and splashy. Beat it well to incorporate some air into it, cover it with a towel and leave overnight, out of the way on your kitchen counter.

In the morning, if your *Biga* looks lively, pour three-fourths of it into your mixing bowl, and store the rest in the refrigerator until the night before your next batch.

Add to the Biga:

1 tablespoon yeast, dry or cake (crumbled)

2 teaspoons fine sea salt

4 cups durum flour

1 cup white flour

2 to 3 cups water at room temperature

Follow the mixing and rising procedures for *Pane Casareccio* (p. 258).

Preheat oven to 450 degrees.

Shape the portioned dough into rounds or oval loaves. For shaping as rounds: Create a clean workspace on the counter and dust the upper reaches of this workspace with flour. Dust the top of one of your portions with flour and place it in the clean, flour-free area. Rub your hands with a little flour and place them over the dough to cover it, letting the outside edges of your hands and pinky fingers rest on the countertop. With a gentle yet firm pressure on the counter and sides of the dough begin a circular motion on the counter. Maintain pressure around the very bottom of the dough with your pinky fingers, as if they were trying to tuck the dough underneath the ball as it travels around its circle. Experiment with large circles and small circles until you begin to feel the skin of the dough stretching downward as the countertop begins to pull on it. *That* is the feeling you want. If the dough begins to stick to your hands, turn the top of the dough quickly in the flour at the edge of your workspace, then pick up where you left off in the clean space. Stop once the skin has attained just enough tension to give the whole ball a sense of its own structure: neither tight like a drum, nor loose and floppy. (*For shaping as oblong, oval loaves:* Follow the shaping instructions for *Pane Casareccio.*)

Once all the loaves are shaped, set them to rise on a floured surface, dust their tops with flour, and cover with a towel or plastic sheet.

Let them rest and rise until the touch test tells you they are ready to go in the oven: Press your finger into the middle of a loaf to a depth of ½ inch.

The impression of your finger should bounce back a little bit, but the impression should remain clear. Gently lay your hand over the whole loaf and wiggle it back and forth: the loaf should feel fluffy and, while it has relaxed somewhat, it still should have some tension and structure in it.

(At this point, take a moment to envision where the loaves must be placed in the oven, and the order in which you will place them. If you are not using a peel, you can slide the rack all the way out of the oven, place the loaves on it by hand, and then slide it back in. *Careful:* Don't burn yourself—my own arms are covered with burn scars.)

Load the dough into the oven: Rub your peel with a little flour to thoroughly coat its surface, and rub your hands, too. Gently wiggle your fingers under a loaf from each end until your fingers touch. Move the dough onto the peel, placing it along one side of the peel, leaving room for another loaf. (A 14-inch-wide peel can load three oblong loaves, or two round ones, at once.) Once the loaves are on the peel, use a serrated knife to slash each one down its center: hold the knife at a 45-degree angle and slash quickly and lightly to a depth of about ¾ inch, starting 1 inch from the end (or side, if the loaves are round) of the loaf to about 1 inch from the other end (or side). Open the oven door and place the peel so that the loaves are where you want them over the stone; now, imagine the sound and motion of a cracking whip: elevate the handle of the peel about 1 inch and smoothly and gently snap the peel out from under the dough. Close the oven door and get your spray bottle, then quickly mist the loaves in the oven and close the door again. Wait 3 minutes and mist the dough again, and again after another 3 minutes.

Bake for 25 minutes, then reduce the heat to 425 degrees and bake until the crust is well browned all over, perhaps as long as another 20 to 25 minutes (watch out, as ovens can vary wildly). In the final few minutes you can spray the loaves again to help make the loaf crustier and browner.

Test for doneness: When the loaves are well browned remove a loaf with a towel and tap the bottom of the loaf: it should feel good and crusty underneath and make a slightly hollow, resonant sound.

Let the loaves cool on a rack or on something else so that their bottoms are not flat on the counter, otherwise condensation will form beneath them and make them soggy. Like I said before: Nobody likes a soggy bottom.

Note: If you are inspired and have the space, this bread is even better if you allow the shaped loaves to age overnight before baking. You will need to do this in the refrigerator, so you'll have to plan carefully. If you have a cool basement space available, or it's cool outside at nighttime, that can work too. The temperature needs to be fridge-cold. In the morning heat your oven, slash each loaf, and load the dough *directly* from the cold environment into the hot oven, mist, and bake. *Do not* allow the dough to come up to room temperature, for it will then over-proof and it has been proofing all night at a much slower pace. To my mind this procedure improves every aspect of this already excellent style of bread, and many of our customers agree (we offer both versions at Pane e Salute). Another advantage of baking in this way is that the baked bread lasts a day or two longer than bread baked the day it is mixed.

Pane al Lievito Naturale

NATURALLY LEAVENED BREAD

WHILE NATURALLY LEAVENED BREADS are enjoying a resurgence through-out Italy, this bread is modeled after one found in Rome, where it is baked as large kilo-sized rounds, simple oblongs, square-cut rolls, and a variety of other shapes and sizes. It is a flavorful and chewy bread that stays fresh for three or four days when baked in loaves of 1 pound or larger. It calls for a greater proportion of starter in the final dough. While the starter is seeded with an addition of yeast at the outset, by the time the starter is ready to be used naturally occurring yeast cells will have taken over. I recommend mixing this wet dough on the mixer; it's just too difficult to develop the structure needed by hand.

Makes enough for 4 to 5 1-pound loaves, plus some rolls or a 2-pound round.

Start the Biga *the morning of the day before you plan to bake:*
Mix together 2 cups white and 1 cup durum flour. Add 2 pinches of dry yeast (or a pea-sized piece of cake yeast, crumbled) and enough cool water to make a slightly thick, soupy mixture. It must not be loose and splashy. Beat the *Biga* well to incorporate some air into it, cover it with a towel, and leave it out of the way on your kitchen counter for 8 to 12 hours.

After 8 or 12 hours (in the evening): Add 2 more cups white flour and 1 more cup of durum to the *Biga,* and stir in enough water to maintain the thick, soupy texture. Again, beat the *Biga* well: at least 50 strokes.

The next morning, if your *Biga* looks lively, pour three-fourths of it into your mixing bowl, and store the rest in the refrigerator until the night before your next batch.

Add to the **Biga:**

4 teaspoons fine sea salt

3 cups white flour

1 cup durum flour

2 to 3 cups water at room temperature

Using the dough hook and the slowest speed on your mixer, mix together the ingredients in the bowl, observing as it comes together how wet it is. The dough you want will be very soft and wet, but not so wet that it doesn't want to try to climb up the hook as it moves around. If necessary, add water (in a slow thin stream down the inside of the bowl) or flour until the proper consistency is reached. The dough will slowly develop its strength and should begin to attempt its assault up the shaft of the hook. Knead the dough on the machine for 4 to 5 minutes, then stop the machine and pull on the dough between your forefinger and thumb: it should stretch easily without tearing and be quite sticky. You may need to add more water as you resume mixing, or you may need to sprinkle in some more white flour. Knead another 6 to 8 minutes until the dough is smooth, silky, and very elastic. Perform the pull test again to assess the strength of the dough. Its structure should now feel well developed compared to the first test.

Remove the dough onto a floured countertop, dust it thoroughly with a light veil of flour, and cover it with a towel or a plastic sheet.

Begin heating the oven and baking stone now to 450 degrees, and let the dough rise until fluffy and well relaxed, anywhere from 30 minutes to 1 hour.

Remove the cover from the dough and dust again with flour, rubbing it gently over the risen dome. Use your dough scraper to cut down through the dough with a single push and then a sideways scrape as the scraper contacts the counter, separating the dough into loaves (the regularity of their shapes is not crucial). Slide your floured hands beneath each loaf so that you can move it either onto your peel or directly onto the hot baking stone *with the cut surface facing up.* Leave about 2 inches between loaves to allow them room to "jump" without cramping one another too much. Once loaded into the oven, mist all the loaves twice in the first 6 minutes of baking.

Bake for 25 minutes, then reduce the heat to 425 degrees and bake until the crust is well browned all over, perhaps as long as another 20 to 25 minutes (watch out, as ovens can vary wildly). In the final few minutes you can spray the loaves again to help make the loaf crustier and browner, if you wish.

Test for doneness: When the loaves are well browned, remove a loaf with a towel and tap the bottom of the loaf: it should feel good and crusty underneath and make a slightly hollow, resonant sound.

Let the loaves cool on a rack leaning up against one another so that their bottoms are not flat on the counter, otherwise condensation will form beneath them and make them soggy. One more time: Nobody likes a soggy bottom.

Variations on the Bread Recipes

UNLESS SPECIFIED OTHERWISE, any of the three preceding bread doughs can be used to make the treats described below. (The final minutes of baking should be monitored closely, especially for the smaller rolls, as the browning accelerates.)

Schiacciatini al Olio—Olive oil flatbreads: Portion tennis ball-sized rolls and shape each one into a rough circle about 4 inches in diameter. Brush with olive oil and let the rolls rise until they are slightly domed. Brush again lightly with olive oil and sprinkle with kosher salt. Bake at 450 degrees until golden brown. These make perfect sandwich rolls.

Schiacciatini alle Olive—Olive flatbread: Just before putting the *schiacciatini* in the oven, press 4 to 6 pitted black Saracene or green Sicilian olives into each portion. Sprinkle with kosher salt and bake. While these are excellent with a young pecorino or fresh goat cheese, most of our die-hard fans demolish theirs—*before* they get back to the car or office—plain.

Schiacciata al Pomodoro—Tomato flatbread: Roll a loaf-sized portion of dough out with a rolling pin to the diameter of a dinner plate and cover the surface with moderately thin, slightly overlapping slices of tomato. Brush the whole thing with extra-virgin olive oil and sprinkle with salt and pepper and a light blanket of dried oregano. Bake at 450 degrees until golden brown all around the edges.

Foccaccia al Rosmarino—Rosemary flatbread: Squish a loaf-sized portion of *Pane Casareccia* dough out with the flat of your fingertips and transfer it onto a lightly floured peel. Brush the whole surface with extra-virgin olive oil and sprinkle the leaves from a 6-inch sprig of fresh rosemary over all. Press the leaves in firmly with your fingertips. Bake at 450 degrees until golden brown.

Panini Quadrati—Square-cut rolls: Let the dough rise on the counter, as for *Pane di Lievito Naturale*. Using a dough scraper, cut 3- to 4-inch-wide strips from the risen, fluffy, and lightly floured dough, and cut these strips in turn crosswise into squares. Transfer by hand directly onto the hot baking stone (they can be quite close together) and bake at 450 degrees for 15 to 20 minutes until lightly browned.

epilogue for now

TWELVE YEARS HAVE PASSED. Twelve years feels like a long time, yet also feels like a brief skip from one date to another. Funny how time works, creating conflicting sensations and perceptions, yet always moving forward. The only instances in which we go backward in time rather than finding ourselves a day, a month, a year older with some surprise is through that multiprismed kaleidoscope—memory. If my husband were writing this, I might tell him he was becoming a bit too philosophical.

But the truth is that so much of what my husband, Caleb, and I do is based on the philosophy of memory—our own memories and those of others. I suppose memories that are not our own become history, a subjective record of time in the past. When we began our mission at the restaurant so many years ago, we began with the notion that we could recreate an experience we had, a mission largely based on nostalgia for a year in our lives that had shown us a world that we previously could not have imagined, a year that revolved around the seasons, the earth, harvest, and gracious hospitality. A day centered on the experience of bounty, or the clever illusion of bounty when there was none, and all this took place on a specific stage, in the kitchen and on the table. At first the notion of opening a particular doorway to an experience of food and taste was born out of the desire to live each day like we had lived each day somewhere else in another country, a notion that was both selfish and generous. We wanted this for ourselves, yet wanted to give and share a similar experience to and with others. What started out as a response to wistful longing became supplanted by another urgency—that of preservation.

What became crucial to us was not only the obvious preservation of a way of life—the quotidian rhythm of provisioning for meals on a daily basis, the support of local farmers, vegetable gardeners, beekeepers, and cheesemakers—but preservation of the code that interpreted and made art out of these ingredients. We became collectors and translators of heirloom Italian recipes and regional and rare Italian varietal wines (Italian because that is where our experience led us, but it could just have easily been France or Germany or China if the dice had fallen differently). We became passionate about keeping alive in our own homeland the old ways that we had learned living in a foreign country. There were connections and there was much relevance. We served these recipes and wines in our restaurant; we focused our attentions on the simple and clear notes that these flavors taught us and our guests. We advocated the notion that this was the closest any of us could come to experiencing history as well as to forging a true link with others in the present. To taste a dish that our ancestors tasted over a hundred years ago is to understand something of their experience, to truly travel back in time and taste history. There is no better way to explain this than through a specific dessert wine that I found and served at the restaurant for a long time.

The wine is called *vin santo*, or holy wine, and has long been custom in Tuscany. Traditionally it is served after dinner with small almond biscotti that are perfect for dipping into a small cordial glass. The wine is honeyed and multilayered with flavors of nut and burnt caramel and candied orange peel. It is a wine made by poor farmers and noble families alike. And everyone makes it essentially the same way. The grapes are picked late and dried in a barn loft to fully raisin before being made into the wine. This wine has been made this way for hundreds, if not thousands, of years. So in it we can taste the same thing that the de' Medici tasted, or Machiavelli, or Dante.

The particular vin santo we served had a particular story. Several years ago the vineyard that produced it began a series of renovations on their outbuildings. Walls and roofs came down for new. In one building the workmen found a series of small wooden casks immured. They were dated 1943. Like so many objects of value all over Europe, this farm had buried their barrels of prized wine in the walls of the barn to hide them from confiscation during World War II.

Those casks of wine were opened, and what was inside—a rich, intense swirl of aromas and yeasts—was used to start the present-day vin santo. The old wine became a *biga,* a mother, for the new wine—not unlike the hundred-year-old yeast mothers that are used in Parisian bakeries, or the centuries-old mothers fed and coddled for making balsamic vinegar in northern Italy. In this dessert wine, not only were we tasting that concept of history, but we tasted something that actually came through time to us from more than sixty years ago. We shared something tangible with the people at the vineyard in 1942 who preserved what they valued most between the lathe and stucco of a barn. This transportation of history where we might sense the artistry of the *contadini* who made the wine, and the noble family who worked alongside the contadini on the night that they hid their barrels, sweating and toiling in the dark so as not to be seen, comes to us through the taste in a glass, not only a sustainable memory, but a living one as well.

So many years ago in the late winter of our first year of running our fledgling bakery and restaurant, that first winter of shaping this mission of preservation, we escaped to a city largely defined by its history through its architecture and its cuisine. We made the long drive to Quebec City on the St. Lawrence River. It was raw and snowy, but since it is a winter city, beautiful and beguiling all the same. We took much from this city: a needed break and needed inspiration. The few days we spent walking the narrow streets and eating *aux Canadienne et Française* reinvigorated us. The experience placed us fully in time. We tasted of the past in the present and that taste would inform our future. A dish simply called Pears Poached in Pernod forms an arc over the last twelve years providing a beginning and a middle. We hope it will still be some time before it winds its way to the end.

We first ate of Pears Poached in Pernod in that venerable Quebecois institution Le Continentale on that first trip away from our first incarnation of kitchen and dining room. This dish captivated our imaginations. The tableside creation of the caramel and the warm pears took us back to one of our first significant restaurant meals when we were very young and living in Manhattan before we were married and before Italy had rerouted us. Watching the creation of the dish took us back to the age-old tradition of the well-schooled professional waiter who could really cook just as well as any chef back in the kitchen. At the same time, the flavors we tasted firmly placed us in the present. We became exceedingly aware of the colors and motion of the dining room: the blue walls, the white fitted jackets on the waiters, the hum and buzz of conversation, and the ballet of the servers between the tables, whipping up the steak tartare or the salad in vinaigrette. Those same tastes projected us into the future where we imagined we might serve this in our restaurant dining room. At the time, we did not realize this house specialty at Le Continentale would also become one of ours.

These pears poached and bathed in the hot amalgam of anise liqueur, sugar, cream, and butter became a pillar of our notion of preservation and that tasting of history. But as the years passed, the bakery became retired, and we moved the restaurant up a flight of stairs and into a corner of a building that seemingly could not exist. Our work at the restaurant intensified and shifted, and we learned that preservation alone can be misleading and not enough. Preservation for preservation's sake in fact can be deadening, locking one in only the past, hobbling ideas and creativity. We saw this in other restaurants that refused, through stubbornness or apathy, to change any of the dishes on their menus as the seasons changed or their guests' palates asked for other tastes (after all, our very human bodies are subject to the seasons and phases of the moon), or refused to change, update, or clarify their style of service. We saw a refusal for reinvention, an element that is crucial in any restaurant. We wanted to keep hold of the initial inspirations, keep hold of those early recipes, but also flex and stretch in new ways, recreating ourselves over again and again. Otherwise, we realized, we would be left only with boredom and work that is no longer relevant or gratifying.

Perhaps even more pointedly, we saw an unbending devotion to replicating the past take its toll in the historical preservation of buildings around us that were not slated to be actual museums, but rather living, working, commercial concerns. The plans for some of these structures had been hidebound by an historical accuracy that rendered them more mausoleum than vital and thriving edifices where history and modernity could coexist. We saw shortsighted village zoning laws block attempts by small and crucial businesses to create sustainability within their own communities. We even saw environmental concerns that could not let go of preconceived notions and see the way to realistic, positive, and maintainable compromise.

While our experience and understanding of our own environment expanded and grew, the explanation of our concepts and the words of our mission became more defined. The desire for preservation became more than just that—we learned from pitfalls. There was the want for revitalization. Our search for heirloom recipes and those regional wines was not to create a museum piece or a simple archive stored someplace safe for posterity, but to create an organic archive that was shaped by our local ingredients and in direct relationship to what our local land could offer. Our kitchen and wine list has become not only preservationist or revitalist with an obvious use of our local bounty, but also *terroir-driven.*

The Vermont terroir offers much. In the past few years local agriculture has exploded. There are more farm gardens, farm stands, farmers' markets, cheese makers, and now vineyards (yes, for making wine) than ever before. At the restaurant we work with ten to fifteen different local farms who fill our larder, as well as partaking of what is available for wild-gathering: mushrooms, dandelion greens, wild leeks, cattail hearts.

As our kitchen has become described by the local terroir, so too have our interests. We own a plot of land, a handful of acres in the rare commodity of open meadow near the ridge of a wilderness called the Chateauguay. For years we have grown flowers, herbs, fruit, and a few vegetables. But in these past years we have become increasingly drawn to more completely husbanding our land and feeding our menu with our own efforts. While we will always support others farming in our area, Caleb has been fueled by the desire to grow specific vegetables for our kitchen: vegetables like wild arugula, radicchio di Treviso, borage, escarole, or agretti, an unusual grasslike green that seems like a cross between asparagus and chive. For my part, I have been compelled to plant a vineyard, working with both cold-hardy varietals proven for our climate, as well as setting into motion the cultivation on my land of almost extinct varietals currently being encouraged in the mountains in northern Italy. Someday these grapes will make our own wine.

As we work within the composite notion of preservation, rivatlization, and terroir, we always return to our touchstone—memory. Caleb and I are nostalgic by nature; we constantly mine our memories for inspiration, and we work hard to create new memories to further feed us. New memories are often created from the return to old, a sort of double inverse of nostalgia. We are driven by the need for pilgrimage (this is another story for another time), and make pilgrimages to places that produce a certain kind of cured meat or a cheese, an unusual wine, an artisanal skill. Often we make pilgrimages to that which is almost lost, and we are always lured by the pilgrimage of return.

In late winter this year, we make the drive once again to Quebec City. The drive is quiet and long, at least five hours from our house to the Vieux Port, but it takes us that much time to go to New York City. The weather has held, the predicted ice storm bypassing us, the roads clear. By the time we are in the wide flat plain above Magog and Sherbrooke, on the last leg of the journey, the sky turns violet and blue, the setting sun over our western shoulder washing the atmosphere in dusk. A large herd of deer graze in a snow-covered field. Sugar shacks hide in maple sugar bushes, dormant and boarded up until the March thaws. Roadside truck stops and *casse-croute* herald two hundred kinds of *poutine*, those gravy-laced fries. Highway traveler hotels are built like castles on the Loire in France. Neat-as-a-pin farms show glowing barn windows suggesting evening milking and warm cow bodies huddled together. The sky darkens to blue, a half-moon lighting the snow fields, and on the radio the talk is of the just-opened Ice Hotel where you can sleep on an ice bed in a down sleeping bag for three hundred dollars per person per night. The lights of the city yellow the horizon ahead.

This time we stay in the old town, down near the water's edge. Though at this time of year the water in the river looks nothing like water. Miles of buckled ice define the river landscape. As we drive down along the bank, the snow begins. Thick, lazy flakes quickly blanketing every surface and obscure all the street signs, so we feel adrift.

Finally we are able to navigate to our hotel, rooms and comfortable lobby with a roaring fireplace built out of an old bank. Our view from our room is twofold, out over the river that once was and the old stone buildings of the old quarter. In the lobby, in front of that fire, we find bright champagne colored ever so slightly with a local cassis, and we plot our return to this city. We arrange to have lunch the next day at Le Continentale. After all, it is late winter, and we hope to eat pears.

The time before lunch is spent meandering up the snow-covered streets, bracing against a bitter cold. It is a relief to enter the doors of Le Continentale on a sleepy Tuesday. The room is plush with quiet, and a few other tables still take lunch—soft voices, and clinking glasses and cutlery. As we hang our coats in the coatroom, a man brushes past. He has a fine network of wrinkles at the corners of his eyes. As he whisks out the door, we see that he is Jean, the waiter we had the first time we came to dine here. I inadvertently touch my own fine crow's-feet stamped at the corner of my eyes. Yes, time has passed. We are all a little older. But we are all still here.

We have a languid lunch of old standbys and old favorites. Caleb is overtired and fighting a winter cold, so he starts with the soup and moves on to a classic herbed omelet. I begin with a duck terrine flecked with pistachios, and eat a main course of snow crab legs in Hollandaise. I am three years old again and eating at some fine restaurant with my parents and sisters. They have ordered for me—Alaskan king crab legs with drawn butter, a trendy dish of the late sixties. Alaskan king crab will be my preferred dish for years to come, the dish I always order when out at that kind of establishment, until Alaskan king crab becomes no more available because it is out of stock and out of fashion. I love that almost forty years later, I am eating a dish from my childhood that is still out of fashion. In Le Continentale style, they still serve these old classics, and while they look back, somehow the energy and the elegance of the space and the food also look forward.

Dessert comes with our lunches, but there are no pears poached in Pernod listed on the menu. I ask our waiter, a young man in that fitted white jacket, if it is possible to order. Also in Le Continentale style, he says, "But of course."

The oldest waiter on staff that day comes to our table, wheeling his tableside carriage. There is the adjustable flame, the copper pan, the bowl of pears, the pitcher of cream, a dish of sugar, one of butter, and a bottle of Pernod. We watch our waiter perform this dance, for it is a performance, an art, a theater of sorts. He makes the same motions that Caleb makes at his stove in our kitchen. I take a series of photographs as the magic of the flame ignites when the Pernod is added and the caramel begins to come together. We reveal our secret—that we have stolen this recipe for our own restaurant far away, but not too far away, and that it is one of the most loved desserts that we prepare. Our waiter does not think of our replication of this recipe as the work of thieves. "No one does this anymore. I am one of the last here who can prepare this dish. The schools no longer teach this. We practice a dying art."

I am seized by melancholy. Will these venerable old dishes someday no longer exist? Will no one know how to make them anymore? I think of opening another restaurant to preserve these recipes and skills, a little restaurant with a clutch of tables. There is no kitchen. Just a larder for storing ingredients. All dishes are prepared tableside, like this, over a hot plate with a flame, the ingredients there for all to see. The process is part magic, part education. Just like the first time we saw this dish made, we were bewitched and taught. We were able to take the *experience* of the recipe back home and duplicate it with our own nuances. We make the dish in autumn from the harvest of a wild pear tree on the edge of the woods. Preservation, revitalization, terroir.

I don't imagine that we have another restaurant in us. This too makes me a little melancholy. I scold myself. Who knows what the future will bring? Already what has happened over the past twelve years could not have been imagined beforehand. At the age of twenty I would not have known that one day I would own a restaurant, craft a garden, feed people. I could not have even seen Italy in my future, let alone a year of honeymoon shaped by hard work and longing. I could not have imagined a marriage in which I worked every day, side by side, with my husband. I could not have foretold that I would acquire some expertise in the field of wine, particularly in the realm of scent and taste. I could not have guessed that someday I would plant my own vines in an unlikely vineyard and make wine myself. I would have been surprised to learn that eventually I would write all this down, like a recipe, as if the retelling of it would offer up the experience again and again, and perhaps not only lead me to the memory of what has happened so far, but also draw me to where I might need to go.

So, twelve years later, we drive the long drive to Quebec City. We will make this drive again. Maybe in early summer or next fall. Perhaps two winters from now. Maybe one time we will come for Carnivale. We will continue to make our pears poached in Pernod as long as we can. We will teach the recipe to those who apprentice with us, or those who care. Our guests will be beguiled by the alchemy of the flavors. We will always think of Le Continentale when we eat this dish ourselves. We will be transported back to that first time, and to the second, and we hope there will be a third, and a fourth, and so on, layer upon layer of memory and sensation. When we taste the anise-flavored and slightly burnt cream over the cooked fruit, we will always be forever in late winter, when we ate pears.

appendix

AFFETTATI (COLD CUTS)

Cold cuts are held in high esteem in Italy and are typically presented by themselves as *antipasti*. They represent long-held traditions within regions and are products characteristic of the *cucina povera*, as the peasant populations up and down Italy depended upon using every part of their livestock for survival. Cold cuts were—and still are today—a way to convert what is typically a short-lived food into something that could be stored for a long time. And of course, over time, Italians have refined the procedures and styles of *affettati* and have elevated them to an art form. Today there are many artisans of the craft, and pride in quality is what drives them.

Just as no two bread bakers make the same bread, no two *salumerie* make the same *salami* or *prosciutti*, even when they come from the same area and are examples of typical *salumi* of that region. Each has his own particular recipes and procedures. In Tuscany the prosciutto *crudo* is generally saltier and more boldly seasoned than that of the Romagna and parts north, but it is important to remember that the bread of Tuscany is saltless, too. Thus the bread and the *cucina* are well suited to one another. (Salt itself represents a whole other discussion of political and economic history, and the *cucina Italiana* is an excellent context in which to set that discussion, and Tuscany a particularly good example.) This is generally true in other regions, as the style of a region's *salumi* reflect the context within which it occurs.

When serving *affettati* it is important to slice them as thinly as reasonably possible. You don't want the slices to be so fine that they fall apart. Given that most of us don't have a deli slicer at home, we depend upon the vendor to slice the meats appropriately. But once sliced, *affettati* aren't meant to be stored for long; they are ready to eat. If you refrigerate them overnight, be sure to display them on plates or a platter and allow them to come to room temperature. Following is a brief description of a variety of *affettati,* some easier to find than others, but all of them worth the trouble.

Prosciutto *crudo*—Cured ham. A number of imported *prosciutti*, from various regions of Italy, are available in the United States, each demonstrating a character typical of its own region.

Speck—Smoked, cured ham from northern Alpine Italy. Excellent with walnuts and fresh goat cheese.

Coppa—A rustic style of *salame* available either sweet or hot.

Sopressata—A finely textured *salame,* often made with peppercorns.

Bresaola—Cured beef from northern Alpine Italy. Excellent with a few drops of lemon juice with an arugula salad alongside.

Salame—Importation of *salame* to the United States is restricted by the USDA. The number and variety of *salame* made throughout Italy is astounding. Fortunately, in this country there are a number of good producers, among whom Molinari in San Francisco and Salumeria Biellese in New York City stand out.

acknowledgments

Thank you:

To Sarah Heekin Redfield for her reading wisdom

To Malaga Baldi for her tenacious belief

To Rowan Jacobsen for stopping one morning for cappuccino and pastry

To Mary Elder Jacobsen for her keen editorial eye

To our families for giving us what we needed

To Ben and Sarah Wood for their patience and encouragement

To Kay Renschler for her iron will, uncompromising standards, and persistent good humor

To Gianfranco who provided

To Renato, Anna, Rosa, Palmira, and Orianna for teaching us

To the Uffreduzzis for setting the table

To those with whom we work and have worked, side by side each day

To all the *gentildonne* and *gentiluomini* of Italy who open their doors and teach us still

To our loyal patrons, friends, and neighbors who make it all possible

index

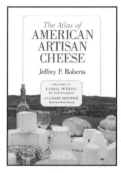

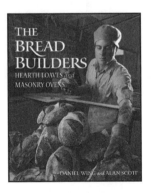
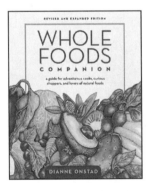